Asserting and Reasserting The Role of Business Education

NATIONAL BUSINESS EDUCATION YEARBOOK, NO. 27

Editor: BURTON S. KALISKI
      New Hampshire College
      Manchester, New Hampshire

Published by:

National Business Education Association
1914 Association Drive
Reston, Virginia 22091

Ministry of Education, Ontario
Information Centre, 13th Floor,
Mowat Block, Queen's Park,
Toronto, Ont. _____ M7A 1L2

ASSERTING AND REASSERTING THE ROLE OF BUSINESS EDUCATION

Copyright 1989 by

NATIONAL BUSINESS EDUCATION ASSOCIATION
1914 ASSOCIATION DRIVE
RESTON, VIRGINIA

$12.00

LIBRARY OF CONGRESS CARD NO. 89-61005
ISBN 0-933964-29-3

Any views or recommendations implied in this book do not necessarily constitute official policy of the National Business Education Association. References to and quotations from this publication are encouraged; however, no part of this book may be reproduced without permission of the National Business Education Association.

Contents

CHAPTER   PAGE

PART I
ROOTS AND ISSUES

1 The Philosophy of Business Education 1
   WALTER A. BROWER
   Rider College
   Lawrenceville, New Jersey

2 Business Education in Years Gone By 9
   PETER F. MEGGISON
   Massasoit Community College
   Brockton, Massachusetts

3 Business Education in the Present Uncertain Times 20
   DAVID J. HYSLOP
   Bowling Green State University
   Bowling Green, Ohio

PART II
STRATEGIES FOR ASSERTING AND REASSERTING

4 Communicating with the Constituencies of
   Business Education 29
   JOHN GUMP, MYRENA JENNINGS,
   and JO NELL JONES
   Eastern Kentucky University
   Richmond, Kentucky

5 Marketing the Entire Business Education Curriculum 41
   HARRIETT J. McQUEEN
   Austin Peay State University
   Clarksville, Tennessee

6 Developing and Coordinating the Business
   Education Curriculum 50
   LANETA L. CARLOCK
   Westside Community Schools
   Omaha, Nebraska

7 Preparing and Updating Professional
   Business Education Teachers 57
   LLOYD W. BARTHOLOME
   Utah State University
   Logan, Utah

PART III
ASSERTING AND REASSERTING BUSINESS EDUCATION AT THE PRESECONDARY LEVEL

8 Keyboarding 70
   LINDA D. KIMBALL
   Portsmouth Senior High School
   Portsmouth, New Hampshire

   PATRICIA MARCONI LANE
   York High School
   York, Maine

9 Presecondary Computer Literacy................................ 77
   ELLA H. FISHER
   East Mecklenburg High School
   Mecklenburg, North Carolina

10 Economic Literacy at the Junior High Level 88
   JOHN E. CLOW
   State University of New York at Oneonta
   Oneonta, New York

11 Job, Career, and Human Relations Skills 100
   SUSAN J. VOGEL
   Fort Madison High School
   Fort Madison, Iowa

PART IV
ASSERTING AND REASSERTING BUSINESS EDUCATION AT THE SECONDARY LEVEL

12 Basic Skills and Core Competencies 107
   BLANCHE ETTINGER
   Bronx Community College
   Bronx, New York

13 Processing Data 119
   EVELYN A. SCHEMMEL
   Cannon's Business College
   Honolulu, Hawaii

14 Owning and Managing a Business 128
   COLLEEN VAWDREY
   Utah Valley Community College
   Orem, Utah

15 Marketing and Distribution 134
   STEPHEN P. SPOFFORD
   Kennett High School
   Conway, New Hampshire

PART V
ASSERTING AND REASSERTING BUSINESS EDUCATION AT THE POSTSECONDARY LEVEL

16 Basic Skills and Core Competencies 138
    ALICE A. TAYLOR
    Northern Virginia Community College
    Woodbridge, Virginia

17 Administrative Support Systems 149
    MICHAEL BRONNER and BRIDGET O'CONNOR
    New York University
    New York, New York

18 Information Systems 156
    THOMAS B. DUFF
    University of Minnesota, Duluth
    Duluth, Minnesota

19 Marketing/Distribution Systems 165
    ROGER W. HUTT
    Arizona State University
    Tempe, Arizona

20 Accounting Systems 174
    ROBERT L. DANSBY
    Columbus Technical Institute
    Columbus, Georgia

    C. DAVID STRUPECK
    Bradley University
    Peoria, Illinois

21 Management Systems 181
    GAIL L. FANN
    Arizona State University
    Tempe, Arizona

Epilogue: Business Education in the Years To Come 189
    BURTON S. KALISKI
    New Hampshire College
    Manchester, New Hampshire

Preface

The past, the present, and the future of business education in our schools is the subject of this Yearbook. Schools at all educational levels, ranging from the elementary school to the graduate school of business, need our attention. They all need our reassertion. The purpose of this Yearbook is to show how business education and its philosophy evolved in our schools, what its current position is and its practices are, and what lies in store for us in the future. We have asserted our role many times in the past; now is a time for reassertion for the future. To do so, we must review our roots and both examine and evaluate current practices. Each chapter of this yearbook is devoted to the common theme of survival.

The chapters of this Yearbook vary in many ways. Some are long, while others are concise. Each of the well-qualified authors has a different way of expressing him or herself. However, all of the chapters appear to be on target, and the Yearbook itself is organized in a logical, and hopefully useful, sequence.

Part I of the Yearbook deals with the roots of business education and the current issues in our field. Part II of the Yearbook deals with general strategies for asserting and reasserting ourselves. Part III of the Yearbook is based on the theme that there is and can be viable business education at the presecondary level—elementary schools, middle schools, and junior high schools. Much of this area of content is new and/or growing for us. The fourth part of the Yearbook takes us to areas with which we are familiar—business education courses and programs in the secondary school. However, the thrust of this part is that there are new strategies for dealing with the problems of secondary business education. The concluding six chapters of the Yearbook form Part V, a section dealing with postsecondary business education.

As you read through these pages, I hope that you will gain some new ideas and then apply them in your setting. Please feel free to comment on the contents of this Yearbook and provide feedback both to me and the NBEA Publications Committee. I wish to thank the Publications Committee for giving me the honor to serve as the editor of this Yearbook and give particular thanks to all contributors and to the chairman of the Publications Committee. I extend my sincere appreciation also to the publications staff at NBEA headquarters.

Burton S. Kaliski, Editor

Part I
ROOTS AND ISSUES

CHAPTER 1
The Philosophy of Business Education

WALTER A. BROWER
Rider College, Lawrenceville, New Jersey

What is business education? What is the mission of business education? What do we really believe about business education? These questions have been asked since before the turn of the century, and in one form or another they are asked today. In the introduction to its 1983 report to the profession, the NBEA Task Force on New Concepts and Strategies for Business Education stresses that business education has been a vital part of our American educational system for over a century and that from its beginnings business education has provided a solid foundation from which we must look to the future. Further, the report emphasizes that business education is education *for* and *about* business and that these two major thrusts are essential components of the curriculum of all schools. Particularly significant in that report is the following, which is the premise upon which its recommendations were formulated:

> Because business education cannot be viewed apart from the society in which it functions, the need is urgent for all business educators—and indeed all who have a stake in business education—to reevaluate all aspects of business education to ensure that the needs and demands for entrepreneurs, managers, and technical workers will be met and that business education will continue to contribute to the general education of all citizens.[1]

Business education in 1989 is experiencing several problems. High on the list is the matter of decreasing enrollments. Changes in graduation requirements for high school students brought about by the emphasis on academic subjects result in students being unable to schedule courses in business education. There are those who stress that in view of this problem and others related to it the need is urgent for business educators at all levels to work together to clarify and to understand the vocational and nonvocational mission of business education not only for today but for the years well into the next century—which is but 12 years away. If we are to meet the challenge of asserting and reasserting what the mission of business education should be, surely a review of some of the pertinent thinking that has evolved over the years about the role that has brought us where we are today may help us in determining what the mission of business education will ultimately become.

---

[1] "Future Directions and Recommended Actions for Business Education: A Report by the NBEA Task Force on New Concepts and Strategies for Business Education." *Business Education Forum* 38:3; November 1983.

SOME EARLY VIEWS

Knepper held that through 1852 no common philosophy of business education had emerged. During this period business education was in its developmental stages, and there is considerable evidence that the vocational emphasis was dominant. It was not until the end of 1873, the period he described as the Business College Period, that Knepper was more specific about the philosophy of business education. He wrote, "Probably for the first time it can be claimed there was a *real* philosophy of business education. There was reasonably unanimous agreement as to *what* should be done, if not *how* it could best be done. Commercial educators tried to anticipate the needs of business and then supply the demand."[2]

Given the fact that business education experienced considerable development during the period of reconstruction following the Civil War and for several years thereafter, especially at first in the private business schools, it is easy to understand why Knepper believed that a philosophy of business education was beginning to emerge. In view of the business and economic growth that took place in the nation at that time, that philosophy continued to be vocational. The advent of the typewriter and the introduction of shorthand had their effect on the growth of business education and prompted him to write that by the year 1893, "What business wanted, the schools tried to provide."[3] Again it is clear that the emphasis was on training persons for employment, thus the vocational purpose of business education continued to be stressed.

In 1904, Herrick wrote that commercial education "is that form of instruction that both directly and indirectly prepares the future business man for his calling."[4] Herrick's definition seemed to emphasize only the vocational nature of business education at that time. However, he went on to suggest that "education for commerce will disappoint if it be planned on narrow lines."[5] Later, he argued that "commercial education is not to be circumscribed by the mere routine of office work," and added that "production, manufacture, transportation, the organization of industry, the principles and facts of both physical and social environments—all these offer a field of intense practical utility and that can be made a means of mental stimulus as well."[6] Although he seemed to be advocating a broader type of business education that goes beyond the preparation for employment, he appeared to be reinforcing the notion that such an education was for those preparing for careers in business.

Lomax added to Herrick's idea when he stated in 1929 that "this thing we call 'business education' is coextensive with all human behavior. There is a business side to every occupation, . . . [and] there is a business side to every

---

[2] Knepper, Edwin G. "A Historical Sketch of Business Education in the United States." *Business Education in a Changing Social and Economic Order.* Seventh Yearbook. Philadelphia: Eastern Commercial Teachers Association, 1934. Chapter 1, p. 3.

[3] *Ibid.*, p. 27.

[4] Herrick, Cheesman A. *Meaning and Practice of Commercial Education.* New York: The Macmillan Co., 1904. p. 6.

[5] *Ibid.*, p. 9

[6] *Ibid.*, p. 13.

social institution."[7] He went on to say that "we must realize more and more in the construction and practice of business education, that our great educational enterprise should be identified with all chief and lofty aspects of life."[8] As a result, it could be argued that Lomax was thinking not only in terms of business education being vocational, but that it was indeed needed in preparing individuals to deal with the economic facts of life that they were confronting during those years of economic turmoil.

A few years later, in 1933, Nichols defined business education as making a contribution to general education as well as having a vocational purpose when he wrote:

> Commercial education is a type of training which, while playing its part in the achievement of the general aims of education on any given level, has for its primary objective the preparation of people to enter upon a business career, or having entered upon such a career, to render more efficient service therein and to advance from their present levels of employment to higher levels.[9]

Although Nichols stressed that the role of business education was primarily career preparation, he went on to say:

> Ability to earn is not enough. Ability to save is quite as important. Wise investing is essential to individual security and social well-being from an economic point of view. People must become more competent in personal, family, and community finance if abiding economic stability is to be achieved. There is no conflict between these two aims—preparation for efficient participation in productive activities and for wise use of resulting financial rewards.[10]

This view appears to express a belief that there is a broadened purpose for business education. He obviously was placing emphasis on the need for individuals to be competent in dealing with economic matters not only in connection with their employment but for personal use as well. Could he have been thinking about a direction for business education that was later to be defined as education *about* business as well as *for* business? From what he wrote one could easily reach such a conclusion.

A BROADENED VIEW OF BUSINESS EDUCATION

Although in the 1930's there appeared to be much thought devoted to broadening the purposes of business education, strong emphasis on the vocational mission continued. This thinking prevailed during and until the end of the Second World War when, in the 1940's, the matter of the mission of business education received considerable attention. Because the vocational purposes of business education were well established and generally understood, more thought was given to the nonvocational aspects of this field. Enterline believed that business education was part of general education and that it

---

[7]Lomax, Paul S. "Editor's Foreword." *Foundations of Business Education.* First Yearbook. New York: Eastern Commercial Teachers Association, 1929. p. ix.

[8]*Ibid.*, p. xii.

[9]Nichols, Frederick G. *Commercial Education in the High School.* New York: D. Appleton-Century Co. 1933. p. 51.

[10]*Ibid.*, p. 62.

had a role to play in economic education. He wrote:
> Certain types of business education, such as general business information, an understanding of business, consumer business education, and social-business education, contribute to the economic well-being of all persons regardless of occupational choice, since all use the services of business or live in a business environment.[11]

Later, Price expressed more emphatically the nonvocational role of business education when he addressed the matter of economic education and wrote, "Regardless of any student's future production activities, he is ill-equipped for life in an economic society unless he has some understanding of how our business system operates."[12] He emphasized that such topics as buying, taxes, insurance, credit, and money management are needed by everyone. Then he added, "Any business education program that is not organized to bear directly on helping young people with these problems is doing only half the job of which it is capable."[13] There can be no doubt what Price had in mind. He held the view that the nonvocational component of business education was a necessity for all students, a view that was later to become more widely held.

According to Slaughter, business education consists of two main functions. He believed that "business education makes not one but two major contributions to the education of youth and indirectly to the welfare of our society. It helps to equip thousands of young people for earning a remunerative and worthy livelihood, and in so doing also contributes to the productivity of our economy. It contributes to the competence of our youth for participation in the social, political, and economic life of our country as citizens and consumers."[14] It is clear from these statements that the two-fold purpose of business education was gaining momentum; much attention was being devoted in the late 1940's and the early 1950's to the nonvocational aspects of business education.

The need for and the importance of the nonvocational purpose of business education was highlighted in 1957 when 12 leading business educators met to consider the need for economic education and issued a report that stressed the need for all youths to understand their business environment and asked the question, Are we giving them the help they need?[15] These educators (Gladys Bahr, Herman Enterline, Hamden L. Forkner, M. Herbert Freeman, James Gemmell, E. C. McGill, William Polishook, Ray G. Price, Herbert A. Tonne, John M. Trytten, Inez Ray Wells, and Theodore Woodward) made a strong case for the importance of economic education and issued a plea

---

[11]Enterline, Herman G. "Trends of Thought in Business Education." Monograph 72. Cincinnati: South-Western Publishing Co., March 1949. p. 5.

[12]"Statements of Belief, Dedication, Creed, Credo, and Faith in the Future of Business Education." *Business Education Forum* 11:39; May 1957.

[13]*Ibid.*

[14]*Ibid.*, p. 41.

[15]*Let's Educate Youth For Effective Business Life.* (A report financed by a grant from the Esso Standard Oil Company given to New York University.) 1957.

to their fellow business educators that the importance of the nonvocational mission of business education be fulfilled. It read:

> Educating our youngsters to understand and appreciate the American economic system is important to us all. Let us all work together to see that every young person is fully equipped to lead an active, intelligent, and successful life.[16]

Also, in 1957, the Soviet Union launched Sputnik into space, and schools throughout the United States were immediately criticized for what was called the preoccupation with educational frills which included typewriting. School administrators began the great push for increased academic requirements for graduation, and enrollments in those courses increased substantially. Throughout this period, business educators continued to stress the importance of the vocational subjects in the business education curriculum while placing increasing emphasis on the nonvocational coursework needed by all students in the high school.

THE MISSION OF BUSINESS EDUCATION CLARIFIED

By 1959 it was clear that there was a need to clarify the mission of business education. A significant step was taken by the National Business Education Association and Delta Pi Epsilon in creating the Policies Commission for Business and Economic Education. The stated purpose of the Commission was to "bring about a better understanding of what constitutes business and economic education and to render any assistance possible to those who are concerned with the total education of young people."[17] The first two policy statements issued in 1961 addressed the mission—the purposes of business education. The first, "A Proposal for Business-Economic Education for American Secondary Schools," states:

> Business education in American secondary schools consists of both general education and vocational preparation for store and office occupations. These two elements of business education are essential parts of secondary education in America.[18]

This statement makes clear that there are two components of business education and stress is placed upon the fact that "We believe it is imperative that *all* young people be adequately prepared to deal with business-economic issues and problems."[19]

The second statement, "This We Believe about Business Education in the High School," emphasized that business education is concerned with two major aspects of the education of youth:

1. The knowledge, attitudes, and nonvocational skills needed by all persons to be effective in their personal economics and in their understanding of our economic system

---

[16]*Ibid.*

[17]*A Chronology of Business Education in the United States.* Reston, Va.: National Business Education Association, 1977. p. 18.

[18]"A Proposal for Business-Economic Education for American Secondary Schools." *Policies Commission for Business and Economic Education 1959-1979.* Reston, Va.: the Commission, 1979. p. 1.

[19]*Ibid.*

2. The vocational knowledge and skills needed for initial employment and for advancement in a business career.[20]

Boggs later addressed the dual purpose of business education and forcefully stated, "Unless we start putting business into business education we shall be fulfilling half of our important task."[21] He added, "This is where we are not doing the job. If we worked as hard here as we do in the skills, I am confident that in time we would see great and vast improvement in the economic strata of our society."[22]

In 1970, the Commission reinforced its earlier beliefs in its statement, "This We Believe About Business Education in the Secondary School," stating that business education achieves its goals by providing "specialized instruction to prepare students for careers in business, fundamental instruction to help students assume their economic roles as consumers, workers, and citizens, and by instruction to assist students in preparing for professional careers requiring advanced study."[23]

In the late 1970's the Commission issued a new statement that specifically addressed the mission of business education and stipulated that the mission is "(1) to educate individuals *for* and *about* business; (2) to provide a continuous program of planned learning experiences designed to equip individuals to fulfill effectively three roles: to produce and to distribute goods and services as workers, to use the results of production as consumers, to make judicious socio-economic decisions as citizens; (3) to provide career information that helps students relate their interests, needs, and abilities to occupational opportunities in business; and (4) to provide educational opportunities for students preparing for careers in fields other than business to acquire business knowledge and skills needed to function effectively in those careers."[24]

From the Tempe (Arizona) Conference held in 1982, which brought together leading business educators from across the country, came a statement titled, "New Concept of Business Education," that stressed the changing nature not only of the world of work but of society in general. The statement declared:

> Individuals need to prepare for effective functioning in employment situations in which information processing and information systems are the central focus of the duties and tasks performed.

It went on to say:

> Other functions of business education will continue to be included with this new thrust. They are: related and background business information, the particular knowledges and skills needed to live successfully in a business oriented society,

---

[20]"This We Believe About Business Education in the High School." *Policies Commission for Business and Economic Education 1959-1979*. Reston, Va.: the Commission, 1979. p. 3.

[21]Boggs, Lohnie J. "Perspective for Business Education—A Viewpoint." *Balance Sheet* 48:62-63; October 1966.

[22]*Ibid.*, p. 63.

[23]"This We Believe About Business Education in the Secondary School." *Policies Commission for Business and Economic Education 1959-1979*. Reston, Va.: the Commission, 1979. p. 21.

[24]"This We Believe About the Mission of Business Education." *Policies Commission for Business and Economic Education 1959-1979*. Reston, Va.: the Commission, 1979. p. 37.

marketing and distribution, and business teacher preparation (preservice and inservice).[25]

This conference called for all interested parties—curriculum builders, association personnel, and others—to develop the appropriate course structure, class levels, and other specifics necessary to implement this new thrust.

Again, in 1985, the Policies Commission issued a statement directing attention to the purposes of business education in the comprehensive high school. Although the major thrusts of this statement are closely related to those expressed in the 1977 statement, the purposes are placed within the context of the role and mission of the comprehensive high school.

From its beginning in 1959, the Policies Commission has not only published statements concerned with the purposes of business education but has issued pronouncements in such areas as curriculum development and planning, research, leadership, career education, professionalism, free enterprise, competency-based education, adult and continuing education, student organizations, computer literacy, word processing, and keyboarding. The purposes and goals of business education as promulgated by the Policies Commission are endorsed by business educators throughout the country and by many professional groups of business educators meeting to consider specific issues confronting our field today. Examples of the latter are the New Directions for Business Education Conference held in Snowbird, Utah, in 1980, the Symposium on Business Teacher Education held at Rider College in 1980, and the National Conference on the Future of Business Education held in Cincinnati, Ohio, in 1985. The work and deliberations of such concerned groups are significant and contribute to the advancement of business education in the United States.

THE FUTURE

In 1986 the Policies Commission looked at business education in the exciting Information Age of today and tomorrow and, taking a futuristic view, stated that the business education curriculum must do the following:

1. Reflect emerging technology such as voice-reproduction systems, electronic mail, networking, teleconferencing, and voice-activated equipment
2. Include such concepts as the electronic cottage, ergonomics, robotics in the workplace, satellite communications, and expert systems and artificial intelligence
3. Incorporate concepts that teach workers to function effectively in a high tech environment
4. Reflect the ethical dimensions of such issues as computer security, software rights, copyright protection, information integrity, and invasion of privacy
5. Incorporate input from business and other community sources
6. Reflect the findings and implications of relevant research.[26]

---

[25] Report of the Tempe Conference on New Concept of Business Education, Tempe, Arizona, 1982.

[26] "This We Believe About the Future of Business Education." *Business Education Forum* 4:13; October 1986.

Sculley, the 1987 Delta Pi Epsilon Distinguished Lecturer, was looking to the future when he said, "I believe it is very realistic to expect that young people will not have one career but many will have three or four or five careers during their lifetime. It means that education, and especially business education, has a responsibility not to end at the boundaries of the institution but to be able to extend beyond the boundaries of the institution and become a lifelong experience."[27] Sculley's thoughts may indeed have far-reaching implications for the future of business education as business educators think more and more about the expanding mission of business education in the coming years.

There are those who today suggest the need to redefine business education believing that the present definition does not project an accurate image of what business education is all about. Sapre believes that business education is in need of such redefinition and that this must include both a new name as well as a reconceptualized mission and philosophy. The compelling arguments he provides to support his contention are:

> Office technology has the potential to eliminate the need for the knowledge and skills taught in business courses.
>
> The emphasis on academic subjects and basic skills challenges us to reaffirm and enhance our contribution to general education.
>
> Preparation for work requires that we do not emphasize narrow and specific skills at the expense of substantive content.
>
> Discovery of new knowledge in such areas as organizational and management information systems has resulted in the fragmentation of our field and in making new demands on us.[28]

In addition, Sapre presents eight propositions he believes should serve as guidelines in the redefinition of business education. Among these are: "integration of basic skills instruction with technology, an understanding of the nature of learning outside school, closer links between teacher education and management education, and emphasis on ethical and moral values."[29]

CONCLUSION

Evidence abounds that business education has kept pace with changes in society and that its contributions to our nation have been numerous and invaluable. Today it is recognized that in the Information Age the need remains for students at all levels to receive the kind of instruction that business education provides. Therefore, today's technological revolution requires that business educators continue to seek to break new ground; that they be willing to change and adapt to new ways of doing things; and that they always be receptive to ideas on defining what business education is if this important area of study is to meet the challenges and demands of a changing world.

---

[27]Sculley, John, "Looking Forward to the Twenty-First Century." *Delta Pi Epsilon Journal* 29:59-66; Summer 1987.

[28]Sapre, Padmakar M., "Toward a Redefinition of Business Education." Thirteenth Annual Peter L. Agnew Memorial Lecture. New York University, March 15, 1988.

[29]*Ibid.*

CHAPTER 2
Business Education in Years Gone By

PETER F. MEGGISON
Massasoit Community College, Brockton, Massachusetts

Some form of education for commercial endeavors can be found throughout the history of education. Even though a type of shorthand was used in ancient Greece, it was not until the development of the Roman Empire that it became widespread. Cicero's secretary, Marcus Tullius Tiro, was the author of a shorthand system that lasted until the Middle Ages and was a forerunner of today's cursive systems.

Bookkeeping, too, has an equally long history. Today's double-entry method can also be traced back to the Middle Ages. Fra Luca Pacioli, considered the father of accountancy, was the first to present this method, commonly referred to as the Italian method, in 1494.

Business education in the United States can be traced back to the very beginnings of colonization, through its formative stages in the nineteenth century, to its present status as an integral component of American education.

COLONIAL FOUNDATIONS

From 1620 to 1640, twenty thousand persons, known as Puritans, arrived in New England. These included college-educated men. A need was recognized, therefore, to establish a formal system of education for youth. This resulted in the establishment of the Latin grammar schools. Their sole purpose was to prepare boys for college. In early colonial America, a college education almost always resulted in a life devoted to ministry.

It was during this time period, however, that a need was seen to provide some fashion of education for persons involved with rudimentary commercial activities. The earliest record of formal training in this area indicates that James Morton taught children to "read, write, and cast accounts" in Plymouth in 1635. Casting was not bookkeeping but more a form of arithmetic with commercial applications. Casting seemed to be a popular course offering in the organized schools that developed in the ensuing years.

Even though formal business education was evidenced during these colonial days, it was through the apprenticeship system that most boys who desired to pursue business careers received their training. As a forerunner of today's cooperative programs, boys were allowed to leave school early and work in stores and offices to gain practical experience in bookkeeping and business practices.

English grammar schools started to develop during the eighteenth century to cater to the needs of young men who did not wish to enter the professions. Bookkeeping was included in the curriculum of these schools. John Green taught the subject in Boston in 1709; George Brownell in New York City in 1731; and Andrew Lamb in Philadelphia in 1733. Records show that it also appeared in Maryland and South Carolina shortly after this. Evening schools were also established during these years which included bookkeeping as a course offering. Handwriting was also offered since it was felt that good handwriting should be possessed by those involved with commercial pursuits.

A different type of education was established with the founding of Franklin's Academy in Philadelphia in 1749. The trustees listed four aims of the academy:

1. To educate boys at home in America
2. To fit bright youths for government positions
3. To prepare the poorer type to become teachers
4. To attract students from the neighboring colonies for the commercial advantage resulting from their patronage of local businesses.[1]

Academies flourished through the mid-nineteenth century, at which time there were over six thousand academies throughout the United States, serving both girls and boys. Since their objective was to assist students not going to college, bookkeeping and other commercial subjects were included in the curriculum. During the latter half of the century, however, public high schools started to take over the work of the academies which, in turn, took over the work of the declining Latin grammar schools whose goal had always been to prepare persons for college.

In the last quarter of the eighteenth century, a number of commercial textbooks were written particularly in the area of bookkeeping. They had a significant impact on the development of business education since they were written by teachers for use in their own classes and later came to be used in other schools as well.

PRIVATE BUSINESS SCHOOLS

The rapid growth of industry in the United States in the early to mid-nineteenth century necessitated the development of an educational enterprise that would more readily meet the needs of businesses than was possible in the other forms of education that were in existence at the time. Private business schools, commonly referred to as "commercial colleges," were established as business ventures to meet this need. Through the rest of the nineteenth century, they remained as one of the chief, if not the major, agencies for teaching business subjects and the preparation of clerical workers.

While it is not possible to pinpoint exactly when or who opened the first business college, James Gordon Bennet, the founder of the *New York Herald*, is credited with advertising the first business college in 1824. The business

---

[1] Haynes, Benjamin R., and Jackson, Harry P. *A History of Business Education in the United States.* Cincinnati: South-Western Publishing Co., 1935. p. 10.

college was to open in New York City; however, if it did in fact open, its duration was short.

James A. Bennett was another leader in the development of the private business schools. An author of bookkeeping textbooks, he developed teaching materials that were the forerunners of today's "practice sets" and "simulations." He used facsimile business papers for recording transactions and felt the schools should replicate, in student practice work, procedures found in counting houses. Two distinguishing features of Bennett's schools were the practice of unlimited attendance and the short-term course, which became very popular since these early schools were comprised mostly of adults. Bennett also advocated the general education values of business training, a precursor of the consumer education movement a century later.

The first "Commercial College" is said to have been opened by R. Montgomery Bartlett, a bookkeeper who saw the need for education in the field, in Philadelphia in 1834. This pioneer of business education was associated with the business college movement for over a half-century. Following his Philadelphia venture, he subsequently opened colleges in Pittsburgh in 1836 and Cleveland in 1838. At this time, "Bartlett's Commercial College" emphasized bookkeeping and penmanship. Following his death, his son continued to manage the College until 1909.

The U.S. Commissioner of Education credited Dolber's Commercial College, which was organized in New York City in 1835, as the first institution in America devoted solely to commercial education. During this period, the private business schools grew rapidly, with schools being located in other major cities such as Boston, St. Louis, New Orleans, and Providence.

These schools filled a very specific need—that of providing clerical training to young men in order to obtain employment. The establishment of these schools showed that this type of training could more appropriately be accomplished through formal school training rather than through the unstructured apprenticeship system. A common criticism of these schools was that the training was very narrow and that broad business concepts were not developed. Since the schools were organized around the profit motive, another criticism was that the owners sometimes exploited students by allowing students to enroll who did not have the ability nor the background to be successful academically.

During the last 50 years of the nineteenth century, the private business schools became so strong that they dominated the entire field of business training. By 1886, there were 239 of these schools in existence in the United States, consisting of both chain schools and individual proprietorships.

Peter Duff, in 1840, established Duff's Mercantile College in Pittsburgh. This institution has the distinction of having the longest continuous existence as a school of business. Today it operates as Duff's Business Institute.

The Bryant and Stratton chain opened in Cleveland in 1853, and within ten years more than 50 schools were operating under their management. The schools used uniform textbooks and provided scholarships that were accepted in any of the schools of the chain.

Among the more notable individual schools of this period were the Eastman

Schools which opened in Rochester, New York, in 1853 and Packard Business College, which opened in New York City in 1858. Shorthand was introduced in the Packard School in 1872, followed by typewriting in 1873.

The private business schools continued to be an important form of education for business through the early years of the twentieth century. The emphasis in many of these schools was on intensive training for accounting and secretarial occupations. Much of the training that was formerly available only through these schools, however, was now being carried on in the high schools and public postsecondary institutions and, therefore, markedly decreased the number of private business schools. Private business schools continue to play an important role in business education in this country. The curriculum today still includes education for secretarial and accounting careers but preparation is also available in specialized areas of automation with applications to particular professions. Long-established schools that continue to play an important role in private business education are the Heald Colleges in the western states and the Katharine Gibbs Schools in the northeast.

BUSINESS EDUCATION IN HIGH SCHOOLS

The first public high school in the United States was founded in Boston in 1821. Known as the English Classical High School for Boys, bookkeeping was included in the curriculum. In 1827 a law was passed in Massachusetts which mandated that every community of 500 or more families establish a high school and include bookkeeping as a subject. During these early years of the development of public high schools, though, only bookkeeping, penmanship, and arithmetic were available for persons preparing for business.

Shorthand, then known as phonography, was offered in the high school at St. Louis in 1862. Issac Pitman published his shorthand system in 1837, and most of the shorthand systems taught in the nineteenth century were a derivative of this system. John Robert Gregg brought his shorthand system, first published in England in 1888, to Boston in 1893. Nearly all schools teaching shorthand in the twentieth century used the Gregg system.

The first practical typewriter was invented by Christopher Latham Sholes and patented in 1868. Combined with shorthand, this provided an impetus for schools to provide training for office occupations and eventually opened the doors to women in securing office positions. Typewriting eventually became the most popular business subject offered in the curriculum and became a graduation requirement in some school systems. Touch typewriting was developed by Frank McGurrin in 1880, and within a few years several textbooks employing his method were being marketed.

Other business subjects, such as commercial law and business correspondence, were also introduced in various schools during the years following the Civil War. Knepper points out:

> What was probably the most advanced curriculum for commercial education offered up to that time (1870's) was the curriculum for the "Commercial Department of the Pittsburgh Public School." Graduates of this department were required to pass an examination in theoretical bookkeeping, practical bookkeeping, commercial law,

penmanship, business forms, business correspondence, and office practice. An elaborate system of offices was provided for practice. These included a post office, a transportation office, a real estate office, a wholesale and importing office, a commission and forwarding office, and a student bank. Each pupil was supposed to do satisfactory work in each of these offices before he could be graduated.[2]

The expansion of practical training for business at the high school level was described by Glass:

> It is a matter of common knowledge that the comprehensive high school had its origin in the first concession made by the academic curriculum to commercial courses of study. When business education had thus blazed the trail to an enlarged secondary program of studies adaptable to both college preparatory and vocational aims the trail became open to other vocational arts curricula. Thus, the comprehensive or democratized high school, which is beyond question the greatest single contribution of the high school to American education, was inaugurated by business education.[3]

The early years of the twentieth century represented a tremendous period of growth in business courses. In a survey completed by Lyon, the number of students enrolled in business courses in the public high schools increased from 15,220 in 1893 to 208,605 in 1915—an increase of 1,270.5 percent.[4]

Data shows that in terms of actual student enrollment, typewriting, shorthand, and bookkeeping—which had come to be known as the "big three"—commanded the largest percent of student enrollment, a trend that would continue for most of the twentieth century. Other business courses such as elementary business training, commercial law, economic geography, and office practice started to find their way into high school commercial programs. Larger high schools were able to develop complete programs of business training with the courses sequenced over a three- or four-year period.

A leading business educator of the late nineteenth century was Edmund J. James of the Wharton School of Commerce of the University of Pennsylvania. As a result of an investigation he conducted of European commercial schools, his influence began to be felt in the development of improved programs and courses. James advocated a four-year commercial curriculum at the high school level. The National Education Association Committee of 1915 advocated two different tracks in the commercial program—one in accounting, the other in stenography.

Prominent businessmen of the time often came to the support of business educators in fighting many of the same problems which today's business educators face. Knepper quotes General Arthur McArthur's commencement address to the Spencerian Business College class of 1888:

> We often hear discouraging remarks about practical education, as if it only enables one to make a living. Well, that is true in a restricted sense; and, even if it did

---

[2]Knepper, Edwin G. "Historical Development of the Business Curriculum." *The Changing Business Education Curriculum.* Fourth American Business Education Yearbook. New York: Eastern Commercial Teachers Association and National Business Teachers Association, 1947. Chapter 2, p. 20.

[3]Glass, James M. "Commercial Education in the Junior High School." *Balance Sheet* 8:3; September 1926.

[4]Lyon, Leverett S. *A Survey of Commercial Education in the Public High Schools of the United States.* Supplementary Educational Monographs No. 12. Chicago: University of Chicago Press, September 1919. p. 2.

no more than that, it would accomplish more than any system of liberal studies known to me; but it means much more than making a living; it means making a life.[5]

Graham analyzed the evolution of business education in the United States. As a result of her study of early aims and curriculums, she identified the following, in rank order, as the ten major purposes of business education as expressed in 47 published statements from 1825 to 1918:

1. To prepare pupils for specific office positions (as clerks, bookkeepers, stenographers, etc.)
2. To give that form of general education which will prepare young people to enter business pursuits (related knowledge)
3. To adapt business education to social and civic life
4. To prepare pupils for later promotion
5. To provide opportunity for mental discipline
6. To fulfill the general objectives of all secondary education
7. To give business information and skills useful to all pupils in personal, social, and civic life
8. To give practical training to boys and girls who cannot meet the requirements of other courses
9. To prepare for university work in commerce
10. To help the United States to win commercial supremacy.[6]

Many of these continued to be key objectives of business education at both the secondary and postsecondary levels. Some business educators, however, recognized that many students did not graduate from high school and that business education had a responsibility to these people who left school without any skills or competencies. Frederick G. Nichols of Harvard University designed a course called junior business training which was intended to offer some training in basic business skills that could be performed by young workers who drop out of school at the eighth or ninth grade. As more and more people completed high school, however, the focus of the course changed into a general business course for economic understandings. The course received renewed interest as a result of the consumer movement of the 1960's. Some states have mandated that consumer education be taught as a required course for graduation. While business education continued to remain predominantly vocational in nature, its dual object of preparing persons to be efficient consumers of goods and services was reinforced by such legislation.

Dykman prepared a history of business education from 1917 to 1967 as observed by business educators who were recipients of the John Robert Gregg Award (an award inaugurated in 1953 by the Gregg Division, McGraw-Hill Book Company, to honor outstanding leaders in business education). The ten most important developments according to these leaders were:

---

[5]Address by Honorable Arthur McArthur, *32nd Annual Graduating Commencement Exercises, Spencerian Business College,* Washington, D.C., May 29, 1888, in Knepper, Edwin G. *History of Business Education in the United States.* Bowling Green, Ohio: Edwards Brothers, 1941. p. 72.

[6]Graham, Jessie. *The Evolution of Business Education in the United States and Its Implications for Business-Teacher Education.* Southern California Educational Monographs 1933-34 Series Number 2. Los Angeles: University of Southern California. pp. 42-43.

1. Development of business teacher education
2. Growth in and recognition of more general education, economic education, and basic business understandings for all
3. The passage of the Vocational Education Act of 1963
4. Development of graduate work in business education
5. Increased professionalization and development of professional associations and their programs
6. Increase in equipment, more equipment, and better equipment
7. Growth in enrollment at all levels
8. Development of computers and electronic or automated data processing
9. The movement of business education from the secondary and private schools into the college and universities
10. Cooperative work experience and coordination of work experience.[7]

Crank and Crank described the growth of business education in this century: "The expansion of the business education curriculum began in the 1920's, continued into the 1930's and 1940's, was halted briefly in the 1950's, and had its greatest growth in the 1960's and 1970's."[8]

The halt in growth in the 1950's was a result of the launching of Sputnik by the Russians. Many educators felt high school students would be better served by "academic" subjects such as science, math, and foreign languages. Thus, business education took a back seat, not dissimilar to its present position in the high school curriculum.

The "back-to-basics" emphasis of the 1980's and the report of the National Commission on Excellence in Education, *A Nation at Risk: The Imperative for Educational Reform*, have resulted in increased requirements in academic subjects. In most cases, these requirements have left little room for occupational courses. In spite of the current negative forces, business education will continue to be an integral part of the comprehensive high school.

Crank and Crank succinctly describe how the high school business education program can serve the needs of today's youth:

1. Occupational and career guidance, career orientation, and exploration of opportunities and requirements in business
2. Development of occupational knowledges, attitudes, and skills that are oriented around job classifications of (a) clerical, (b) stenographic, (c) bookkeeping and accounting, (d) data processing, (e) marketing and sales, (f) business ownership and management
3. Development of consumer knowledges, attitudes, and skills that permit one to make appropriate and reasoned decisions in the selection, buying, and use of consumer goods and services
4. Development of understandings regarding the organization and operation of the nation's economic system that will permit one to make personal economic

---

[7]Dykman, Dorothy. *A History of Business Education from 1917 to 1967 as Observed by Selected Leaders.* Doctor's thesis. Fort Collins: Colorado State University, 1969. p. 93.

[8]Crank, Floyd, and Crank, Doris. "Historical Perspectives of Education for Business." *Curriculum Development in Education for Business.* Fifteenth Yearbook. Reston, Va.: National Business Education Association, 1977. Chapter 1, p. 5.

decisions that are appropriate for the economic system as a whole and cast votes for elected officials who are most likely to promote the best economic interests of the nation
5. Development of personal-use skills that will permit one to become a fully functioning individual in the personal business activities of life
6. Course offerings that serve as the basis for advanced study in business.[9]

COMMERCIAL HIGH SCHOOLS AND VOCATIONAL SCHOOLS

The first commercial high school was opened in Washington, D.C., in 1890. Shortly thereafter, they were established in other large cities and by 1925 there were 20 such schools in the United States. The chief aim of these schools, obviously, was to prepare students for careers in business, even though their programs were not too different from those found in the comprehensive high schools. Sequential programs, covering a three- or four-year period, were found in most of the schools. Specialized options included bookkeeping, secretarial, and merchandising sequences.

Although these high schools did flourish for a short time, they were eventually discontinued in most cities. Critics felt that their objective was too narrow and that youth could be better served by affiliating with a comprehensive high school. The few high schools of commerce that continue to exist today are more comprehensive than was their original intent.

Within recent years, however, the original concept of the commercial high schools has been revived with the establishment of vocational-technical schools. A major difference from the commercial high school is that these vocational centers are intended to include a great many occupational areas. In addition, the vocational-technical centers are designed to serve several different communities, thereby reducing the need to provide expensive equipment for occupational training at each local high school. Business education programs in specialized secretarial areas, data processing, and office automation are among those that can be found in area vocational-technical schools.

COLLEGIATE BUSINESS EDUCATION

While colleges and universities offered commercial course work as early as the mid-eighteenth century, it was not until 1881 that the first successful school of business was established at the University of Pennsylvania. Known as the Wharton School of Commerce, it led the way in the establishment of other Schools of Commerce at major universities throughout the United States. In 1898 Schools of Commerce were opened at the University of California and University of Chicago. The subject matter taught in these schools was broad and included topics such as banking, accounting, finance, and economics. In 1916 the American Association of Collegiate Schools of Business was established to set standards and monitor practices of member schools.

---

[9]*Ibid.*, p. 12.

University education for business emphasized the managerial aspects of business and many of the original schools of commerce changed their names to schools of business administration. Such programs are now found in more than 2,000 colleges and universities in the United States.

The first public junior, or two-year, college was Joliet (Illinois) Junior College, which was founded in 1902. Junior colleges were established in many cities throughout the country in the ensuing years, and by 1930 there were about 500 junior colleges in the United States. By 1960 the number had risen to 650. There was great progress in the junior college movement during the 1960's. State-supported two-year colleges had come to be known as community colleges after a model plan that was first developed in California in the 1950's. Today there are approximately 1,250 two-year colleges in the United States.

A vast array of business programs has always been offered in the two-year colleges. Some are designed to prepare persons for immediate employment after two years of concentrated study. Typical associate degree programs have included secretarial science, accounting, business management, data processing, and specialized business areas. In addition, the two-year colleges have offered programs of transfer that parallel the courses offered during the first two years of a traditional four-year college program. Upon completion of two years of prescribed courses at a two-year institution, students are able to transfer to a four-year institution with a minimum, if any, loss of credit. Two-year colleges, in addition to attracting the recent high school graduate, are also attractive to nontraditional learners.

BUSINESS TEACHER EDUCATION

Little, if any, formal training was available to teachers of business subjects until the beginning of the twentieth century. Prior to that time, teachers of business secured their training through practical office work experience on the job, through the private business schools, or through self-instruction. The first collegiate institution to offer a program of preparation for business teachers was Drexel Institute in Philadelphia in 1898.

Business teacher education experienced a slow growth during the first 20 years of this century. By 1923, only 37 schools had started courses for training commercial teachers. Some of the outstanding programs were found at the state normal schools at Salem, Massachusetts; Whitewater, Wisconsin; Plattsburg, New York; Trenton, New Jersey; Albany, New York; and Willimantic, Connecticut.

During this period, business teacher education programs were also being established in private universities. One of the first to offer such a program was New York University, which shortly thereafter started to offer graduate course work in business teacher education. As programs started to become somewhat standardized, attempts were made to develop curriculums where there was a balance of requirements in general education, business content, education, and specialized business education methods courses. Most business teacher education programs offered, and continue to offer, various options to prospective business teachers. These included concentrations in accounting, secretarial skills, data processing, basic business, or a combination thereof.

By the mid-1960's over 400 collegiate institutions were offering programs of business teacher education. During the last 20 years, however, many of these programs have been eliminated due to declining enrollments, lack of administrative support, and pressures from outside accrediting agencies.

BUSINESS EDUCATION PROFESSIONAL ASSOCIATIONS

The first professional organization for business teachers, known as the Business Educators' Association, consisted of mostly private business school teachers and was established in 1878. This group published monographs on various business education topics. At a meeting of this association held in Chautauqua, New York, in 1892, the association accepted an invitation of the National Education Association to become a department of its organization. The early leadership of this group was weak although the Department did publish model business education curriculum guides for both private and secondary schools.

In these early days, private business school leaders began withdrawing from the Department of Business Education of the National Education Association and eventually formed the National Commercial Teachers Federation, which appears to have been a return to an independent association for business education. S. S. Packard, a long-time leader in the private business school movement, served as the first president.

The Eastern Commercial Teachers Association was founded in 1897 to serve business teachers on the Eastern Seaboard. Fifty years later the association changed its name to the Eastern Business Teachers Association. This association became widely known for its yearbooks on selected topics of importance to business educators. A similar group, the Southern Commercial Teachers' Association, was formed to serve the needs of business teachers in the South in 1922. In 1934 it changed its name to the Southern Business Education Association.

In 1923 Pi Omega Pi was founded by Paul Selby at Northwest Missouri State Teachers College. This national undergraduate honorary business education society promotes scholarship and ethical ideas in the field. Delta Pi Epsilon, the national graduate honorary business education society, was founded by Paul S. Lomax at New York University in 1936. The goals of the society include the advancement of business education through research and professionalism. Its annual publication, the *Business Education Index*, is a listing of books, research studies, and periodical literature in the field for a particular year.

In 1927 a group of college business educators formed the National Association of Commercial Teacher-Training Institutions. Later, this group became the National Association for Business Teacher Education, a division of the National Business Education Association.

In 1933 the various business education professional groups unified by forming the National Council for Business Education. This Council merged with the National Education Association's Department of Business Education in 1946 to form the United Business Education Association, with Hollis Guy as its executive director. This new association began publishing the *Business Education Forum* the following year. Within the next few years, regional associations affiliated with the United Business Education Association in an effort to unify the existing organizations for business teachers. United Business Education Association changed its name to the National Business Education Association in 1962 and currently has five regional affiliates—Eastern, Southern, North-Central, Mountain-Plains, and Western. O. J. Byrnside, Jr., was appointed executive director of the association in 1968.

FEDERAL LEGISLATION AFFECTING BUSINESS EDUCATION

The first federal legislation that affected business education was the Smith-Hughes Act of 1917. Wanous describes the purposes of this act:

> One of the provisions of the Smith-Hughes Act made federal money available for the organization and maintenance of part-time classes in order to give business training to employed persons. Reimbursement for instruction could not be obtained for regular high school business courses.
>
> Provision was also made for conducting studies and making reports on business jobs and their requirements, problems of administering vocational schools, and development of courses of study.[10]

The George-Deen Act of 1937 and the George-Barden Act of 1946 allocated funds for distributive education programs.

The Vocational Education Act of 1963, and its subsequent amendments, have had the most profound affect on the funding of business education programs. Vocational education, for the first time, included business and office occupations. The Act was amended in 1968, and funds were made available for teachers to improve existing programs and to develop new ones which included cooperative ventures, simulated offices, and individualized programs. This legislation was intended to benefit high school students who would not be entering college as well as unemployed or underemployed adults. The amendments also called for the inclusion of career awareness concepts throughout the school program.

Since 1983 each state has been given the responsibility of developing its own plan for the expenditure of federal funds for vocational education.

CONCLUSION

Many forces have impacted business education in the United States from the colonial days up to the present uncertain times. Institutions that have provided education for and about business have changed as the needs of society have changed. However, the dual objectives of providing education for occupational competence and economic efficiency have always been and will continue to be what business education is about.

---

[10]Wanous, S. J. *A Chronology of Business Education in the United States.* Reston, Va.: National Business Education Association, 1977. p. 10.

CHAPTER 3
Business Education in the Present Uncertain Times

DAVID J. HYSLOP
Bowling Green State University, Bowling Green, Ohio

Current trends in business education portray a picture which can be interpreted in various ways. The tradition and philosophy of the discipline, as described in Chapters 1 and 2, have without question created a foundation of acceptance and excellence for business education. Business education programs, in order to achieve success, have fulfilled societal needs and assisted students in their career growth and development. However, the current status of the profession is being challenged by a variety of forces—some within our profession and others reflecting changes in our society. The challenges our discipline faces, as excellence is sustained, revolve around understanding these current trends and adopting change strategies which will be successful.

The purpose of this chapter is to review the current status of business education, particularly stressing the challenges which must be evaluated and addressed. Through gaining an understanding of these key challenges, our profession can develop a targeted response to ensure a continuation of past successes.

A LOOK AT BUSINESS EDUCATION

Types of programs. To accomplish the major goals of business education, a variety of courses and programs are currently offered at all educational levels. The traditional "skill" courses such as typing and shorthand are still evident, but exist with significant content changes and enrollment demands. Typing has progressed into keyboarding, which is being increasingly taught at presecondary levels and encompasses a wide variety of computer applications. Shorthand is in a similar state of flux; enrollments are decreasing significantly although some employers still request or require this skill when screening prospective employees. Also, the use of dictation/transcribing equipment—the progression of written shorthand—is emerging into computer shorthand.

The scope and breadth of business education courses and programs is difficult to assess. If one were to list the titles of courses currently offered, the list could easily extend into three digits and cover the alphabet—at least from A to W (accounting to word processing). A similar pattern is evident in the number of business education programs available. Several recent classifications have categorized business education courses/programs into areas such as accounting, basic business and economics, communications, entrepreneurship, information processing, keyboarding, marketing, and office procedures. Others have developed more generic categories, such as basic skills, processing text, and processing data. Regardless of the classification scheme being used, it is apparent that business education courses and programs have evolved into a "systems" approach focusing on computer technology and applications. Changes in the quantitative aspects of business education (e.g., enrollments, graduates, job placement) have been accompanied by changes in the qualitative aspects, such as improved curriculums, innovative instructional design, or more effective course/program planning.

Delivery systems continue to focus on the options of specific learning activities, courses, or programs. In some settings, emphasis is more directed toward the vocational aspects of programs, while in others it is focused more on the general understandings and competencies *about* business education. In some cases enrollments in vocational programs have remained stable or decreased. However, enrollment demands have increased for many basic business education courses, especially those courses being offered above high school level.

Emerging curriculum models. To address the many changes occurring in business education, new programs and curriculums have developed in every segment of the discipline. These innovations reflect several goals as outlined in the policies statement, "This We Believe About the Future of Business Education" issued in 1986 by the Policies Commission for Business and Economic Education.[1] These goals focus on students being able to:

- Refine traditional communication skills of writing, speaking, listening, and reading
- Expand and improve computational skills
- Identify and solve problems
- Develop critical-thinking, reasoning, and decision-making skills
- Improve and refine interpersonal skills.

One focus of curriculum development has been to develop more integration of career education concepts into courses and programs. Learning experiences which enhance career awareness, career identification, career preparation, and career assessment are stressed in meeting both the career development and occupational needs of students.

Another direction in curriculum development is the development of course/program competencies. Although competency-based business education is not a new concept, the current use of this approach reflects the critical societal and occupational trends which impact on student success. A recent publication of the National Business Education Association, *Database of Competencies for Business Curriculum Development, K-14*, outlines performance objectives for the entire business education curriculum from

---

[1] Policies Commission for Business and Economic Education. "This We Believe About the Future of Business Education." *Business Education Forum* 41:14; October 1986.

kindergarten through grade level 14.[2] This publication lays the foundation for designing curriculums and determining course content and program objectives.

Reflecting business education's movement toward information technology and the systems approach, a model curriculum for office systems education has been developed by the Office Systems Research Association.[3] This curriculum, based on office automation skills and competencies, outlines the courses and content which should be part of an "office technology" program. The model curriculum involves the components of (1) general education courses, (2) standard business courses, and (3) office systems core and optional courses. Learning experiences within these courses include planning, implementing, and evaluating office systems. Moving to this curriculum will further change the traditional orientation of business education and move the discipline into greater focus on information processing technology.

Relating business education to changing employment trends. Without question, many significant employment trends have affected the current status of business education. In addition to changes in the duties and responsibilities of business education graduates, there have been important changes in social, economic, and demographic factors in our society. These changes have prompted business education to assess our programs and curriculums, who we educate, when we educate, and how we educate. As a discipline, business education has been moving to serve the needs of traditional and non-traditional students, expand programs and courses into the entire K-adult spectrum, and integrate new techniques of classroom instruction and management. Reacting to these widespread changes in employment patterns has required our discipline to challenge the concept of "business as usual" and create new learning experiences within and outside of classroom.

A comprehensive summary of the significant employment trends and changes as they affect business education is contained in the 1987 NBEA Yearbook, *Business Education for a Changing World*. In addition, recent reports from the Bureau of Labor Statistics show a continuation of trends established in the early 1980's.[4] The BLS projections up to the year 2000 reveal continued opportunities for occupations within the business education field, but also reflect change in the training and job duties for these emerging positions.

CHALLENGES FACING BUSINESS EDUCATION

The major challenges facing business education can be categorized into either those internal to our profession or those reflecting changes occurring in public education or society in general. Some of these challenges represent a continuation of trends beginning several years ago (e.g., the back-to-basics

---

[2]National Business Education Association. *Database of Competencies for Business Curriculum Development, K-14.* Reston, Va.: the Association, 1987. p. 4.

[3]O'Connor, Bridget N., and Thomas, Edward G., editors. *The Office Systems Research Association Model Curriculum for Office Systems Education.* Cincinnati: South-Western Publishing Co., 1986.

[4]Bureau of Labor Statistics. *News.* Washington, D.C.: U.S. Department of Labor, June 1987.

movement, accountability, integration of computer technology) which are still impacting on business education. The strategies that our profession adopts in meeting these challenges will, in many respects, define the role and importance of our discipline for years to come.

Societal trends and demands. A fundamental change in education in the United States has occurred as more policies and educational leaders have advocated the strengthening of the academic preparation of students. *A Nation at Risk*, the report by the National Commission on Excellence in Education, has fostered widespread support on curriculums and courses enhancing students' academic achievements. Curriculums in most schools have been revised to strengthen the typical student's background in math, English, physical science, social science, and fine arts. As of 1987, a total of 32 states had adopted curriculum changes reflecting the above areas as part of high school graduation requirements. Many states have also encouraged college preparatory programs which have been supported by higher education institutions within the state or region.

Programs and courses in business education, particularly vocational business education, are directly competing with the academic stress being adopted by public schools. Within the limitation of the number of courses a student can complete during an academic year, pressure is placed on students when selecting courses or programs in their career preparation.

To cope with this challenge, business education courses and programs must contain the appropriate experiences and standards expected by our society. Further, our profession must increase its respectability by continuing to focus on the goals developed in 1986 by the Policies Commission for Business and Economic Education. The student outcomes of communication competence, computer literacy, critical thinking, and problem solving need to be further integrated into the learning activities of all courses and programs.

International dimensions of education. Our country's role in international events has broadened the education needed to function effectively in many business careers. Trade practices and the worldwide economy have forced our nation to better understand how to conduct business and interact with countries and cultures in all parts of the world. Increasingly, our educational system is being modified with the goal of giving students sufficient background in international affairs as necessary for business success.

To meet this international thrust, changes in existing courses or the creation of new courses are under way in a variety of educational institutions. For example, courses in economics, management, and marketing have been examined to incorporate concepts reflecting international trade and business policies. There is also a national trend to strengthen the foreign language background of students through requiring one or more languages. In a similar way, this societal change will impact on business education—both in the programs being planned and the course content of existing programs. The teaching of concepts "for and about" business will, of necessity, need to integrate international aspects of trade, business policies and practices, and cultural awareness into the curriculum.

To meet this international thrust, changes in existing courses or the creation of new courses are under way in a variety of educational institutions. For example, courses in economics, management, and marketing have been examined to incorporate concepts reflecting international trade and business policies. There is also a national trend to strengthen the foreign language background of students through requiring one or more languages. In a similar way, this societal change will impact on business education—both in the programs being planned and the course content of existing programs. The teaching of concepts "for and about" business will, of necessity, need to integrate international aspects of trade, business policies and practices, and cultural awareness into the curriculum.

Institutional and teacher accountability. The issue of accountability came to the forefront several years ago as a result of studies and conclusions regarding the success of our public schools. This concern was magnified when data from several national studies showed a significant downturn in the academic achievements of students at a variety of levels.

Because of the perceived need for improvement in education, many policies and practices have been enacted which require greater accountability, both in our institutions and in teacher performance. Some of the measures that have been adopted include:

- Stricter qualifications for teachers to earn certification
- Competency testing of teachers entering the field and of those currently teaching
- Greater use of performance standards when developing or evaluating courses or programs
- Stricter control on teaching methodology
- Increased assessment of student learning
- Greater collection and use of data on student achievement by educational leaders.

The use of accountability measures in business education, as in other areas, results in greater external control and evaluation of course and program success. Further, it requires greater use of quality standards in the formulation and evaluation of learning activities. Although not all teachers and educational organizations endorse the use of accountability measures in evaluating teaching, the trend has been widespread enough to result in the use of additional external controls for measuring student achievement and helping to increase the quality of our educational system.

Back-to-basics philosophy. Educational traditionalists have advocated this philosophy as a return to an earlier teaching methodology which they feel produced greater results. The back-to-basics philosophy reflects a return to a core set of student competencies and a more structured approach to teaching. A national movement to develop a core curriculum stressing basic skill areas has been under way and adopted at some institutions, both secondary and postsecondary.

Through the use of this approach, curriculum development would be centered around ensuring that all students are well educated in the agreed-upon competencies. For business education, this approach requires a review of curriculums and a more focused approach to learning systems. This focus could, in many ways, require more emphasis on the general education component of business education and less emphasis on the vocational aspects.

Development of critical-thinking and problem-solving skills. The writing of many futurists has established a pattern depicting the many changes we will face in the next 20 to 30 years. These futurists project a continuation of the trend toward information technology and the need for people to know how to adapt to the technology. They also stress the need for people to have the capability to "learn how to learn" and be analytical, able to think critically and solve problems in a logical manner.

Similarly, educational theorists have advanced the notion that our schools need to teach critical thinking and problem solving in a more sustained way. A planned program in which students are required to exercise their analytical skills should be a part of every curriculum, according to these theorists. The same concept has been reiterated in the philosophy and employment practices of business employers as they select and promote employees who possess the analytical skills important for success.

For a number of years business education has endorsed the need for and desire to provide critical-thinking and problem-solving skills for students. This support has been evident in a number of policy statements from professional organizations within the discipline. However, implementing this belief requires change—both in the philosophy of each teacher and in the development and use of appropriate learning activities. Business education has many areas in which critical-thinking and problem-solving skills can be easily and clearly integrated: communications, word processing, data processing, and office procedures, to name a few.

CHALLENGES WITHIN THE PROFESSION

The challenges presented in this section are ones which are more narrow in scope than those given previously. These may vary to some degree based on the unique philosophical and organizational elements which impact on business education programs at any institution.

Maintaining program enrollments. Without question, some business education programs are scrutinized because of enrollment trends. And when a pattern of declining enrollments is evident, educational policy makers are quick to examine the relative contribution of a program when allocating resources. Many traditional business education programs, most notably vocational programs at the secondary level, have experienced enrollment declines or shifts away from specific courses or programs. When this occurs, program effectiveness is challenged and a negative image may persist. The vitality of business education, in part, rests on the belief that our programs are needed, relevant, and attractive to students. In a time when our discipline must compete with other courses or programs, maintaining enrollment stability becomes even more difficult.

A significant challenge, therefore, is to develop appropriate strategies to maintain and/or increase enrollments. Many of the strategies included in the following chapters can be of significant help in achieving this goal.

Integration with other disciplines. Through its course content and program goals, the field of business education is linked with other disciplines. The areas of business communication, math, and English, for example, interact with courses taught in other content areas by other departments. Further areas of overlap may be found in consumer economics, data processing, and keyboarding. This linkage represents both a challenge and an opportunity. A challenge is present because of the competition for students, for control over course content and staffing, and over resource allocation. Business education, in order to enhance its credibility and visibility, must seek out the boundaries of the discipline and obtain a degree of excellence within this boundary.

The opportunity to build greater integration and increased coordination with other disciplines is evident. Through working with other departments, sharing goals, and developing curriculum that integrates business education concepts with other content areas, this opportunity can be realized.

Program acceptance and professionalism. The public image of most programs is established in the mission and value of the program, and in the quality of the personnel responsible for the program. Program acceptance in business education is an important goal, not only within the school setting but also externally. A positive image can help in many ways: recruiting students, obtaining resources, developing curriculum, motivating staff, and achieving goals.

Building on the strength of our current degree of professionalism is the challenge to be addressed. Continued efforts are needed to communicate the value and successes of business education to others outside of our field. Greater professionalism—as viewed by administrators and the public—can only be achieved through the process of building quality programs, strengthening staff development, and working toward excellence in every respect.

Curriculum and teaching innovations. The current trends in information technology and office systems have affected business education significantly. As mentioned earlier in this chapter, these trends have required our profession to reevaluate program goals and course content along with reexamining how we should be teaching. Traditional programs need to be phased into emerging technological areas, reflecting the knowledges and skills other institutions and employers wish our students to have. Concurrently, our curriculum will need to contain those core content areas expected of all students for personal and career development.

The issue is one of constant evaluation and change. No longer can business education proceed in a "business as usual" fashion and yet respond appropriately to the societal, institutional, and pedagogical thrusts being forced upon it. Program and curriculum development must reflect the most current information technology, but still retain those areas in which our profession has the expertise and society demands. There are many content areas in which business education has assumed a proper leadership role and can continue to do so—as long as quality is maintained.

The focus of curriculum changes is, of necessity, one in which evaluation must occur on what is taught and how it is taught. Innovations in teaching are occurring constantly, and business education has long been a leader in implementing these innovations. There is every reason to assume that additional changes will be forthcoming, perhaps at even a faster rate than we have already experienced. Our profession can meet this challenge through remaining current, evaluating our goals/programs/courses, and being open to change and renewal.

Broadening the student base. Business education can achieve growth through expanding the curriculum to meet the needs of students at different age levels or in nontraditional areas. For example, students in the elementary and middle school levels can be served by providing courses in typing/keyboarding, computer applications, word processing, and others. This area represents a major opportunity for expansion as students at the K-8 level are encouraged or directed to develop information processing skills as part of their development.

At the secondary level, business education can expand its base through providing learning experiences for students in non-business curriculums, especially those in a college preparatory program. The knowledges and skills taught in many business education classes are applicable for students regardless of their personal or career development plan. Several states, in their recent research into the number and type of courses offered at the secondary level, report the courses currently most popular are those enrolled heavily by non-business education students.

Another opportunity for growth rests in developing courses and programs for adult or nontraditional learners. Employees or individuals wishing to enter the business field and have a need to develop additional skills or keep up to date on information technology could be served by business education.

Implementing research findings. The body of knowledge in any profession is constantly being updated as a result of new information or technology advances. In many ways the vitality of a profession is reflected in how well the profession seeks out this new information and uses it. Business education is no different; the discipline must continue to study emerging trends and conduct research to improve efficiency and effectiveness. Research can be a powerful change agent as it reveals the need for change and presents evidence in a factual, analytical manner.

The degree to which research is used in business education to effect change represents a significant challenge. During the last several years, a number of national studies have pointed out actions business education could take to maximize its effectiveness and success. However, the research is only of value when used by teachers and administrators in formulating change or innovation. For change to occur, an openness and degree of flexibility must be present among business educators.

Another important aspect is the profession's willingness to keep current on research studies and conduct research projects when appropriate. Participation in professional development activities—workshops, seminars, conventions—is necessary to learn new ideas and share concepts with other professionals. The information gained from these development activities can help in conducting research or implementing recommendations from other studies.

Developing a coordinated plan of action. Because of the diversity in business education, it is sometimes difficult to obtain common agreement on our mission or how to progress toward building excellence in our programs or courses. The profession has, in some cases, been fractionized based on vocational vs. nonvocational interests, skills vs. content courses emphasis, or secondary vs. postsecondary focus, to name a few.

In a time when business education needs to respond in a collective manner to obtain community, institutional, and political support, having a comprehensive philosophy is critical. The mission of the profession can be best served when there exists a common belief among professionals—which creates a feeling of direction, commitment, and purposeful behavior. Business education teachers, administrators, professional organizations, student organizations, and support personnel must develop this coordinated plan of action if maximum success is to be achieved.

SUMMARY

As the title of this chapter denotes, there is a degree of uncertainty today in both education in general and in business education. The challenges given in this chapter represent some of the reasons for this uncertainty. However, with every challenge there can be an opportunity. Through examining these challenges a set of strategies can be developed and implemented to guide business education toward greater excellence.

The task is very clear: business education's strength and vitality will only continue when strategies are pursued to build a future foundation for professionalism in every respect.

Part II
STRATEGIES FOR ASSERTING AND REASSERTING

CHAPTER 4

Communicating with the Constituencies of Business Education

JOHN GUMP, MYRENA JENNINGS, and JO NELL JONES

Eastern Kentucky University, Richmond

Communication between business educators and their constituencies is essential for the continued development of business education. The primary ingredients of effective communication are working together, sharing resources, sharing ideas, developing common priorities, coordinating plans, learning from one another, reducing duplication, and avoiding working at cross-purposes. With the limited resources available today, communication is essential.

Business educators traditionally have communicated effectively among themselves through professional organizations, meetings, and publications. But communicating within the profession is not enough. Business education has many other constituencies who should be included in the communication network. The constituencies of business education are (1) internal constituencies—administrators and guidance counselors, faculty, and students; (2) external educational constituencies—elementary and secondary schools, technical and vocational institutes, community and junior colleges, and four-year colleges and universities; (3) governing constituencies—school boards, state departments of education, and legislators and governors; and (4) business and community constituencies—business and industry, community and professional organizations, and parents and alumni groups.

The purpose of this chapter is to identify and discuss strategies for communicating with the various constituencies of business education. Because a single strategy seldom accomplishes a goal, communication with these groups must be planned and consistent. Communication that is planned assures that all constituencies will be included.

COMMUNICATING WITH INTERNAL CONSTITUENCIES

Business educators communicate with three basic groups of internal constituencies—administrators and counselors, other teachers, and students. While some communication strategies with internal constituencies will be highly personalized, other strategies are also required to enhance or support the personalized communication. Personalized messages to the appropriate administrator (dean, department head, principal, guidance counselor), teacher, and student might be interesting and helpful; but more formalized strategies could also be necessary.

To be able to support a business program, the internal constituencies must be informed about the goals of the department, the achievement of the program and the students, and the course offerings. A series of well-planned strategies might be required to convince the administrators, counselors, other teachers, and students of the goals. Some strategies are useful for communicating with all internal constituencies. The following strategies are especially appropriate when communicating with administrators, counselors, and other teachers:

- Show proof of the business education courses which include the basic survival skills, and show this proof in writing, on video, and/or through personal testimony from students.
- Provide copies of and interpret the statements of the Policies Commission for Business and Economic Education.
- In subject area where curriculum changes are requested, show need for employment. Utilize current government reports such as those from the Department of Labor, Bureau of Labor Statistics, and current newspaper advertisements for projected manpower needs.
- Be flexible in adjusting to new names for courses for the traditional and the nontraditional business education programs—computerized shorthand, computerized accounting, keyboarding, communication for business and nonbusiness students.
- Be flexible and recognize time constraints with length of courses and with scheduling to avoid conflicts.
- Establish a regular meeting time and place to bring new ideas, to evaluate, and to reevaluate curriculum. Listen, take notes, and follow up on questions and/or suggestions.
- Phrase all communication positively. For example, instead of "Only 80 percent . . .," say "Eighty percent. . . ."
- Brag about and be proud of your students and their achievements. Share student ACT, SAT, and other scores (use group numbers and percentages, not individual scores) to indicate the level of students, especially when the scores are above average.
- Invite administrators and counselors to participate in field trips.
- Share a video of an open house, a field trip, and/or a special class activity.
- Promote a professional image of students. Utilize one day each semester for students to demonstrate their ability to dress for success by asking the students to dress for a job interview, for a business meeting, or for a typical work day. This activity provides an opportunity for discussion and critiquing. Advertise this day well in advance so that all school personnel can appreciate the students' efforts.
- Participate in other departments' and other schoolwide activities to show your cooperation and school spirit.
- Speak and dress like a professional business educator and leader. Other teachers and administrators, as well as students, respect professional opinions that are expressed clearly, courteously, coherently, and correctly when those opinions come from educators who look like professionals.

- Share equipment with other departments.
- Show willingness to teach new topics and new courses to traditional and nontraditional students.
- Utilize school newspapers and bulletin boards to report activities.

In addition, these strategies are effective when communicating with and about business students:

- Announce, present, and recognize student awards, certificates, and honors in an open forum. Place the awards in an academic trophy case or in a high profile area.
- Work with student business organizations such as Future Business Leaders of America, Business Professionals of America, Distributive Education Clubs of America, Phi Beta Lambda, and Pi Omega Pi.
- Utilize students in business organizations as guides or ushers for special school events—graduation, assemblies, athletic events, and alumni functions.
- Offer minicourses to assist the nontraditional or the nonbusiness student to gain special skills and knowledges.
- Request that students be given the opportunity to learn and practice office skills by working in the school system—answering telephones, keyboarding, filing, and calculating.
- Provide students an opportunity to converse with special guests on a one-to-one basis. Specifically, students can (a) be at the parking lot to ensure that the speaker has an approved visitor's permit, (b) help carry supplies, (c) direct the way to the classroom, (d) assist in the setup and takedown for the speaker's presentation, (e) introduce the speaker, or (f) escort the speaker back to the parking lot and car.
- Be friendly but not familiar. Students need a professional who can be objective, knowledgeable, and kind—not a pal.
- Establish homework clubs. At the secondary level, selected and approved students can assist younger students at the middle or elementary school in reading comprehension, vocabulary, mathematics, and grammar. Also the upper division students in the four-year colleges and universities can assist freshman and sophomore students in specialized or basic skill courses. This program is somewhat like shadowing or big brother, big sister clubs. These homework clubs provide younger students with good role models and provide excellent recruiting opportunities for the business education program.

COMMUNICATING WITH EXTERNAL EDUCATIONAL CONSTITUENCIES

Business educators also communicate with a number of external constituencies—educational, governing, business and community. This section discusses communication strategies with external educational constituencies such as elementary and secondary schools, technical and vocational institutes, community and junior colleges, and four-year colleges and universities. Although they are both public and private, these educational institutions have similar external communication needs to maintain and to improve their curriculums. The external communications are primarily vertical, although they can also be lateral.

Some of these strategies for communicating with external educational constituencies are traditional and well used; some are very new, using the newest technology:

- Access information on students, curriculums, and/or computer software through electronic networking, electronic mail, and electronic bulletin boards. Many educational constituencies have access to electronic networks at the local, state, regional, and national levels.
- Establish a regional articulation plan for transfer of credit, including cross-references for other majors.
- Join professional education organizations and participate in leadership development programs. Some of these organizations include National Business Education Association, American Vocational Association, Association for Business Communication, Delta Pi Epsilon, and Phi Delta Kappa.
- Interact with other educators at professional business education meetings at the local, state, regional, and national level.
- Write for publication in business education and other educational periodicals with colleagues at different educational levels. Even unpublished work strengthens the business educator's knowledge, confidence, and awareness—thus a better business educator emerges.
- Accept leadership positions in subject areas and in local, state, regional, and national professional organizations.
- Give recognition for outstanding service, teaching, and research that makes a contribution to business education programs.
- Participate in teacher exchange programs or teacher loan programs where postsecondary business educators exchange time and workplace with a secondary business educator. Teacher exchange and loan programs provide excellent opportunities for articulation of curriculum, motivation, goodwill, and recruiting of students.
- Participate in classroom and curriculum-related research, both laterally and vertically.
- Sponsor contests for students at lower or comparable levels of the educational institution. Provide incentive prizes such as free tuition for a course or semester, reference books, computer software, office and school supplies, gift certificates, or money (cash or savings bonds).
- Print and circulate brochures, booklets, or flyers advertising and explaining specific business education programs.
- Work with elementary and middle school teachers in developing keyboarding and other business-related courses or topics.
- Develop and accept competency tests for skills and knowledges obtained at other educational institutions.
- Provide a series of mailings about business education topics to be sent to other business educators in the state or region.

COMMUNICATING WITH GOVERNING CONSTITUENCIES

At every level of policymaking and governance from the local school board to the national Congress, nearly every decision that affects education is a political one. Business educators can influence the direction of business education by communicating with political constituencies. This section will focus on communicating with the local school boards, state departments of education, and legislators and governors.

Business educators have a responsibility to communicate jointly or individually with these governing constituencies. Not to do so creates great risks. Recent political decisions as a result of reports such as *A Nation at Risk* and *High School: A Report on Secondary Education in America* have critically affected business education at all levels. So important have political constituents become that the Policies Commission for Business and Economic Education believes that business educators must consider legislation and the legislative process a major concern to be addressed.

School boards. School boards make decisions that are crucial to business educators. It is the school board that appropriates funds, approves budgets, and provides facilities. Because the educational backgrounds of school board members are likely to be other than business education, members may not understand completely the business education program, the curriculum, or the goals. Communicating with the school board means more than asking for funds. Communicating also means providing the board with information about the program and the accomplishments of the students and listening to and understanding the decisions of the board. The following communication strategies will assist the board to become a more knowledgeable partner of business education:

- Get to know the members of the school board, and if possible, attend the board meetings at regular intervals.
- Request approval from the administration for placing a presentation on the agenda of a meeting of the school board. This presentation could include other constituencies—students and graduates—or it could include video or documentation.
- Invite board members to visit the school to tour the business department and/or to see a special activity in action.
- Ask board members to complete an evaluation form of the business program based on the presentation and/or tour of the business department. Not only will the evaluation provide feedback, but it will also provide the board members an opportunity to think actively about the program and to contribute to the structure of the program.
- Prepare and send a document to the board illustrating how business courses integrate and reinforce basic skills. In this period of educational reform with emphasis on basic skills, board members welcome methods to help students improve in the basic areas.
- Prepare and send board members a document about the career opportunities that business education provides. Because board members may be business persons too, they should be interested in having an effective local work force. Use articles from the newspapers, magazines, and business education journals and statistics from the Department of Labor and the Bureau of Labor Statistics to support your statements. Current information is convincing.
- Distribute to board members the results of a follow-up survey of business

graduates. Capitalize on the successes and on the high placement and/or promotion rate of the graduates.
- Invite board members to attend activities honoring employers of cooperative education students, advisory boards, and the like. Ask a board representative to extend greetings.
- Invite board members to tour student cooperative education sites.

State departments of education. Both state departments of education and business educators share in the responsibility of communicating. State departments of education have many responsibilities to communicate with educators including (1) distributing curriculum designs and resource information; (2) providing materials and information about such topics as working with advisory committees, developing a public relations program, working with student organizations, identifying employment opportunities in office and marketing occupations, developing program standards, and the like; and (3) informing educators of the decisions of pertinent committees related to business and vocational education.

However, insuring the improvement and growth of business and vocational education must be a team effort. As part of the team, business educators may use the following strategies for communicating with state departments:
- Request information about bills that will have an impact on business and vocational education, about membership of special committees related to education, about names of people to contact about special issues, and about suggestions for means to communicate with state legislators.
- Show a willingness to serve on advisory committees.
- Keep in touch with appropriate state education officers. New state and federal laws may create changes in programs and funding.
- Obtain a copy of any new laws, since state departments interpret and determine the types of programs that will meet the new guidelines. Business educators who have unique knowledge of local programs and resources of which state officials may not be aware can then be better able to anticipate and plan for changes rather than to react to the changes.
- Inquire about opportunities for writing proposals which provide possibilities for funding, for curriculum development, and for policymaking.
- Talk with other state agencies dealing with special education, adult education, manpower education, and sex equity. The Carl Perkins Vocational Education Act specifically relates these areas to vocational education more strongly than previous legislation has provided.

Legislators and governors. Governors and legislators at both the state and national levels spend much of their time seeking information from informed and credible sources to help them make decisions. Because business educators are knowledgeable and skilled in communicating, they are credible sources. Communicating with political constituents is an opportunity for business educators to inform, to learn, and to listen. The Policies Commission for Business and Economic Education states that business educators must become actively involved in developing positive relations with their legislators and that "these relationships should provide opportunities to—

- explain the goals and purposes of business education
- enumerate the benefits of business education to the students and to the community
- cite the contributions of business education to the economy
- describe the needs of business education and suggest ways of meeting them
- seek support on legislative issues
- influence educational policy."[1]

The following are some specific strategies that may be used for communicating with legislators:

- Get to know the district representative. That person, even if not on key committees, can provide information about those who are. Furthermore, the business educator may wish to seek the representative's support on some issue in the future.
- Identify the legislators who affect educational policies. If possible, learn something about their backgrounds. Learning about them will help to establish some common ground.
- Make an initial contact with the selected legislators on a businesslike basis. Identify yourself and your professional status both verbally and in writing. Let legislators know that business educators are interested in the welfare of the education program. Be willing to listen to their opinions about education—especially business education—policies.
- Establish some form of regular contact with these legislators. However, appreciate the time constraints of both legislators and their staffs.
- Invite appropriate legislators to the school, the department, or the classroom to speak to students and to become more familiar with the program and activities.
- Stay abreast of the political activities of the selected legislators, and use that information to show interest in them.
- Contact the legislators and express positions when education issues are being discussed. If it is appropriate, propose a solution. Supplement oral presentation with written material. Whenever possible, support positions with facts and figures; they are persuasive.
- Write appreciation letters to legislators to acknowledge their consideration and/or action.
- Make reasonable requests of legislators. Expect and accept reasonable compromise.
- Use good human relations. Never demand a commitment or threaten a legislator or a staff person. Legislators react to many conflicting pressure groups and usually cannot make a commitment until all information has been studied.
- Offer to help the legislator by providing information; build a working relationship.
- Maintain detailed documentation about the business education program and its accomplishments, and be ready to provide specific information to the appropriate legislators.
- Do not give up if you lose on an issue.
- Join political action committees (PAC's) or support lobbying efforts of professional organizations. Support and encourage coalitions that share an interest in business

---

[1]Policies Commission for Business and Economic Education. "This We Believe About the Role of Business Educators in Influencing Legislation." *Business Education Forum* 41:13; October 1986.

and vocational education. While the individual effort of one business educator is important, legislators are usually more impressed when an entire educational group or coalition supports a particular piece of legislation.
- Support legislators through a personal campaign contribution or contribution to the appropriate PAC when possible.

Often in the past, the relationship between the governor and educational associations consisted of legislative program presentations to the governor or the governor's staff or an occasional speech by the governor to an educational association. Now, however, many governors realize they can benefit from the experience and expertise of educators and seek information and suggestions. They have seen that education and economic growth are directly related.

Many of the same strategies for communicating with legislators may be used for communicating with governors. In addition, business educators may wish to consider the following in planning their communication strategy with governors:

- Focus on results. Because governors have limited time to achieve results, they prefer concrete suggestions.
- Support education initiatives from the governor. Governors are constantly looking for allies who will help them build support for new ideas among the public, the media, and the state legislature.
- Understand that governors generally will not support actions that require large budget or tax increases unless measurable results will occur.
- Utilize the link between economic development and an educated, skilled work force.

COMMUNICATING WITH BUSINESS AND COMMUNITY CONSTITUENCIES

The link between business education and the business community is indisputable. Business and industry need skilled and knowledgeable employees, and business education exists to supply those employees. Furthermore, a solid link between parents and the educational system must be formed if students are to reach their full potential. Regular and planned communication with business, parents, and other community groups improves the image of business education and the morale of the teachers. This communication keeps teachers abreast of the latest office technology, the labor needs of business, and the qualifications for employment. It also informs these constituencies of the educational programs and the educational needs and opens the doors for job opportunities for business graduates. Specific strategies will be discussed in this section for establishing and maintaining effective communication with business and industry, professional and community organizations, and parents and alumni groups. In addition, news media personnel are included since some form of the news media is frequently used to transmit the communication between business educators and each of their constituencies.

Business and industry. Formal school/business partnerships have been established in some big city school districts where large corporations are located. Through these partnerships, businesses have delivered needed services to schools, provided cash contributions, built reservoirs of understanding and support for the educational staff, and even worked for more tax support for the schools. Some smaller school districts use an arrangement called adopt-a-school program where a specific company is paired with a specific school. These types of school/business alliances are most successful when they involve an exchange of human resources and services. Schools should not emphasize the materialistic approach, even though cash contributions or equipment subsidies may follow once a trusting relationship has been established. Business and industry feel comfortable to offer assistance in the areas they know best, for example, food service, payroll processing, security, public relations, auditing, and budgeting.

School/business partnerships and adopt-a-school programs sometimes evolve into associations for specific short-term or one-time projects. Through these projects, schools and businesses interact on a more limited basis; but these associations help strengthen the channel of communication between the school and the business community. The project approach is possible for all business departments to consider, even those in schools without formal school/business partnerships. Below are some strategies that may be used for communicating with business and industry.

- Establish a businessperson of the week (or month) program. A business educator might invite a personnel director, secretary, legal assistant, manager, or other employee to school for lunch and informal discussion with a small group of students and faculty.
- Utilize advisory committees. These committees should be composed of business and industry leaders, business education faculty, guidance counselors, principals, and nonvocational faculty. Regular and planned round table meetings help business educators promote the general education value of business courses as well as the specialized skills. Advisory committees also provide information to strengthen existing programs and establish new programs or courses to meet the needs of all students.
- Conduct business research. Businesses may contract with business educators and/or students to conduct consumer research. In addition, educators may conduct research to determine current hiring practices, employment needs, or equipment usage. Through research business educators establish contact with businesses and show that they are staying up to date with technology and business needs.
- Incorporate student work-experience programs. These programs may be offered as internships or under cooperative office education. Through the business supervisor's evaluation of the student worker's performance, a business educator obtains feedback about the student's training and the relevancy of the educational curriculum.
- Participate in faculty/employee exchange programs. In one day the participants gain first-hand knowledge of the other person's work. Business employees become more aware of the needs and problems encountered in the classroom. Likewise, the faculty members can participate in the actual business work and relate it to the curriculum.

- Utilize business volunteers. These volunteers may assist in specialized instruction, demonstrate equipment operation, or speak to classes or student groups. Representatives from business are excellent positive role models for students.
- Offer minicourses. Saturday or evening minicourses may be offered at a computer sales center or other large business for teachers or students who have no access to hands-on experience with computers or word processing equipment in the classroom.
- Participate in summer employment. Business educators benefit from some full-time experience in the business environment to enhance their teaching and to keep the curriculum up to date.
- Organize field trips. Trips to businesses allow teachers and students to observe operations and to view the latest equipment and technology.
- Utilize videotapes. These visuals of office equipment and business personnel in action may be used as alternatives to field trips and help supplement classroom discussion.
- Establish employment centers. These centers help match qualified graduates with job openings.

Most of the above strategies involve services offered by individuals. After businesses and industries become aware of the facilities of local schools, they frequently make cash contributions toward the purchase of equipment or toward a needed improvement, or they sponsor awards for contests or high achievement. With this financial assistance business education departments have been able to equip computer laboratories; conduct Business Teacher-of-the-Year contests; offer scholarships to deserving graduates; send students to regional, state, and national meetings of student organizations; obtain certificates and prizes for student contests; and fund consumer and educational research. With effective communication, business and education can be partners in the training of future employees and consumers.

Professional and community organizations. Professional business organizations give educators the opportunity to meet and interact with practitioners in business and office occupations. Through membership and active participation in associations such as Professional Secretaries International, the Association of Records Managers and Administrators, Data Processing Management Association, American Management Association, or any of the other specialized associations, business educators learn about current business practices and technology. Communication abounds through the various publications of these associations and at conferences and conventions where members meet to exchange ideas, concerns, and solutions to problems.

Local business, service, or community organizations such as Lion's Club, Kiwanis, Rotary, and Business and Professional Women's Club provide other opportunities for interaction between educators and the community and between students and the community. The members of these groups are often involved with the business community; therefore, they are interested in the educational programs which prepare students for employment in the business sector. Business educators who are participating members in one or more of these groups are able to establish a communication network with these community leaders. Even without membership in an organization, business educators may volunteer to speak to service clubs about their specialty areas or on topics of interest to the general membership, such as protecting rights of consumers or changes in ergonomics.

Students and student organizations can also offer many services to local community groups, especially charitable organizations such as United Way, March of Dimes, and Rescue Squad. These services may capitalize upon human relation skills as well as business skills and may be offered weekends, after school, during a student's free time, or as part of one or more classes. Examples of these services are (1) answering telephones during a telethon; (2) preparing a large mailing; (3) typing newsletters; (4) campaigning and canvassing door to door for charitable contributions; (5) distributing books and magazines to prisoners or nursing home residents; (6) playing games and performing skits at hospitals, nursing homes, or day care centers; (7) visiting and doing grocery shopping for shut-ins and senior citizens; and (8) adopting a needy family. These service activities get the business students into the community; bring attention to their programs; and show that the students are skilled, conscientious, civic-minded, and capable of doing good work.

Parents and alumni groups. Studies show that parents want to be kept informed of their children's progress and of educational policies and procedures. Parents prefer direct, personal contact with educators, for example, scheduled parent/teacher conferences, personal visits to schools, teacher notes or telephone calls, meet-the-teacher nights or school open houses, school newsletters, and report cards.

Other strategies for communicating with parents and alumni groups that have been successful include the following:

- Operate a miniclassroom in a shopping mall so that parents, alumni, and others can see school in action without going to the school building.
- Display student work in public places such as restaurants and libraries.
- Establish a "people library." Identify parents, alumni, or others in the community who can be used as guest speakers, volunteer aides, or personal learning resources for students.
- Initiate a Swap Day. Parents or "borrowed" adults from the community attend classes for the day while students stay home.
- Organize a specialized parent/teacher group to support the business department. The goal of this group would be to promote excellence in the business curriculum.
- Establish an advocacy group consisting of parents and alumni to promote the business education curriculum.
- Send letters to parents highlighting business education activities and student accomplishments.
- Establish an alumni foundation. These foundations are common at the postsecondary level and are also possible at the secondary level.
- Invite alumni to become members of an Ambassadors Program to serve as ambassadors of the school in the business community.
- Schedule a special meeting time and place for former business students who are attending class reunions. Alumni enjoy returning to the school, seeing the changes

that have taken place, and talking with former faculty and other business graduates.

News media personnel. Finally, business educators use the news media as one way to communicate with their external constituencies. News releases keep the name of the department in the public eye. Announcements or feature articles are used to report activities, to discuss new courses or programs, to describe success stories, to explain departmental needs, and to increase enrollments in a course or program. Thus, business educators should remember to utilize the news media when communicating with their external constituencies.

SUMMARY

Business education constituencies consist of internal and external educational groups such as administrators, other teachers, students, and educators at other institutions and other levels of education; governing bodies such as school boards, state departments of education, legislators, and governors; and business and community groups which include the business and industry segments, community and professional organizations, and parents and alumni. The primary ingredients of effective communications are well-planned and consistent messages which present business educators as knowledgeable, cooperative, and caring about meeting the needs of their constituencies.

Communication means action, and business educators who are communicating are actively listening and interacting with their constituencies. Business educators should be attending and speaking at professional meetings; conducting research and sharing the results with other educators, legislators, and business leaders; interacting with legislators at political forums; exchanging ideas with business leaders, administrators, and other teachers at advisory committee meetings; and informing parents and students about the business programs. Business educators need to share with, listen to, and learn from their constituencies.

CHAPTER 5

Marketing the Entire Business Education Curriculum

MARRIETT J. MCQUEEN
Austin Peay State University, Clarksville, Tennessee

Business as usual? Hardly! Business education is being bombarded by change as never before. But the same changes that impact business education also impact every organization—both profit-oriented businesses and nonprofit oriented. These changes have brought about new products and services and new marketing strategies to increase the number of customers who will avail themselves of the products and services.

Just name a company or organization which is experiencing success. The awareness of that company's products or services resulted from a successful promotional strategy. No organization that has a product or service to offer would consider eliminating its marketing activities. Successful promotional strategies result from well-developed marketing plans; thus business educators would do well to examine the elements of marketing plans which have led to marketing success.

Marketing activities to promote the entire business education curriculum must be developed around the value and benefits of business education. Simply having a strong program does not guarantee success. However, adopting marketing strategies which have been successful for both profit and nonprofit organizations can generate a renewed interest in business education.

THE MARKETING MIX MUST BE CONSIDERED

The components of marketing, generally referred to as the marketing mix, are *product, place, price, promotion,* and *people.* The assumption of this study is that the successful marketing of the business education program will happen only when the marketing mix is considered in terms of the effects of a changing environment. The elements of change focused on are the declining population of high school and college-age young people, increasing requirements for college entry, the renewed emphasis on liberal arts, the changes in the workplace brought about by the impact of computers, the continued demand for office workers, the continued increase in skill levels needed for office work, the training needs of business and industry, and the need for basic business skills to function intelligently in an information society.

The *product*, business education, traditionally has been the most popular elective in the high school curriculum. Marketing specialists generally define a product as something that has benefits, physical features, and services which are designed to satisfy the needs of people or a market. A description of the product, business education, would be a group of courses with a twofold purpose—developing marketable skills and providing knowledge needed to function as a citizen or consumer in a market-oriented economy. Certainly the benefits have always been obvious—hence the popularity of business education as an elective. The benefits to students are preparation for living and earning a living, and the benefit to the employer is having a well-trained employee. The physical features are identified in the titles of the courses making up the curriculum. Today, the physical features of business education programs are less well defined because of the impact of technology and the ability of the individual school to make adjustments in the curriculum.

Teachers and administrators have been faced with the development of a new product in order to respond to environmental changes and to protect the image enjoyed by business education. In describing the product, business education, the points listed by the American Vocational Association to describe the image of vocational education are fitting:

1. It is educational.
2. It is professional.
3. It opens options for young people in careers, in educational enrichment, and in learning styles.
4. It is a good way to test an interest.
5. It is a good precollege program.
6. It is a good way to finance college.
7. It is challenging.
8. It is exciting.
9. It is socially desirable.
10. It is vital to our economy.[1]

The well-designed marketing strategy for business education will have these 10 points as its basis.

Place as an element of the marketing mix suggests that business education must be conveniently located and must be available to all students who want it, when they want it. Business education programs have long been a part of the high school curriculum as well as two-year and four-year college programs. Changes in the environment suggest new opportunities for offering business education in nontraditional settings and mandate deviations from traditional ways of making the product available to changing customers.

What are the *price* questions that must be considered in marketing business education? Currently students are asking if their time is better spent enrolling only in academic courses; some employers have even suggested that voca-

---

[1]Brodhead, Charles W.; Cogan, Howard S.; and Sharp, Deede. *Achieving a Desired Image in Vocational Education Resource Guide.* Alexandria, Va.: American Vocational Association, 1985. p. 11.

tional business skills can best be developed by business and industry. Return on investment is a measure of value, thus the value of business education is determined by the results of having enrolled in it. Lynch suggests that psychological pricing may be the greatest barrier to enrollment in business education.[2] The price decision is based on what is given up in order to take business education courses.

The *promotion* of business education competes for the prospective student's attention at a time when young people are bombarded with messages. Promotion is synonymous with communications. Thus to communicate effectively, business educators must be result oriented; that is, goals for the promotional strategy should be measurable and should dictate the blend of activities which will be used to communicate the benefits of business education to prospective students, parents, and administrators.

The *people* element of business education obviously includes teachers who teach the classes, students who enroll in the classes, and administrators who oversee the business education programs in various settings. People involved in business education also include employers who prefer well-trained employees and parents who want the best programs for their children. Today parents are insisting on having their questions answered and want to know the value of any course in a child's educational program. Likewise, the community (who pays the bill for education) is demanding accountability. Each audience must be considered in the marketing strategy for business education.

ENVIRONMENT IMPACTS MARKETING STRATEGY

In order to successfully market business education, teachers must develop a clear concept of the factors brought about by environmental change which affect it. Minimizing the importance of these factors may very well sound the death knell for the business education program.

Declining number of young people. The "baby bust" is impacting secondary business education programs and will shortly impact postsecondary programs. The *Chronicle of Higher Education* predicted that by 1995 the number of traditional college-age students would decline by 25 percent. Obviously the declining high school population means fewer high school students available to enroll in the business education program. Employers have already recognized the impact on the availability of entry-level workers and are mapping out strategies for ensuring their access to a sufficient number of qualified entry-level workers. Retailing establishments, fast-food restaurants, grocery stores, and other industries which have depended heavily on young people for both part-time and full-time jobs are finding themselves affected by the drop in the teenage population.

But, to the teenage population, this is a very positive phenomenon; the scarcity of young people means more individual opportunity for those who develop skills needed for success in the business world. The message to these

---

[2]Lynch, Richard. *Marketing Your Business Program.* Atlanta: Gregg Division/McGraw-Hill Book Co., 1986. p. 37.

young people is that business education does develop skills needed for success whether employment is sought immediately after high school or whether the goal is a college education. Students must be made aware of the opportunities provided through business education instruction which prepare them for employment.

Collegiate business training enjoys unprecedented popularity; approximately one-fourth of the baccalaureate degrees granted are in some area of business. However, the discipline of business education does not always share this success. In many areas, the employment market demand is very high for those with business and office education preparation, yet enrollments are declining. Thus, both high school business education programs and business education at the collegiate level must be creative in designing a marketing strategy to attract sufficient numbers of the declining youth population into programs which provide the training for the occupational cluster which continues to have the most opportunity for entry-level employment.

Increasing requirements for college entry. American education is still reeling from the report, *A Nation at Risk*, and other such studies which rebuked the inadequacies of education in America. Consequently, not only is business education impacted by a declining population of youth, but young people today are facing more rigid requirements in the high school curriculum in order to enter college. Many educators do not see business education as being important to preparation for college entry. As an elective subject, business education has had to redesign programs. The result has been that those students who do elect to enroll in business education spend far less time in these classes than their counterparts did a few years ago. Today, as never before, the value to the student enrolling in business education courses must be communicated as part of the marketing strategy. Charles Brodhead, a marketing specialist, suggests several messages which should be communicated to students, parents, counselors, employers, and other teachers:

1. Business education students are able to obtain good jobs upon graduation from high school.
2. Business education classes are fun, relevant, and exciting.
3. Business education graduates find out early what they want to do in life.
4. Business education can enrich a college-bound student's background.
5. Business education teaches basic skills in the context of career interest.
6. The business education graduate has greater wage-earning potential to pay college expenses.
7. Business education trains people for in-demand jobs.
8. In many cases, the academic grades of students improve when enrolling in business education classes.
9. Many of the employment skills and attitudes developed through participation in business education are transferrable to the universal workplace.
10. Business education offers an opportunity to many students to develop leadership skills.[3]

---

[3]Brodhead, Cogan, and Sharp, *op. cit.*, p. 6.

The percentage of jobs requiring training beyond the high school level is increasing. Thus the value of business education at the high school level for the college-bound student must be stressed. Likewise, opportunities for higher level employment available to students who pursue collegiate and postsecondary business education programs must be communicated. At the same time, the opportunities to provide training to nontraditional learners must be seized if business education is to remain viable in a changing world.

Renewed emphasis on the liberal arts. The criticism that both high schools and colleges are graduating students with poor communication skills is accompanied by an increased awareness of the importance of liberal arts studies in preparing for a career. According to the *Chronicle of Higher Education,* liberal arts graduates in 1986 enjoyed a 28 percent increase in employment opportunities, while students who held degrees in specialized areas met declining employment opportunities. Daniel R. DeNicola, provost of Rollins College, noted that both large and small businesses thrive when employees are talented, committed, and possess the ability to learn.[4] Without question, the ability to read well and write well is a must for success in business occupations. However, businesses need employees who can imagine; who can recognize, define, and analyze a problem; who can research and synthesize solutions; and who can present and evaluate results effectively. Perhaps the key to success in today's changing world is the ability of the employee to learn new things in order to adapt to change. DeNicola notes further that one fundamental missing from the job description is a "liberal" education.[5]

Are these characteristics for success developed only through a "liberal" education? The enhancement of basic skills is a component of basic and vocational business education courses which are traditionally a part of the high school curriculum. Collegiate business education requires a liberal arts core which comprises 50 to 60 percent of the baccalaureate requirements. Thus a message which business educators must communicate to fellow educators, administrators, students, and employers is that business education is not just a narrow sort of training. Furthermore, the business education curriculum and course content must be modified so that the demands of employers which have been mentioned will be met.

The changing workplace. No invention parallels the computer for its impact on the way work is done. Literacy no longer refers to reading and writing; literacy also includes the ability to operate a computer and to understand robotics. Another dimension added to the definition of literacy is to learn, unlearn, and relearn. Chester Delaney, vice-president for system human resources at Chase Manhattan Bank, in an address at the 1988 annual meeting of the Office Systems Research Association, noted a number of factors that emphasize continued change in the workplace. For example, for the person who is 50 years old in the year 2030 (born in 1980), 97 percent of what is known will have been discovered in his or her lifetime. Burford and Wilson

---

[4]DeNicola, Daniel R. "Liberal Arts and Business." *Nation's Business* 74:4; March 1986.

[5]*Ibid.*

noted that in 1984, 60 percent of the work force was employed in information processing and that the number was predicted to increase to 80 percent by 1990.[6] They wrote of the applications of artificial intelligence in decision-making processes which can be routinized and noted processes in the office for which artificial intelligence will be useful.

These facts support the notion that if business education is to survive it must be relevant. Thus, business educators must sell to administrators and school boards the needs for relevancy—the need for the business education curriculum to be based on up-to-date knowledge, skills, and attitudes which are identified for success in the business environment. Business educators must maintain a liaison with employers in order to know which skills students should have when leaving high school or college programs and which skills should be reserved for on-the-job training.

Continued demand for office workers. Perhaps the key message of any marketing strategy developed by business educators is the abundance of job opportunities for office workers. According to the Bureau of Labor Statistics, office workers account for 65 percent of the total work force in the United States; this labor force is growing at a rate of 1.3 million a year. Furthermore, the Bureau also predicts a continued increase in the employment of secretaries. While business education does serve a general education role, preparation for gainful employment has always been considered the primary objective. Clearly, those students who select programs of study for vocational purposes want assurance of job opportunities. Business education teachers should create a marketing message emphasizing the demand for office workers as a central theme.

Because of the shortage in the teenage population, many office jobs in the near future will be filled from the nontraditional sources—groups who are currently underutilized in the work force. As these people enter the work force, their needs may be different from those of the traditional white male entry-level worker. Motivational techniques which have worked well with the traditional work force may require modification to meet the needs of a changing work force. Internships and cooperative work experience programs will prove valuable as businesses rely more heavily on nontraditional groups to meet the demand for office workers. The astute business educator who works to develop these cooperative relationships not only meets the needs of employers but markets the business education program as a vital link in bridging the gap between school and the world of work.

During the past two decades, office costs have spiraled and office productivity has been low, increasing only four percent. Business managers have targeted the office for special emphasis in order to increase profits by cutting costs. Automation of office processes becomes the key to cost cutting. Whether or not business education can play a key role in this process will be determined by its image—the beliefs that employers and students have

---

[6]Burford, Anna M., and Wilson, Harold O. "Artificial Intelligence: Its Impact on Accounting." *Business Education Forum* 42: 11-12; March 1988.

about it. Images are based on previous experiences; a good image is essential to effective marketing.

More skills needed for entry-level jobs. According to *Workforce 2000*, a national study published in August 1987 by the U.S. Department of Labor, by 1990 three out of four workers will need technical training beyond the high school for their jobs and one-third of the jobs will be held by college graduates, as opposed to 22 percent today. This federal report also notes that 90 percent of all new jobs will be located in metropolitan areas, and only 4 percent of these jobs will be held by persons with minimal skills, compared to 9 percent today. By 1990, in order to be functionally literate, individuals will need a twelfth grade education. New jobs expected for 1990 will be in the technical, managerial, sales, and service industries. The number of lawyers, scientists, and health professionals is expected to double or even triple, thus suggesting a commensurate increase for administrative support personnel.

These work force facts may have a negative impact on high school business education programs. Certainly the two- and three-hour blocks of instruction in a day are no longer realistic. However, business and office education at the postsecondary and collegiate levels should expect to increase enrollments as high levels of skills are demanded. In order to market programs, teachers at all levels must work together to develop articulation agreements and to sell the value of high school business education in pursuing collegiate or postsecondary training. This is best accomplished by creating opportunities for college teachers to visit high schools and talk to students. Bright students who either are presently enrolled in business education programs or have completed business education programs and are successfully employed are valuable assets often underutilized. These students can be invaluable in enhancing the image of business education and can many times get the attention of the high school student in ways that a teacher cannot.

Increased need for training for those already employed. The rapid change which characterizes the workplace and the increasing dependence on nontraditional workers compound the need for ongoing training for those already employed in jobs in business and industry. The amount of money being spent by business and industry for training—$40 billion annually—suggests that business educators should explore ways to become involved in meeting these training needs. The training provided by business and industry generally falls into three categories: basic skills training (to combat the illiteracy problem); training to update skills (such as is required when processes are automated); and developmental (that which prepares the employee for management responsibilities). Training may occur on site, or the trainee may be sent to schools, seminars, and other training located away from work. Business educators may market business education by working with industry representatives to design programs to meet their training needs. Such cooperation creates a favorable public image and builds goodwill for the school and for the program—something that must not be overlooked in the marketing strategy.

The importance of intelligent consumerism. While business education must be marketed as critical in the development of a qualified work force, consumer skills are a must as citizens are bombarded with demands for their money and time. Already, many students have discretionary buying power resulting from summer jobs and part-time work.

Hardly a business educator would quarrel with the inclusion of a basic business class as a requirement for high school graduation, but the success in marketing this idea has been marginal at best; yet no student should leave school without a knowledge of the impact of taxes, the costs of credit, the need to budget, the expenses of ownerships, the need for insurance, and other topics associated with basic business. Can business educators sell this idea to administrators? It has been done!

FACULTY UNITY NEEDED IN DEVELOPING A CREATIVE MARKET PLAN

The forces of a changing environment require that business educators know their product and their market better than ever before. Unfortunately, today's teachers of business education subjects can't just sit back and wait for students to seek out their classes. Numerous case studies in business cite successful companies who stumbled when they forgot that the market is paramount. Business educators must identify market needs and satisfy those needs by using ingenuity, understanding demographic changes, and listening to customers—students who enroll in their classes and employers who hire graduates.

Lynch suggests that applying the marketing mix involves work.[7] A marketing plan should be developed and implemented to provide structure and direction for marketing business education. The marketing plan includes what is to be done, who is to do it, and when it is to be done. Before that plan is developed, an analysis of the market is necessary as well as an analysis of the business education department—strengths and weaknesses of personnel and programs. Other elements of the business education marketing plan include:

1. Benefits of the program and courses
2. Ways to correct identified weaknesses so that benefits result
3. A description of target audiences
4. Specific, realistic objectives for a defined time period
5. Benefit-oriented messages for targeted audiences
6. Choices of media
7. A promotional budget which prioritizes media based on a cost-benefit analysis as well as identified funding resources
8. The techniques for evaluating results.

Many business teachers may be thinking that they chose a career in teaching—not in selling. However, the status of business education today

---

[7]Lynch, *op. cit.*, p. 72.

is putting the teacher in the posture of a salesperson as well as a teacher. For many teachers, recent years have been a painful experience. Enrollments have declined; programs have been attacked for not teaching relevant skills. The image of business education deteriorated when students graduated who were ill prepared to read, write, listen, and follow instructions. Furthermore, the discipline is fragmented as teachers identify themselves as vocational or nonvocational, or with a subject rather than the discipline.

Alert business educators will not wed themselves to old methods which have outlived their usefulness. Business educators must seek unorthodox solutions to orthodox problems in order to inject vitality into dying programs. Vision in planning and marketing the business education curriculum can result in fantastic returns.

CHAPTER 6
Developing and Coordinating the Business Education Curriculum

LANETA L. CARLOCK
Westside Community Schools, Omaha, Nebraska

As the twenty-first century approaches, business educators must reexamine the mission of business education, maintain an up-to-date curriculum to meet the needs of students enrolled in business education programs, and improve teaching effectiveness. Business education is an integral part of the total American educational system. It represents a broad and diverse discipline that is included in all types of our educational delivery systems—elementary and secondary schools, one- and two-year schools and colleges, four-year colleges and universities, adult day and evening schools, and vocational centers.

Business education can begin at any level, can be interrupted for varying periods of time, and can be continued throughout the lifespan of an individual. Business educators believe their mission is to educate people *for* and *about* today's business and to show *how* business affects the lives of everyone. The business education curriculum includes education for office occupations, marketing and distributive occupations, business teaching, business administration, economic understandings, and computer literacy. It is imperative, therefore, that business education be uniformly conceived, promoted, evaluated, and improved.

This chapter will address the following questions: (1) Why does business education need a coordinated curriculum? (2) What are the articulation problems between levels of schools? (3) How can a coordinated curriculum be developed? (4) Who is responsible for a coordinated curriculum? (5) When can the needed changes be implemented? and (6) Where are the resources to help meet these needs? It is hoped the information provided here will help business educators keep business education on the cutting edge in American education.

NEED

Why does business education need a coordinated curriculum? Curriculum coordination is a dynamic process. The *what*, *why*, and *how* of relating people and programs must be a part of this process. The term "coordination" suggests in a positive sense the smoothness with which articulation and transfer of knowledge can happen. Because business education is found in some form at literally every educational level, some kind of coordination is a necessity.

The rapidly changing business environment requires a continual modification and evaluation of the business curriculum. The curriculum must provide skills to meet the requirements of individual interest, changing attitudes, legislative requirements, technical knowledge, and employment. The business and industry community, and indeed the community itself, play an important role in keeping the business curriculum relevant. Again, there is need for coordination.

To prepare students to function well in the emerging society, it is necessary for business educators to see the big picture context in which program offerings exist—and to understand the economic, social, and demographic changes happening today in the United States. We are entering the age of technology/information/services. The work force is changing, and this shift in employment opportunities clearly indicates the growing need to prepare entry-level employees with quite different skills than in the past—and to initiate and develop retraining programs for displaced workers. Business education is the key to preparing students for the roles they will be assuming in this new society. However, the key will unlock doors of opportunity only through the development of a balanced and coordinated program which enables students to adapt quickly to the changing requirements of new technologies and to benefit from lifelong education.

The day of the static business education curriculum is over. The day of a business educator knowing and teaching every subject in the business curriculum is over. Today, there are hundreds of different influences on course content and sequence. If business education is to be on the cutting edge of education, we must network together closely and coordinate our curriculums at all educational levels.

ARTICULATION PROBLEMS

If we recognize the need for a coordinated business curriculum at all educational levels, the next question obviously is, What are the articulation problems between levels of schools? Clearly there are many—as will be pointed out in the following paragraphs—but they are not unsolvable problems for business educators willing to adapt to change.

Elementary level. First, there is the problem of articulation from the elementary school program. Efforts have been made to include business subjects in many elementary schools. Career awareness, career orientation, and career exploration are meant specifically for the elementary schools. Often, business educators are asked to assist in this instruction. Another area of instruction in the elementary school where concepts related to business are infused is the economics dimension of the social studies program. Economic understanding, consumer education, business principles, and attitudes toward work are being integrated into the elementary curriculum. Here too, business educators are asked to assist in this instruction. The third area of curriculum at the elementary level which is causing articulation problems is typewriting and/or keyboarding. On the one hand, there is a growing number of computers in our elementary schools. On the other hand, there are growing numbers of elementary school children who do not have the keyboarding skills and parallel language arts activities to operate these computers skillfully.

The articulation processes involved in the successful implementation of these curriculum programs at the elementary level are not easy processes. Most business educators have dealt with secondary and/or postsecondary students; many are afraid to take the leadership role at the elementary level. Teacher certification is an additional problem in some states as most business teachers do not have the elementary school certification. Sometimes principals and/or school supervisors assume that professionally trained teachers automatically or intuitively know how to teach elementary students the basic principles of career, economic, and computer education. If business teachers do not take the leadership role in the articulation process at the elementary level, we shall find more and more students at the junior high or middle school level who are not able to transfer their business skills knowledge. Taking a leadership role does not mean that business teachers must deliver all of these services at the elementary level. It does mean, however, that business teachers act in an advisory or consulting capacity and offer inservice training and workshops to elementary school teachers. The business teacher can be the "expert" in providing necessary background material to the elementary school teacher in the different curriculum areas. An organized, systematic design for including the teaching of business concepts in the elementary curriculum must be done.

Junior high/middle school level. Second is the problem of articulation from the junior high or middle school programs. The philosophy underlying the development of the junior high school was that grades 7-9 should provide students with exploratory experiences and give them opportunities to examine their interests. The junior high school was conceived as the bridge between the elementary school and the high school—meeting the needs of young people in the critical transitional stage of adolescence. Keeping this same philosophy, business education at the junior high level was to provide students with experiences that would allow them to explore opportunities available in business, to create an awareness of the senior high school business curriculum, to instruct in personal and consumer skills useful in everyday living, and to set the foundations for further study in business.

However, in many schools, the junior high became like a miniature senior high school—complete with departmentalization and scheduling. For some, the exploratory role of the junior high was forgotten and a return of the 8-4 organizational plan was seen. For others, the belief that young adults in early and preteen years have special needs, interests, and problems led to the development of the middle school. Student enrollment declines in some districts have also contributed to the reorganization and concept of providing a program that encompasses grades 5 through 8 in a 4-4-4 educational pattern or grades 6 through 8 in a 5-3-4 pattern. This new middle school pattern is still evolving. The philosophy behind the middle school recognizes that students mature earlier physically and socially. Students are being exposed to multifaceted educational experiences as early as fifth grade.

Two business courses most frequently offered at the junior high/middle school level are typewriting/keyboarding and some form of basic business. Career education is the third most popular offering. Other scattered offerings such as business mathematics, business English, consumer education, and exploratory business are also found. With the technological changes facing today's students, recommendations are now being made to expose middle school level students to four broad areas of microcomputer technology if they are to be prepared to move to higher level courses at the secondary level. These four areas are keyboarding, computer awareness, introduction to computers, and disk operating system (DOS). Specific areas to integrate within these broad areas include computer-related terminology, computer-aided instruction, and software programs.

Business educators are once again the teachers who must take the leadership role to see that students have the business transfer skills from their elementary curriculums to move into the junior high/middle school curriculums and on to the next level.

Secondary level. Third is the problem of articulation from the secondary school programs. Every year about two-and-a-half million young Americans leave school and enter the job market. Many of these young people have little career preparation. They are not all dropouts; most are high school graduates. Is it not possible for every secondary school to provide opportunities for students to prepare for the world of work? The sequence of learning experiences from all educational levels should be planned so that the student will achieve his or her highest occupational competency upon completion of any program. The senior high school business education program must meet the needs of all ability levels of students.

Business education at the secondary level is for all students: those whose formal education will end with high school graduation, students who will enter a two-year college or technical school, and students preparing to enter a four-year college or university. The business education program must offer courses for students that will orient them to careers in business, make them economically aware, equip them with life skills, prepare them with work skills, make them contributing citizens, and provide them with information to fulfill their personal needs and responsibilities. To do this, courses must be comprehensive, relevant, and build upon the learnings already accomplished by students at the elementary and junior high/middle school levels of education. Technological changes have affected every facet of business as well as our personal lives. Thus, focus must be given to instruction for business literacy, the computer, current entry-level job preparation, communication skills, and analytical skills. It is recommended that efforts be made to integrate technological changes into existing courses at the secondary level, i.e., microcomputers and software, and offer technology-based courses such as word processing and computer applications. The need for a coordinated curriculum becomes even more important at the secondary level. But the articulation problems do not end here; they continue to the postsecondary level.

Postsecondary level. The fourth problem of articulation comes at the postsecondary level. This might be a one- or two-year school or college, a four-year college or university, an adult day or evening school, or a vocational center. Each of these institutions is unique in its mission. For example, the primary mission of two-year postsecondary schools and colleges has always been to serve the needs of business, communities, and a wide variety of students—from teenagers to octogenarians. Some people consider the two-year postsecondary institution the capstone of a public educational system. Others consider the role to be that of serving as a foundation of higher education. Still others perceive this institution to be an entity unto itself. Regardless, ever-increasing numbers of students are attending these schools, and serious attention must be given to their role in the total educational system. Certainly, there must be coordination with the secondary school programs; it is also needed with the four-year colleges and universities and with business establishments.

The four-year college or university has the responsibility to prepare competent business teachers for the nation's elementary, secondary, and postsecondary schools. Frequently, questions like these will arise: Do we waive this class because of earlier training at another educational level? Do we give competency tests? Do we give credit for lower-level classes that are bypassed?

The adult day or evening school and/or vocational centers also have unique missions in the educational system. The need and demand for lifelong learning opportunities has increased dramatically in recent years and the trend continues. Business education has historically played an important role in adult education. Business educators are needed now to take a leadership role in this growing field of education.

HOW, WHO, WHEN?

How can a coordinated curriculum be developed? Who is responsible for a coordinated curriculum? When can the needed changes be implemented? These three questions will be addressed together in the following paragraphs.

The development of a coordinated curriculum takes time. The planning procedures involve identifying problems, developing needed studies, proposing solutions, and reaching agreements or implementing recommendations. Many techniques are used by institutions to articulate with each other. These might include committees, advisory councils, conferences, publications, interinstitutional visits, tours to visit other schools, exchange of faculty and facilities, periodic meetings, and invitations to former graduates to speak. The list is limited only by one's imagination and resourcefulness. A list of resources at the end of this chapter might also be useful in planning the development of a coordinated curriculum. The importance, too, of using established criteria for building successful curriculums must also be reviewed. A continual evaluation program must be implemented. Frequent surveying of business, industry, and government agencies to determine present and future community employment needs must be done. Maintaining close relationships with professional associations is also considered vital to the success of curriculum planning and coordination.

No one individual can undertake the responsibility of developing and coordinating the business education curriculum. Faculty, administrative personnel, and advisory committees must be actively involved in the planning process if the coordination is to meet with any success. It may even be necessary to work with curriculum specialists and members of professional associations who are competent in specific areas. Business educators need to share information and assist one another. Curriculum needs differ between parts of the country, and often within a city itself.

As teachers develop instructional programs, they consider the type of students they serve, their culture and background, their career objectives, and their learning styles. They reflect on the type and amount of instructional equipment available, supply and equipment budgets, and other details. To serve students, curriculums must be designed around student needs. When the needs vary, the curriculum must reflect these differences. We must rely upon local schools to select the course content that is appropriate for their instructional environment. We must then network and coordinate programs with one another, and with our different educational levels, if the articulation problems are to be solved.

When should we do this? Now. Waiting until tomorrow will be too late. If business educators do not develop and coordinate the business curriculum at all educational levels, there will be nonbusiness educators teaching the business courses. Waiting could also mean the dropping of many business courses from the various curriculums. Business education course content will continue to evolve at a rapid pace. Students cannot succeed in business without the basic skills of reading, writing, and computing. Flexibility is the key, but the time to begin implementing the needed changes to develop and coordinate the business education curriculum is now.

RESOURCES

The curriculum must be designed so that the student can progress through successive stages with a minimum amount of duplication of effort and maximum opportunities to achieve career goals. Business educators must continually examine and reexamine their curricular offerings. This task can be made somewhat easier if there are established guidelines or criteria to follow. There has always been an expressed concern that someone might propose, and actually put into place, some sort of national curriculum. Our democratic system has no interest in a dictated curriculum proposed and enforced by outside agencies. However, there are many resources available to help each local school develop curriculum to meet its needs and still coordinate with other programs as well. Some of these resources are listed here:

1. *Database of Competencies for Business Curriculum Development, K-14.* Reston, Va.: National Business Education Association, 1987.
2. "Future Directions and Recommended Actions for Business Education: A Report by the NBEA Task Force on New Concepts and Strategies for Business Education." *Business Education Forum* 38:3-11; November 1983.
3. "This We Believe . . ." Statements by the Policies Commission for Business and Economic Education.
4. *An Action Agenda for Business Education.* A Report of the Proceedings and Recommendations from the National Conference on the Future of Business Education, Cincinnati, Ohio, August 11-14, 1985.
5. *Handbook for Business Education in Nebraska.* Lincoln: Nebraska Department of Education, 1984.
6. *Model Curriculum Standards, Grades Nine Through Twelve.* Sacramento: California State Department of Education, 1985.
7. *Postsecondary Business Education Basic Curriculum Guide.* Little Rock: Arkansas Department of Education, 1984.
8. *Skills for a Changing Workplace: A Business and Office Educator's Guide.* Columbus: National Center for Research in Vocational Education, 1985.
9. *Standards for Excellence in Business Education.* A project of the school of Technology, East Carolina University, Greenville, North Carolina, and the U.S. Department of Education, 1985.
10. *Business Education Competencies.* Santa Fe: New Mexico State Department of Education, 1985.
11. *Business Education for a Changing World.* Twenty-Fifth Yearbook. Reston, Va.: National Business Education Association, 1987.
12. *Career Education Guide—K-Adult.* Palo Alto: Science Research Associates, 1973.

SUMMARY

Business educators will be constantly faced with the challenge to review curriculum content to keep up to date with changing technologies. Education is a lifelong process, and preparing students for career changes is an important need in the business education curriculum. Developing and coordinating the business education curriculum is not an easy task, but it can be done. This chapter addressed the questions of why a coordinated curriculum is needed and what some of the articulation problems are. How and when a coordinated curriculum can be developed and who is responsible were also discussed, and a list of available resources to help in this endeavor was provided. Indeed, if business education is to be on the cutting edge in American education, business educators must be the leaders in developing and coordinating the business curriculum at all educational levels.

CHAPTER 7
Preparing and Updating Professional Business Education Teachers

LLOYD W. BARTHOLOME
Utah State University, Logan

Education has been and will continue to be a source of controversy—controversy because most adults have children to be educated and they want their children to have the best education possible. The purpose of this chapter is to provide some background on the current status of public education as well as business education and to use the information to make recommendations for preparing and updating business teachers. What competencies are necessary to prepare quality business teachers? How are these competencies affected by outside forces such as accrediting agencies, social and economic forces, and various governing boards? Who should prepare business teachers and how should business teachers be kept up to date? One cannot discuss business teacher education in isolation. The subject should be viewed from the total perspective of the status of public education.

REPORTS ON THE STATUS OF PUBLIC EDUCATION

A Nation at Risk. The first of the present series of reports on the status of education in the United States was published on April 26, 1983. T. H. Bell, then Secretary of Education and formerly superintendent of the Granite School District in Salt Lake City, Utah, appointed David P. Gardner, then president of the University of Utah, to chair a National Commission on Excellence in Education. This appointment was made in 1981. There were 18 members on the Commission with 15 of those members having a background in education. Business was not represented except for one person who was a retired chairman of Bell Telephone Laboratories. The report had a tremendous impact on public school education, especially on requirements for high school graduation.

On the basis of testimony gathered throughout the United States, the Commission on Excellence in Education found that expectations in the nation's public schools were not as high as they should be, and that students were not taking the so called "solid subjects." The commission provided five recommendations. However, the most far-reaching recommendation was:

> ... that state and local high school graduation requirements be strengthened and that, at a minimum, all students seeking a diploma be required to lay the foundations in the Five New Basics by taking the following curriculum during their 4 years

of high school: (a) 4 years of English, (b) 3 years of mathematics, (c) 3 years of science, (d) 3 years of social studies, (e) one-half year of computer science. For the collegebound, 2 years of foreign language in high school are strongly recommended in addition to those taken earlier.

The report had a widespread impact, and by the end of 1984, over 40 states in the nation had increased high school graduation requirements to meet the general intent of the recommendations.

One can readily see the impact of this report on business education. O. J. Byrnside, executive director of the National Business Education Association, summed up the report best when he said:

> One should seriously question the wisdom of recommendations that prescribe the same courses for graduation for all high school students with little or no regard for the aspirations, interests, and abilities of individual students. Schools that do not serve the needs of individual students are not serving the needs of society.
>
> Most of the recommendations ignore the need for occupational preparation for the 80 percent of all public school students who will never complete a course of study in a college or university.

Many college governing bodies immediately responded to the report by raising admission requirements and/or requiring foreign languages. The open-door policy to a college education was beginning to close. Other reports supporting and refuting the *Nation at Risk* report began to appear.

The Unfinished Agenda, The Role of Vocational Education in the High School. This report was written because members of the vocational education community including the U.S. Department of Education, Office of Vocational and Adult Education, felt the *Nation at Risk* report did not adequately deal with the role of secondary vocational education in addressing the problems of quality in American education—especially the fact that secondary school students are a diverse group varying in background, ability, and aspirations. A National Commission on Secondary Vocational Education was appointed in January 1984. After testimony from many individuals and groups, Commission members concluded that access to secondary vocational education is becoming increasingly limited primarily because of increased emphasis on academics, consolidation of programs, time scheduling, and inadequate or inaccurate student knowledge of vocational education. The Commission suggested a balance in the curriculum to better serve students' needs so that both academic and vocational courses become more permeable, more related, and more integrated. The Commission provided six recommendations including the recommendation that "states should not mandate curricular requirements that restrict students' opportunities to participate in vocational education experiences." Unfortunately, there is little evidence that this report has had an impact on secondary education in the United States.

A Nation Prepared: Teachers for the 21st Century. In January 1985, the Carnegie Corporation established a forum on education in the economy. The purpose of the forum was to look at the preparation of teachers. The result of this report (and other reports) is the move to restructure the teaching profession and require a bachelor's degree in the arts and sciences as a prerequisite for the professional study of teaching—a specific recommendation of the Carnegie Forum. The forum members recommended that graduate schools of education provide a specific curriculum to provide a master of teaching degree based upon a systematic knowledge of teaching including internships and residencies in the schools. This report has had some effect on how teachers are prepared—including business teachers—but the recommendations are currently being debated in teacher education institutions.

Subsequent reports on the preparation of students in the public schools and the preparation of teachers for the public schools continue to appear, with many states in the nation producing reports. All of these reports provide data on which to further debate education in the public schools and the preparation of teachers for the public schools. What has occurred and will occur in business education?

PREPARING BUSINESS TEACHERS—AN OVERVIEW

The past. Most of the pioneer business teachers in America learned their subject matter by private instruction or work experience. Many teachers came directly from England where they had served as apprentices. Little attention in the 18th century was provided in the profession of teaching. Business subjects were taught for vocational purposes only.

During the 19th century, there was an increased interest in the teaching of business subjects such as bookkeeping, penmanship, and arithmetic. By the later part of the 19th century, private business schools were expanding rapidly and business subjects began to be introduced into the high schools. Teachers were either high school graduates with a few months of training in business, university business school graduates who were well trained in subject matter but had little expertise in teaching, or normal school graduates who had some preparation in teaching but little expertise in the business subject area.

The real awakening of the need for professional business teachers did not come until the 20th century. F. G. Nichols reports that between 1900 and 1920, 30 normal schools professed to prepare business teachers, but not more than six were really making a serious effort to prepare business teachers for the public schools. However, by the end of 1930, there was definite evidence of a trend toward providing business teachers with academic and appropriate professional education as well as the technical subject matter of business. In 1957 it was reported that the National Association of Business Teacher Training Institutions led the way in the preparation of business teachers. This association is now known as the National Association for Business Teacher Education, a division of the National Business Education Association. By 1957 business teachers were certified to teach only after completing four years of preparation for teaching in an accredited college or university. In some instances, permanent certification required a fifth year of preparation, much as it does today. Business teacher education has its roots in experiential education, and occupational work experience has been and continues to be recommended and, in many cases, required for the preparation of business teachers.

The present. Because of severe inflation in the 1970's and early 1980's as well as a back-to-the-basics movement triggered by the *Nation at Risk* report, and because of small enrollments with a lack of funding at some schools and refusal to emphasize the computer technology in business, many business teacher education programs have been eliminated. In most cases these programs have been programs with very small numbers of students. In other cases priorities in business schools and schools of education have been such that the business education programs have received lower priority and, thereby, a lack of funding or elimination. However, during the last two-to-three years, there has been more stability in the business teacher education programs. A recent NABTE survey found only four respondents of 144 institutions indicating that their business teacher education programs would probably be discontinued within the next two years.

Future. The back-to-the-basics movement, especially the movement by state boards of education to increase high school graduation requirements as a result of the *Nation at Risk* report, has potentially decreased the number of business classes being taught in the secondary schools. However, the *Nation at Risk* report did contain a recommendation for computer literacy as a requirement for all high school students. Thus, business teacher education programs that are including an emphasis in microcomputer and computer instruction as well as an emphasis in information systems are finding the job outlook for their graduates to be excellent. Microcomputer/microchip technology has virtually eliminated the use of the electric typewriter. IBM and other companies are no longer producing electric typewriters. They are producing electronic typewriters which are based upon the microcomputer chip technology. Also, with the advent of very easy-to-use microcomputer word processing software packages, the microcomputer is tending to eliminate the use of even the electronic typewriter for many office purposes. Office education is not what it was five to ten years ago. Office education is now a part of the whole computer information systems movement. Business education teachers who recognize this will not only continue to survive, but they will continue to thrive.

In 1979, the first conference on the future of business education as related to the new technology was held at Snowbird, Utah. About 50 business educators met to discuss new directions for business education. They recognized that several forces were affecting business education. These forces were (1) an economic recession in the United States that forced public school education and higher education to cut back programs, (2) an information revolution in the United States comparable to the industrial revolution in the late 1900's, (3) a series of reports criticizing teachers and teacher education, and (4) a general decline in the birth rate in the United States. One of the recommendations of the resulting report, *New Directions for Business Teacher Education*, was that a new curriculum should be developed for business education and that this new curriculum must define a subject matter base more closely related to business in order to increase enrollment and gain professional credibility. Another recommendation was that the curriculum must be flexible in order to expand career options for business education students to include the technological breakthroughs that continue. An additional recommendation was that there should be a focus on a new direction for curriculum and a new direction for preparing business teachers.

During the fall of 1980, another conference was held at Rider College. Forty business educators from across the United States discussed the future of business education. An outgrowth of this conference was the prediction that the next five-to-ten-year period would determine the nature and quality of business education for the following 50 years. Members of the conference also agreed that business education was not an "island" of its own, and that the future of business education is highly political and the result of power exercised by state and federal legislative bodies as well as by accrediting agencies. The Snowbird and Rider College symposiums were intended to make business teachers aware of problems related to business education.

There was a follow-up to the Snowbird conference held at Arizona State University, Tempe, in February 1982. The position paper which resulted from that conference recommended a new thrust in business education. That thrust was to be information processing and information systems. The position paper was published in several business education periodicals, and it was adopted by the National Business Education Association. Subsequently, an NBEA task force on new concepts and strategies for business education was appointed. After several meetings this task force recommended that NBEA develop new curriculums for business teachers at all levels of instruction. NBEA President G. W. Maxwell then appointed two task forces to develop these curriculums. One task force was charged to develop a subject matter curriculum for business instruction for levels K through 14. Another task force was charged to develop a professional business teacher education curriculum. Both of these task forces were to include recommendations for a curriculum in word processing and information systems and to develop curriculums to prepare business teachers and business students for the information age.

NECESSARY COMPETENCIES FOR BUSINESS TEACHERS

In February 1985, members of the two NBEA task forces, K-14 and Business Teacher Education, met in Inglewood, California, at their own expense to decide a strategy for developing curriculum guides. Members of the task force for the business teacher education model curriculum decided that the curriculum guide should be competency based and should include the results of research completed in the field. Members met again in August 1985 to write the first draft of the report. After several versions with input from NABTE institutional members and state specialists for business education, the final guide was adopted and published by NBEA in July 1987. Several states have already adopted the guide as a requirement for developing new business teacher education programs. Necessary competency statements for quality business teachers are recommended for each of the following areas.

Curriculum development. Competent business teachers must be able to develop a curriculum based upon sound philosophical, social, psychological, and economic bases. The curriculum should be consistent with the school and community philosophy. The curriculum should also consider (1) current and emerging occupations and careers in business including self-employment as entrepreneurs, (2) intelligent participation in our economic system as consumers, producers, and citizens, and (3) advanced education in business. Curriculum development should be continuous, and the new technology should be included in curriculum development.

Instruction. Instruction is teaching. Good teachers can bring about desired changes in the behavior of the students. To be competent instructors, teachers must be able to identify objectives, select and organize content, use appropriate methods and techniques, select and develop appropriate materials, and effectively evaluate student learning. Good instruction emphasizes methodology of teaching including different methods of presentation, communicating knowledge, and instruction in skill development. Good instruction also includes a mastery of the subject matter. A good teacher has acquired subject matter mastery when there is insight into the process by which learning occurs in that specific subject matter.

Evaluation. Evaluation is an important part of the instructional process and as such should have special consideration. Teachers should be able to evaluate students so that the extent to which student learning is occurring can be determined systematically and reliably. Conducting sound evaluation is as much a professional obligation of the teacher as providing instruction. Evaluation includes the mastery of the subject matter and the ability to apply valid knowledge about educational measurement devices and the interpretation of the data. At least a basic statistics course should be required of all business teacher candidates so that a background can be secured in the evaluation process.

Management. To be a successful business teacher, one must practice positive and effective management techniques within the classroom and outside the classroom. It is crucial that business teachers be familiar with and apply the general principles of management relating to planning, organizing, motivating, controlling, and evaluating. It is especially important that effective business teachers operate smoothly functioning classrooms where students are highly involved in the learning activities and where there is little or no student disruption or chronic misbehavior. Business teacher managers who are judged to be the most effective and productive in an organization concentrate on managing their units well. They are supportive of the general objectives of the school and the district, and they are aware of how their teaching contributes to these objectives. They are also communicative with students, school administration, and parents.

Guidance. Good business teachers must take an interest in their students and help them in the guidance process. They do not have to consider themselves as guidance specialists, but they should have an understanding of appropriate counseling and guidance procedures. In the business teacher education setting, guidance seeks to help students adjust and function effectively in that educational environment. Guidance also includes providing information to students about their chosen careers and how to enter these careers. The teacher's role in guidance is to help students shape their personalities, help them make informed decisions, and help to prepare them for the realities of life. In order to be effective in guidance, the teacher must have a genuine interest in the students.

Communication. A good business teacher must be a good communicator. A teacher must be able to transmit information, ideas, and feelings through verbal or nonverbal means to students, parents, and administration. The ability to communicate effectively is perhaps the major determinant of an effective business teacher. Communication requires knowledge about the process and elements of communication, proficiency in the use of the language, and a highly developed sense of empathy that enables one to receive subtle messages—especially nonverbal ones.

Leadership. The good business teacher must be a leader—a leader in the classroom, a leader in the school, a leader in the district, and a leader in the profession. One way to develop this leadership is to provide student organizations for business teacher candidates to practice their skills. Student organizations can provide a vehicle to explore career interests, learn and refine citizenship, and develop a commitment to the business teaching profession. Business teacher candidates must also learn the role of an advisor for leadership organizations since they will want to sponsor business student organizations when they become business teachers.

Professional development. Professional development is the continual process of acquiring knowledge, skills, and insights that result in the improvement of professional practices. For business teachers there are four dimensions. These dimensions are:

1. To keep up in the knowledge
2. To search for accurate new knowledge about the discipline
3. To continually refine teaching skills and practices
4. To serve the professional organizations.

Some leaders may be born, but leaders can also be developed. It is a primary responsibility of business teacher educators to develop business teachers to assume leadership roles in the business education profession.

Subject competencies. Business teachers must be expert in the subject matter which they teach. They also must possess a broad general business background. Only in this way can business teachers understand how the specific subjects they teach relate to the total business enterprise. Teacher education curriculums must include a broad background of all business skills and knowledge as well as specialty business skills taught in the public schools. Business teachers must stay current in the subject matter areas after they graduate from school.

In addition to subject matter knowledge, successful business teachers must have relevant occupational experience in the area taught. The number and hours of experience is not as important as the quality of experience provided. Summer internships for practicing business teachers are an excellent way to stay current in the subject area. The American Assembly of Collegiate Schools of Business has identified five broad background areas of subject matter expertise. All business teachers should have classes in these five areas. In addition to special expertise in the subjects which they teach, general subject recommendations for the public secondary schools are provided in the NBEA publication, *Database of Competencies for Business Curriculum Development, K-14.* Because the five broad background areas required by AACSB are so important, they are stated below along with the suggested classes in which these areas are taught.

Area 1: A background of the concepts, processes, and institutions in the production and marketing of goods and/or services and the financing of the business enterprise or other forms of organization. (production, marketing, finance)

Area 2: A background of the economic and legal environment as it pertains to profit and/or nonprofit organizations along with ethical considerations and social and political influences as they affect such organizations. (micro and macro economics, law, business and society)

Area 3: A basic understanding of the concepts and applications of accounting, of quantitative methods, and management information systems including computer applications. (accounting, statistics, computers and information systems)

Area 4: A study of organization theory, behavior, and interpersonal communications. (organizational behavior, business communications)

Area 5: A study of administrative processes under conditions of uncertainty including integrating analysis and policy determination at the overall management level. (management, policy)

SPECIAL COMPETENCIES OF THE PRESECONDARY BUSINESS TEACHER

Competencies mentioned in the preceding section relate to all business teachers. However, most business teachers teach in the secondary school and the competencies stated are generally for preparing business teachers to teach in the secondary schools. There are some special competencies required of elementary teachers who teach certain business topics.

With the introduction of the microcomputer in the elementary school, it is necessary to teach keyboarding skills at the elementary school level. Elementary school teachers should be able to keyboard and should be proficient and knowledgeable so that they can teach introduction to the keyboard and keyboard skill development. If business teachers assist elementary teachers in this very important skill, they should have knowledge of how pre-adolescents learn. Elementary school teachers should be required to be credentialed to teach keyboarding at the elementary school level. This credentialing should be done by business teachers and business teacher educators. Elementary teachers must also have some knowledge of the various career options in business and the basics of our economic system.

SPECIAL COMPETENCIES OF THE POSTSECONDARY BUSINESS TEACHER

Postsecondary business teachers must be able to serve the needs of many kinds of students from teenagers to octogenarians. They must be at the forefront of the educational and technological society and must be leaders in the changing and restructuring of curriculum and teaching delivering systems. Postsecondary teachers must have a broad background in business but have great expertise in specialized subject areas of business including computers and business literacy. The office is changing and the change is being brought about by computers and information systems. Postsecondary teachers who have formerly specialized in office systems must now specialize in the use of computers and information systems and lead out in the instruction of computers and information systems at their respective institutions.

PREPARING PRESERVICE BUSINESS TEACHERS

Many forces are affecting the preparation of preservice business teachers. These forces include accrediting agencies, state departments of education, the federal government, and various political groups. Business teacher educators must be aware of and understand these forces so that they know how to balance the forces and provide potential business students the best education possible.

Accreditation forces. There are three major accrediting agencies related to the preparation of preservice business teachers. These agencies are the National Council for the Accreditation of Teacher Education (NCATE), the National Association of State Directors of Teacher Education and Certification (NASDTEC), and the American Assembly of Collegiate Schools of Business (AACSB).

NCATE. NCATE is the sole agency for the accreditation of university teacher education programs. NCATE allows various divisions of teacher education programs to use their own professional standards. The National Association for Business Teacher Education (NABTE) has developed a list of standards for business teacher education, and NCATE recommends the NABTE standards.

NASDTEC. NASDTEC is represented through each state office of education. NASDTEC consists of state certification officers from the various states. The NASDTEC teacher certification requirements contain requirements for business education teacher certification.

AACSB. AACSB is the sole accrediting agency as identified by COPA (Council on Program Accreditation), an arm of the federal government, to evaluate business schools. AACSB is controlled primarily by deans of business schools in the United States. AACSB guidelines are fair and appropriate for business teachers. However, sometimes business deans use AACSB guidelines as the reason for eliminating or cutting back business teacher education programs. This is not a fair evaluation of AACSB, and when business deans use AACSB incorrectly, direct contact should be made with AACSB representatives.

Dealing with outside forces. The NBEA *Business Teacher Education Curriculum Guide* includes recommendations by NCATE, NASDTEC, and AACSB as well as NABTE. Furthermore, the curriculum guide task force took into consideration standards for excellence developed at East Carolina University under a U.S. government project.

Other forces affecting business teacher education include local institution situations and state mandates and directives. There is currently a move to require basic competency testing of all teachers prior to admission to teacher education programs, and competency testing of teachers upon graduation from business teacher education programs. All of these forces must be considered. Business teacher educators must resist those forces which do not enhance the business teacher education programs and work hard to incorporate aspects which enhance programs.

Other ingredients of a good preservice program. The NBEA curriculum competencies apply to *all* business teachers—preservice and inservice. There are several other ingredients required of a good preservice business teacher education program.

1. There should be a pool of bright, energetic high school graduates who wish to have careers as business teachers. Present business teachers should encourage bright students to pursue careers as business teachers. Most schools require SAT or ACT scores for entrance to the university. Students majoring in business education should have entrance test scores similar to or better than the average of the rest of the university.
2. As previously mentioned, students should have a broad background in all areas of business. They should be known as the "business teacher" and not the "typing teacher" or the "shorthand teacher."
3. Students should emphasize in their college programs one or more areas that are taught in the public secondary schools. These areas might be computers and information systems, accounting, economics, etc. Students should have a background in all areas, but they should have at least one or two subject specialty areas.
4. In today's technological world, almost all business programs in the secondary schools include or should include instruction in computers and information systems. Therefore, this is an imperative area for business teachers to emphasize in their college academic programs.
5. Students should be well versed in the methodology of their subject matter and understand that there are two basic methodologies—one methodology for skill learning and the other for concept and theory learning. Whether these methodologies are all in the same class or different classes is immaterial as long as students understand how to teach both skill and theory learning.
6. Potential business teachers should culminate their programs with at least one quarter or semester of full-time student teaching in a school district. Stations should be found so that the teacher candidates can be under the mentorship of qualified business teachers who keep close contact with the teacher education institution. The student teaching experience should be closely coordinated between the university and the local school district teachers.
7. Upon graduation from a certified preservice business teacher education program, students should be given a provisional certificate, and the university should be provided funds to further supervise the candidates for at least one or possibly two additional years.

8. Candidates should have access to university business teacher educators for professional development and should continue to be formally evaluated by the teacher educators and the local school district for at least two years after graduation.

UPDATING INSERVICE BUSINESS TEACHERS

The teaching of business subjects is dynamic especially with the new technology in today's business. Business teachers must update in many ways.

Conferences and workshops. School districts should encourage and assist in the funding so that business teachers can attend their state, regional, and/or national conferences. Universities and school districts should work together to provide workshops and seminars for practicing business teachers. Universities should also provide inservice graduate classes either via telecommunications, independent study, or traditional means when possible.

Renewal of certification. In many states, business teachers are no longer required to renew their credentials in order to continue teaching. This is unfortunate because business teachers need to continue to update themselves. Therefore, positive incentives must be provided for business teachers. These incentives include additional funds for business teachers who are identified as leaders and who can assist beginning business teachers. Funds should also be provided to attend university classes. Salary schedules should be such that positive incentives are given for summer work experience. In many schools, graduate credit can be given for summer work experiences. This should be done when possible.

Change or don't survive. Sometimes business teachers are unwilling to change. University personnel, school district personnel, and other administrators should provide positive incentives so business teachers can update their teaching and subject matter competencies. When business teachers do not react to positive incentives, they should be counseled and, if necessary, encouraged to change professions rather than teach outdated material.

ALTERNATIVE MODELS FOR PREPARING BUSINESS TEACHERS

As shortages of teachers occur, many states have moved to alternative ways of certifying teachers via vocational certification or certification in single subject areas. This credentialing is a very dangerous procedure. Often, candidates are excellent in the subject matter but have no interest in students or how to teach. If handled correctly, there are two alternative models for preparing business teachers.

Subject matter changes for good teachers. Teachers who are already experts in teaching can change subject matter expertise by taking additional classes and getting additional work experience in the fields for which they are preparing to teach. This method is occurring in the computer field where many teachers are computer experts but don't know how computers are used in business. They are expert teachers as well. These teachers need to take the broad background of business subjects and understand how computers are used in business before they teach business students.

Recruiting from business and industry. Many states allow vocational accreditation. The usual procedure is to allow people with six or more years of industry experience to teach with a provisional vocational certificate. They are then required to get educational pedagogy as they begin their teaching. This method doesn't appear to make too much sense because normally the teacher needs at least three years to get the educational pedagogy. In the meantime they have taught for three years without understanding how to teach. The model can work quite well if people in business and industry are given the educational pedagogy first and then required to student teach—just like preservice business teachers.

THE PREPARATION OF BUSINESS TEACHER EDUCATORS

Are preservice business teachers always prepared under the tutelage of business teacher educators? Do business teacher educators have the appropriate background to prepare preservice business teachers? Perhaps preservice business teachers are not being properly prepared.

Who prepares preservice business teachers? Usually one of the following three models is used to prepare preservice business teachers:

1. Business teacher education departments with a major in business education
2. Secondary education departments which may or may not provide a major in business education
3. Schools of business where a business degree is earned and the candidate then receives the professional education from a college of education.

The requirements for business teacher educators. Business teacher educators should first and foremost have taught in the public schools. They should also have a background of subject matter and educational pedagogy at least similar to the students they are preparing. In addition, they should have recent work experience in business and industry. The competencies required for business teachers should also be required of business teacher educators, with a heavy emphasis on an understanding and empathy for students and the ability to communicate with students.

Role of the business teacher educator. Business teacher educators should be the leaders of business education in their state and region. They should be a liaison with the state office of education and should be change agents for business instruction in the public schools. Business teacher educators should be active in at least regional and national business education associations and should be able to identify potential new leaders in business education and nurture those potential new leaders. Business teacher educators should also be active on their university campuses and serve on university committees so that their program will be viable and visible on campus. Business teacher educators are the single most important influence for viable, energetic, and growing business teacher education programs; *or* they can be the single most important reason why business teacher education programs wither and die.

SUMMARY

Historically, outside forces have generally influenced education and will probably continue to do so. Recent reports on the status of public education such as the *Nation at Risk* report, the Carnegie report, *Teachers for the Twenty-First Century*, and other reports have focused on problems in public school education. State boards of education have responded by increasing requirements in the basics to graduate. Consequently, elective areas such as business education could potentially suffer. In addition, various certification agencies such as NCATE, NASDTEC, and AACSB influence business teacher education. Business teacher educators and business teachers must be able to balance all of the outside forces influencing education and provide the necessary competencies for successful business instruction. A task force of the National Business Education Association has developed a list of necessary competencies for business teachers. These competencies have been officially adopted by the Executive Board of the National Business Education Association as the recommended curriculum for business teachers. Guidelines include competencies in curriculum, instruction, evaluation, management, guidance, communication, leadership, professional development, and subject matter. The AACSB five areas of business expertise have been included in the curriculum among the required subject matter competencies for all business teachers.

We must have capable, understanding business teacher educators with a business and a public school teaching background to properly prepare preservice and inservice business teachers at all levels. Many states have adopted other means to enter the teaching profession rather than through the traditional business teacher programs. These means can be dangerous if candidates are not qualified and do not get their expertise prior to their teaching instruction. Business teacher educators, business teachers, state specialists for business education, local school districts, and students must all work together to improve the instruction of business in the public schools. There must be valid preservice programs following appropriate accreditation and curriculum guidelines, and there must be valid inservice programs for practicing business teachers. The future of business education depends upon well-prepared business teachers who are willing to accept responsibility for improving the profession.

Part III
ASSERTING AND REASSERTING BUSINESS EDUCATION AT THE PRESECONDARY LEVEL

CHAPTER 8
Keyboarding

LINDA D. KIMBALL
Portsmouth Senior High School, Portsmouth, New Hampshire
PATRICIA MARCONI LANE
York High School, York, Maine

Keyboarding is learning the correct manipulation of keys on a computer/typewriter keyboard and using that keyboard for basic data input. The importance of keyboarding has been emphasized by the Policies Commission on Business and Economic Education. In its 1984 statement on keyboarding, the Commission states, "With the rapid expansion of computer usage, primarily microcomputers, educational institutions should require that all students develop keyboarding skills." By the 1990's there will be over ten million computers in public schools, and keyboarding skills are essential in learning to use a computer efficiently.

As students begin using the keyboard, they form lifelong habits where correct techniques are extremely important for efficiency. Being a cumulative skill, keyboarding requires the perfecting of initial techniques upon which further skill can be built.

Everyone will soon need to know how to keyboard and how to make proficient and productive use of this skill. At some point all of today's students will use computers in the school, in the home, for recreation, and on the job. Keyboarding proficiency will be necessary within almost any occupational area. It is for this reason this chapter addresses the importance of keyboarding in grades K-8.

In order to obtain up-to-date information on keyboarding instruction, we devised a questionnaire which was mailed to a random sampling of one elementary and one middle/junior high school instructor in each of the 50 states. The purpose of this survey was to determine the following:

- Instructor's area of certification and training
- Curriculum, methodology, and duration
- Evaluation techniques
- Equipment and materials.

Fifty percent of the instructors surveyed responded to our questionnaire, and this chapter is based upon the tabulated results.

INSTRUCTOR'S AREA OF CERTIFICATION AND TRAINING

Our survey shows astounding and unbelievable statistics about an issue that can no longer be ignored—51 percent of all keyboarding instructors now teaching keyboarding at the elementary and middle/junior high schools are not certified! Of the remaining 49 percent, 12 percent are certified at the elementary level and 37 percent at the middle/junior high school levels for teaching keyboarding. Thirty percent of the certified elementary and middle/junior high school keyboarding instructors are certified in business education. The respondents state that their keyboarding preparation comes from in-service workshops provided by business and computer departments, observations and training by business instructors, and courses in typing and computer literacy. Of significant importance is the fact that 28 percent of our respondents have no formal or informal training to teach keyboarding.

A teacher who is responsible for providing keyboarding instruction for elementary and middle/junior high schools should be trained in methods and techniques for teaching keyboarding. It is most important that teachers receive training in the traits, needs, and interests of the student age group with whom they will be dealing.

CURRICULUM, METHODOLOGY, AND DURATION

The results of our survey show that formal keyboarding instruction is most frequently given daily in the sixth grade for 40-45 minutes for nine weeks.

Curriculum. Keyboarding skills should be taught to students at the time they use computers with frequency. In early elementary (K-2), the goal of instruction may simply be to aid students in locating keys on the keyboard. These younger students' attention spans are too short for proper learning of the keyboard, and their hand size and level of finger dexterity are drawbacks. Students in grades 3-6 have longer attention spans, better dexterity, and the greater maturity that is necessary for learning to keyboard. Studies have shown that third-grade students are physiologically ready to learn keyboarding and can become keyboard proficient. Thus, a formal development of correct keyboarding techniques could be introduced at the beginning of the third grade, focusing on the alphabetic keys. The primary goal at this level should be to develop increased efficiency in computer keyboarding through learning touch-keyboarding techniques.

At the middle/junior high school level, the purpose of learning how to keyboard is not an end but a beginning to using introductory word processing, database, and graphing software programs. Students will use word processing skills for the purpose of written communications with the introduction of proofreading and editing software. Middle/junior high school students will also engage in computer activities which will facilitate the development of the problem-solving skills of logic and logical thinking.

As a result of keyboarding instruction, students should improve skills in the following areas: listening, following directions, attention to task, fine motor skills, eye-hand coordination, self-concept awareness, speed-up mode of expression, and language arts. Keyboarding should be considered as a communication tool or skill and should be considered as part of any language arts program within the elementary and middle/junior high school curriculum.

Methodology. Each day's instruction begins with warm-up drills on previous instruction. Then new material for the day is introduced with adequate time given for practice. Keyboarding practice should consist of real words, phrases, and continuous prose. At all levels it is important to have a variety of activities and occasional rest periods. In dealing with elementary students it is especially important to keep activities short. The instructor should demonstrate proper fingering techniques frequently to the entire class and to individual students when appropriate. The instructor may need to manipulate student fingers to pattern various reaches with which students have difficulty. At the end of each class the student should receive a printout of everything he/she has keyed for that day. Each student then has tangible proof of his/her accomplishments. A keyboarding program with immediate feedback and reinforcement is advisable. Keyboarding instruction ideally should be expanded upon each year.

Duration. In most cases, time for keyboarding instruction is part of the language arts program. The keyboarding program consists of daily lessons over several weeks. Ideally for third- and fourth-grade students, the course should be 20-30 minutes daily for one quarter of the year. For middle/junior high school students, the course should be 40-45 minutes daily for one quarter of the year. Daily instruction could be interspersed with short rest periods utilizing oral language arts activities. The most appropriate time for learning to keyboard would be when students are fresh and raring to go. Less appropriate times are when students' attention levels are low, such as before lunch or at the end of the school day.

EVALUATION TECHNIQUES

Eighty-eight percent of the respondents from our survey evaluate students on proper keyboarding techniques. These techniques include correct fingering, posture, and key memorization. Speed and accuracy are used as evaluation measurements by 81 percent of the respondents: 40 percent evaluate by other means of testing such as written tests and appropriate setup of completed tasks. These statistics are based on the fact that some instructors evaluate on more than one criteria.

Evaluation should focus on correct technique through observation of students *as they key*. A pass/fail basis of evaluation could be used if grading is a necessity. To generate enthusiasm, build interest, and increase motivation, rewards such as certificates, stars, and stickers for accomplishments could be given daily and/or weekly to students. After the keyboarding unit, a certificate of completion could be given to each student.

EQUIPMENT AND MATERIALS

Equipment. From our survey we determined that 51 percent of our respondents teach keyboarding solely on computers. Typewriters are still used by 28 percent. Twenty-one percent of the instructors use both computers and typewriters for keyboard instruction.

Whether a computer or typewriter is used for demonstration, be sure the students are able to see proper keying techniques. An important consideration often overlooked is furniture for the keyboarding classroom. To insure that the students can reach the keyboard properly, both tables and chairs must match student size.

Materials. According to our survey, computer software is used exclusively by 42 percent of our respondents. Publishers' textbooks are used by 37 percent. Both computer software and publishers' textbooks are used by 14 percent. Seven percent create their own instructional materials. The selection of audiovisual aids should be based on size and print to accommodate the grade level of the students.

ROLE OF BUSINESS EDUCATORS AT PRESECONDARY LEVEL

As we know, not just anyone can teach keyboarding. Therefore, it is now or never for business educators to take the time to show our expertise in the correct techniques necessary for using computers properly. Business educators need to provide the subject matter expertise and leadership in local school districts. We need to educate school administrators and the public on the importance of keyboarding skills. Business educators can no longer wait to be called upon to assist in the development of the keyboarding curriculum.

Business educators must assist noncertified personnel who are instructing K-8 keyboarding classes. Business educators should plan and implement inservice programs to educate K-8 teachers in keyboarding methods. It is also important for business educators to work as a team with the elementary and middle/junior high school teachers. Keyboarding teachers should be given release time from their schedule to observe the appropriate methods utilized by experienced business teachers. In particular, the following techniques would be observed: the presentation of the keys, the variety of activities used, the length of the instructional period, and the teacher-student involvement. It is of the utmost importance that the business educator also be given release time to observe the K-8 teachers in their keyboarding classes to ensure that proper keyboarding techniques are being taught.

SUCCESSFUL KEYBOARDING STRATEGIES

Make keyboarding fun as well as a meaningful learning experience by trying some or all of the activities provided by the respondents to our survey. We hope that these strategies and helpful hints will add to the success of your keyboarding class.

1. Eliminate screen watching by turning off the monitor.

2. Cut out the shape of a mask from black construction paper, paste the picture of a small computer where each eye should be, staple elastic to each edge of the mask, and voilà—you have a computer mask that the students enjoy wearing and they cannot see the keys!

3. Play tag. Student A is chosen to walk around to try to catch another student (B) using an incorrect technique at the computer. Student A "tags" student B. Student B then tries to find another student to tag using an incorrect technique.

4. Take a picture of each student at his/her computer to use on the cover of his/her progress report.

5. Leave a keyed message in each student's computer indicating something you want accomplished.

6. Play musical computers. Each student creates one line of a story, then moves to another computer to add another line to the story. A different story would be composed at each computer.

7. Key from advertisements such as cereal boxes, candy wrappers, cookie boxes, and anything else you can find with large letters.

8. Have the teacher dictate a word and students key rhyming words.

9. Complete a sentence started by the teacher.

10. Key an animal for each letter of the alphabet.

11. Dictate a word and the student lists things this word reminds him/her of within a given time limit.

12. Reward and praise constantly. Use stars, stickers, and certificates as well as a "pat on the back."

13. Construct a keyboarding chart of blank keys using posterboard. As new keys are introduced, place a large letter in its proper position on the chart.

14. Sing the alphabet song along with your students as they key the letters.

15. Create a newsletter containing the students' own compositions of poems and stories.

16. Tape a piece of paper to the keyboard to cover the keys. This will enable you to test the student's knowledge of the keyboard.

17. Divide the keyboard at the correct position with a piece of yarn or string to illustrate right and left hand usage.

18. Upon completion of the keyboard, have students key complete sentences in which they are given a choice of a correct and incorrect spellings of a word.

19. Key sentences using vocabulary words. Have students key a synonym, antonym, and homonym when applicable.

20. Have students compose stories about activities in which they are interested—television, hobbies, etc.

21. Have an upper-level student act as a helper "patrolling" in your class to check for correct fingering, no peeking, eyes on copy, etc.

22. Synchronize dictation with musical beats.

23. Give 30-second technique timings—no looking at keys!

24. Attach a poster (that is of interest to the particular age group you are teaching) to a bulletin board. Divide the poster into segments progressing up the poster from good to excellent. Give timings for accuracy and/or speed

improvement. Move students' names up as students improve.

25. Make a poster of your state including names of cities and/or points of interest. Number each location starting at the bottom as number one and working your way to the top of the state. If you have 10 locations on your map, then you will need 10 sentences for students to key. Students key five perfect lines of sentence one to get on the map at location one; students key five perfect lines of sentence two to move up to location two on the map, etc.

26. Make a collage of computer terms or parts.

27. Prepare a one-page report on important men/women in the history of computers.

28. Make a pictorial poster of computer definitions.

29. Construct a mobile showing computer parts/terms.

30. Prepare a poster with explanations of community uses of computers that students have supplied.

31. Devise a crossword puzzle of computer terms.

32. Key pictures as a change of pace (typing mystery).

33. Be patient! Instruction may take three times as long in explaining a mechanical concept.

34. At Christmas have students compose and key a personal business letter to Santa Claus.

35. At Thanksgiving assign students to key an editorial on "Thomas T. Turkey—Should He Be Eaten for Dinner or Not?"

36. Have students key a half-page personal note to anyone in the class.

37. Exchange "computer-pal" letters with another computer class in a different school.

38. Ask students to compose, arrange, and key their own announcements on brightly colored paper.

39. Make a copy of an actual-size keyboard for each student to use for practice in learning key location at home.

40. Give a weekly "Best Effort Award" to an often neglected student.

41. Have students actually key real words on the first day to get them excited (as, dad, fad, etc.).

42. At the end of the course, have a graduation ceremony.

CONCLUSION

Keyboarding skills are important for students to effectively develop one of the basic tools of computer literacy and of communication itself. Today's students will use computers at some point in their lives, and many students will be required to operate a keyboard with proficiency at least part of the time in a job-related activity. For those reasons as well as the fact that computers are now in the entire K-12 educational system, it is essential that we properly prepare our students to use computers effectively.

How can this be achieved? One way is by requiring *all* education majors to have successfully completed a keyboarding methods course. This methods course should be geared to the grade level of students in which the instructor will be trained. These instructors may be called upon to teach keyboarding.

In fact, our survey shows that instructors with the following educational majors are presently teaching keyboarding at the K-8 grade levels: special education, art, physics, music, natural sciences, French, biology, Latin, social studies, English, mathematics, library science, administration, and counseling. Therefore, it is vital that proper methods for teaching keyboarding be used. Even after this requirement is instituted, all future business educators must be required to successfully complete a methods course in keyboarding for levels K-12. This should be a prerequisite for graduation of all business educators as they should be and will be called upon to help implement and continually update keyboarding programs in the elementary, middle/junior, and high schools.

In the initial steps of keyboarding, students must be monitored constantly and given immediate praise and/or constructive feedback on techniques. How one practices and what one practices are more important than how much one practices. Students must be encouraged to use proper techniques so that bad habits are not formed. Computer time is too costly to be wasted while students "hunt and peck." Students enjoy using computers, and they themselves recognize many of the benefits. Keying information sparks an interest in proper spelling, punctuation, and capitalization and develops organizational and writing skills.

The time is now—in the Computer Age—for keyboarding to take its rightful place in the elementary and middle/junior high schools. All over the world computer keyboards are being used from elementary students to business executives. Everyone needs basic touch keyboarding skills to make efficient use of computers. The educational basics of today are reading, writing, arithmetic, and keyboarding!

CHAPTER 9
Presecondary Computer Literacy

ELLA H. FISHER
East Mecklenburg High School, Mecklenburg, North Carolina

Computers have permeated all areas of business, industry, and society. As a result, computer education should permeate all areas of the educational curriculum, beginning with computer-aided instruction at the pre-elementary level, computer-aided instruction and keyboarding at the elementary level, computer awareness and computer literacy at the middle school level, and continuing with concentrated computer studies at the secondary and postsecondary levels. Computer education, then, should be a continuing process throughout each student's educational career.

As computer-aided instruction and keyboarding shift down into the elementary grades, more time will be available at the middle school level for computer awareness and computer literacy courses. Computer literacy at the middle school level begins with computer awareness, defined as an orderly picture of computers and how they fit into schools, society, and industry. Most computer awareness courses at the middle school level consist of a nine-week course available to all students. Major content areas include a brief history of the computer industry; impact of computers on individuals and businesses; social issues involved with computers; a survey of existing computers, data, storage, and memory; computer and computer-related terminology; and an introduction to simple, user-friendly software, including low-level graphics.

From computer awareness, middle school students move farther up the ladder in their development of computer literacy, usually to a second course. Often this second course is called introduction to computers, a semester course designed to introduce the basic concepts of information processing and to develop further the students' computer literacy. Major content areas include a survey of computer languages and equipment, technological terminology, input/output media and devices, computer and computer-related careers, the uses and effects of computers in areas other than business, the disk operating system (DOS), and an introduction to such software programs as word processing, database, graphics, and utility programs.

CURRENT STATUS OF COMPUTER LITERACY

While the history of mainframe and minicomputers spans several years, the microcomputer, used by most middle schools, is relatively new on the market. Considering the microcomputer's brief history, educational institutions have made amazing progress in integrating it into the schools, particularly in the business area. Though a great deal of progress is being made, much is yet to be accomplished.

According to Bonnie White of Auburn University in Alabama, who conducted a national mailing in 1987-88 asking for suggestions and ideas for integrating computers into computer and noncomputer courses for the NBEA Computer Education Task Force, there are "pockets of sophistication" in computer literacy and computer education across the nation. Outside the "pockets of sophistication," there are many areas where computer literacy is almost nil or barely thriving.

Just prior to White's mailing, Emma Jo Spiegelberg of Laramie High School in Laramie, Wyoming, conducted a 24-question survey of all states for the NBEA Computer Education Task Force to determine the extent computerized accounting was used in accounting classes and the extent spreadsheet software was used at the secondary level. Most of the 160 responses from the states indicated that there were too few computers and too little software available in all areas at the secondary level. Her survey also indicated that instructors shared computers and computer labs, students shared computers, and instructors rotated students. A variety of kinds of computers was used, generally microcomputers with two disk drives, but no prevailing standard existed among the respondents. Many classes had little hands-on time on computers in accounting classes or other computer classes at the secondary level. As indicated by teacher remarks from the respondents, teacher training was lacking in many areas of the country.

On the optimistic side, many states have devised and adopted state guides for computer awareness, introduction to computers, word processing, computer applications, and computerized accounting. Some states are involved in networking and desktop publishing. Other states, such as California, Oklahoma, Virginia, and Washington, have prepared and adopted state guides for keyboarding at the elementary level. Others states are in the process of preparing keyboarding guides as is the NBEA Computer Education Task Force.

From these two recent surveys, from magazine articles, and from presentations, some assumptions can be made regarding the current status of computer literacy: educational institutions over the nation are making efforts to obtain equipment and software, to write curriculum guides, to train teachers, and to integrate computer literacy and computer education into new and existing classes; a lack of funds to purchase equipment and software inhibits teachers from pre-elementary to postsecondary in moving quickly in the computer area; the lack of training and interest of many business teachers inhibits their abilities and enthusiasm to establish new computer courses and to update existing courses; and a lack of understanding of and priority for computer training by school administrators inhibits computer training in many schools. Although the two surveys were addressed to a greater extent to secondary teachers than to middle school teachers, it may be assumed that those obstacles to computer literacy and computer education are even greater at the middle school level than at the secondary level.

REASSERTING LEADERSHIP IN PRESECONDARY COMPUTER LITERACY

What can business teachers at the middle school level do to assert or reassert themselves in leadership roles? Concentrated teacher training must come first, and business teachers must take the initiative to become trained. As in most fields, retraining opportunities occur often. Among the sources available are the following:

1. Professional organizations, which present training workshops, lectures, and demonstrations and predict current and future trends in computer areas
2. Professional magazines, which provide a host of articles on teaching methods, curriculum guides, equipment, and software
3. Computer magazines, which evaluate and critique hardware and software and answer questions asked by most business personnel and teachers
4. Local computer workshops and courses at community colleges, universities, or educational staff development centers
5. Summer workshops conducted by state departments and computer materials and curriculum guides prepared by them
6. Individual learning, which may be accomplished by walking through a software package using either the software documentation or learning guide or by using a book explaining the software package
7. Visits to computer stores to talk with vendors, to try out the equipment, and to spend time with demonstration software
8. Visits to computer repair shops to gather damaged disk drives, memory boards, and keyboards as learning tools and for student displays
9. Visits to local businesses to determine the kinds of equipment and software used and to observe computerized office procedures
10. Summer work in a local business involved with computers
11. Purchase of a home computer, which will provide time for learning and experimentation.

Once training is under way, the second step is to start integrating computer training into classes. If no computers exist, integration may be as simple as exposing students to computer terminology or to the damaged hardware obtained from a repair shop. In the meantime, contact your state department of public instruction and request any prepared materials involving computers. Ask to become a part of one or more of the groups working on computer curriculum guides. Request of administrators that computer classes become a part of the curriculum. Further, ask to teach the classes. Apply for a grant from your local school or your state department to conduct a pilot program in some area of computer training. If your school system has a minigrant program, apply for a minigrant to work on some phase of computer training.

To obtain interest from co-workers, offer computer classes to the co-workers after school or on teacher workdays. Invite administrative personnel to attend the classes. If your school system or state does not have a plan for teacher computer competency, start one. Provide training and testing. When the teachers become computer literate, give them or help them make Level I Computer Competency Certificates to hang on their walls.

As business teachers become computer competent and follow some of the suggestions provided, they will be asserting themselves as leaders in the computer area, promoting business education, and promoting the integration of computers into the curriculum. Most of the suggestions are very inexpensive except for time, but retraining in any field takes time. Not only is computer training valuable for use in the classroom, but it is valuable on a personal level in dealing with businesses and other aspects of society.

COURSE OF STUDY

The following course of study is intended for a one-semester introduction to computers course at the middle school level; however, it may be adapted to a nine-week computer awareness course by deleting parts or all of some of the units:

I. Computer concepts and terminology
II. Hardware
III. Software
    A. Word processing
    B. Programming language(s)
    C. Graphics
    D. Disk operating system (DOS)
    E. Database
    F. Utility programs
IV. Computers in business and society
V. Computer ethics
VI. Computer and computer-related careers
VII. Brief history of computers
VIII. Future computer developments

CLASSROOM COMPUTER EQUIPMENT

When selecting classroom computer equipment for the middle school, a number of areas must be considered. A wise step is to determine what software will be used, then purchase the equipment most suitable for use with the software. The local secondary schools, community colleges, and businesses should be surveyed to determine the predominant kinds of software and equipment in use to ease student adjustment to secondary classes and later into local colleges or business. Since the American society is transient, take a hard look at national trends so that students will be prepared to cope with schools or occupations in other cities. Another consideration is whether or not purchased equipment can be easily upgraded as new software becomes available; and cost, of course, is always a factor.

The ideal computer classroom would contain 24 to 30 two-disk drive computers and a printer for every two computers, with the two computers connected to a switch box for printing ease. Because software requires more and more memory, computers should have 384K to 512K of memory, especially if resident utility programs are introduced at the middle school level. If only 15 to 20 computers are available, students generally have to share them. While sharing is acceptable, there tends to be some loss of student time in the classroom unless the teacher provides expert plans each day.

COMPUTER LITERACY TEACHING METHODS AND STRATEGIES

For efficient use of student time and for sufficient coverage of all topics in the suggested course outline, some doubling of units is desirable, and attention is called to these areas. All suggested methods and strategies have been tested at least once, and some of them have been tested up to 10 or more times. The instructor must use judgment, based upon student abilities, as to how fast particular classes can move.

If the introduction to computers course is started with a display of damaged disk drives, memory boards, and keyboards, students will quickly get the necessary hardware terminology under control, especially if they are allowed to disconnect and reconnect cables, extract and replace computer chips, and take items apart. At this time, a chip test may be administered, giving the student full credit if no legs are broken off the chip. A computer toolbox and chip extracting and replacing tools will be useful. To reinforce the terminology, pictures depicting the terms should be posted on a bulletin board or wall. Small, interesting, and colorful posters may be found at any school supply store for a minimal cost. Keyboard handouts or a keyboard/hardware tutor will aid the students with unfamiliar keys once hands-on work is started. A teacher demonstration on the printer and proper paper loading is usually sufficient to teach printing techniques.

Once the hardware is under control, start students immediately with an easy-to-learn word processor. To gradually integrate student training on the disk operating system (DOS), allow students to format or initialize their own data diskettes for use with the word processing program. If data is stored on the teaching diskette for use with the word processor, allow students to copy the data onto their diskettes, thereby teaching DOS copying features. Provide students a walk through the features of the word processing program and give sufficient time for them to feel comfortable with it. Once they feel comfortable, select computer concepts or terms and have students write a paragraph about each on the word processor.

A descriptive paragraph about the computer chip might be handled by using the cluster writing strategy along with a brainstorming session. Before beginning the brainstorming session, prepare a sheet of paper with a large circle in the middle. Write inside the large circle "computer chip" or "silicon chip." Cluster small blank circles around the top of the large circle, connecting them together and to the large circle with lines. Cluster another set of small blank circles around the bottom of the large circle, also connecting them together and to the large circle with lines. Give each student a copy of the prepared sheet. During the brainstorming session, write the descriptive words on the chalkboard as students call them out. Students write all the descriptive brainstormed words in the small circles at the top of the page. Connective words to pull the sentences together should be written in the small circles at the bottom of the page. Review the structure of a paragraph with the students. Give students seven minutes to write a rough draft of a well-constructed descriptive paragraph on the computer chip and seven minutes to refine the paragraph. Have them key the paragraph on the word processor, then return to the top of the page to insert a centered title in all capital letters. By using time in this manner, students learn computer terminology and concepts of word processing as they refine their writing skills. Use a variation of this method or other writing strategies to continue with several more paragraphs concerned with computer terms or concepts that need to be taught immediately.

Once the paragraphs are under control, proceed to teach larger and more complex computer concepts. An example is the impact of the computer on society, a subject which can be handled on the word processor with a five-paragraph theme such as students use in their English classes. After student readings and class discussions, provide students with the structure of a five-paragraph theme. Detail for them precisely what area should be covered in each paragraph. For example, paragraph one should be an introduction, paragraph two may cover the impact of the computer on society and on the individual, paragraph three may cover the impact of the computer on businesses, paragraph four may cover the impact of the computer on crime, and the last paragraph should be the summary paragraph. With this method, students learn further concepts of word processing, relate the learning to writing and their English classes, and reinforce communicating skills. Students should be encouraged to use the word processor for writing assignments from other classes.

Near the end of the course, use the same five-paragraph theme method or a variation to review the word processor, but use other computer concepts such as computer or computer-related careers, the history of the computer, or future computer developments. If two word processors are to be introduced, hold the second until near the end of the semester. After a walk-through, use the five-paragraph theme method to reinforce the word processing concepts as other computer concepts are taught.

As word processing programs are introduced, inform students of the use of spell checks included as a part of most word processing programs. At this time, other utility programs may be introduced, such as a proofreader and writing style analyzer, a thesaurus, a desktop organizer, or any one of the pop-up clocks, calculators, or calendars that will enhance the introduction to computers course.

Upon completion of the word processing unit, introduce students to the BASIC programming language, using the structured concept. Before beginning to write the BASIC programs, give students a handout borrowed from a drafting teacher to practice penmanship, and discuss with them the importance of accuracy in the written programs. Provide them with additional DOS training by having them reformat their data diskettes (with the system) and by having them copy the BASIC and BASICA programs onto their diskettes.

The purpose of this introduction to the BASIC programming language is not for competency, but to give students a taste of the concepts of programming to determine if this is a field in which they are interested and to provide enough expertise for students to modify simple programs in the future to fit their own needs. To accomplish this purpose, keep programs short and simple. A workable plan is to help students write the first six programs, introducing a different concept in each program. Assign students to write an additional six programs patterned after the first six. For example, the seventh program would be patterned after the first program, the eighth after the second program, and so on. Through this kind of exercise, students learn to write simple programs quickly. To impress upon the students the importance of good documentation, the first BASIC program statement in each program should include the student's name, period, and program name. If programs are named PROG1, PROG2, etc., students will not forget the names of their programs. The second BASIC program statement should state the purpose of the program. For each group of programs, provide students with a sign-off sheet listing program names and lines for the instructor's initials. If printers are not available for all students, the instructor can initial completed programs without having students print the programs. If printers are available, students initial their own programs on the sign-off sheet and attach a listing and execution of each program. If students must share computers, each student should be responsible for all handwritten programs, but in order to conserve computer and printer time, one printout or sign-off for the two students or the group should be sufficient.

Follow the same pattern for the next group of twelve programs, introducing a different concept in each of the first six and having students write the last six. At this point, introduce flowcharting, and have students flowchart each of these twelve programs, attaching the handwritten programs and the flowcharts. Again, each student should be responsible for written programs and for flowcharts; however, when working in groups, one listing and one execution of each program should be acceptable.

Gradually increase the difficulty of the programs as students move to the third group, perhaps going to a payroll program that uses simple subroutines and the PRINT USING keyword and then building to programs using the relational operators. For the last group, select debugging programs, sound programs, and graphics programs which require BASICA. Students enjoy the sound and graphic programs. After students have been introduced to a program which draws circles with the CIRCLE keyword, they can generate any number of interesting programs. By efficient use of time in class, these 48 programs can be written and executed in only a few days, especially if students write some of the programs out of class. Ask students to write, without help if possible, an additional two programs of a creative nature.

A second programming language such as Pascal or COBOL should consume a shorter period of time with approximately 20 programs assigned. Keep in mind that the Pascal programming language provides excellent training in structure and there is an easy-to-use Pascal compiler available. However, when deciding upon the second programming language, survey the secondary schools into which the students feed to see which programming languages are included in the curriculum; then select the language based upon your findings. Again, have students prepare their own diskettes by using a reformatting/copying process to review the DOS commands.

Once the programming languages have been finished, walk students through one of the simple database programs. Have students prepare a form detailing the kinds of software on the market or the kinds of computer careers available. A form on the database program for careers might consist of the career title, pay scale, required education, job responsibilities, and other data of the instructor's choice. A form for software might list the title, publisher, vendor, category (word processing, database, graphics, spreadsheet, system, utility), cost, and other selected data. Some research skills may be added to a project of this nature, if desired, by requiring students to research computer careers or the software market.

Move to a graphics software program upon completion of the database unit. Should the selected graphics software program produce graphs and charts, introduce it at the same time that students deal with the uses and effects of computers in areas other than business by having students graph a science project from a biology class or an instructor-prepared science project in addition to graphing a business project such as a sales analysis.

An example of a teacher-prepared science research project consists of charting the affects of acid rain on a small flowering plant such as the duckweed, which grows in pond water in most areas. Assume the research started with 20 plants in each of four beakers. If tested in pond water and well water with no acid rain added and in each kind of water with acid rain added, the project would have four variables. Four observations could be charted by testing once each week for four weeks. Chart the survival rate of the plants each week in each kind of water. An assumption can be made that all or most plants survive in pond water, and about 60 percent survive in well water. The survival rate of the plants in the beakers to which acid rains was added can be expected to drop to zero survival rate during the first or second week of observation. This kind of graphing project will lend itself to bar or stacked bar graphs or to line graphs. Grid lines may be added for special effects. With some graph programs, students might print four small pie charts with exploded slices for the highest survival rate of plants or any number of variations. After completing this project, students will be able to relate computers to other areas while learning a graphics software program, and they should be encouraged to apply their knowledge to assignments in other classes.

Should students be exposed to a drawing or sign-making software program rather than a graph program, have them concentrate on advertising a product or a cultural event through their drawings. This project will allow students to relate the computer to both business and uses other than business as they veer off into the advertising area. Students may also be encouraged to draw maps for a social studies class as drawing programs lend themselves readily to map drawing. Should a low-level desktop publishing software program be used, a variety of activities tying the computer to uses other than business can be incorporated into student activities.

While computer ethics may be inserted at any time during the semester, it is appropriate to have students discuss ethics during the time they are working with the computer and its effects on the individual, society, and business. Group work, however, does not fit into the course structure if the class is writing themes on the impact of the computer on the individual, society, and business; therefore, this unit may be inserted elsewhere. For student involvement and to teach effective team cooperation and communication, the instructor may wish to place a number of computer ethical discussion questions or situations in a box, divide the class into groups of three or four, and have a group member draw a question or situation from the box. After the group has elected a spokesperson, allow students 15 to 20 minutes to discuss the question or situation and arrive at opinions and conclusions to be presented to the class by the spokesperson.

A suggested situation to use is as follows: A law enforcement center, which is networked to a national database where information may be obtained on any individual, has a rule that law enforcement personnel may obtain information about an individual on a "need to know" basis only. One curious policeman obtained information on his neighbor, which he spread about in the neighborhood. The angry victim learned the origin of the information and proceeded to take action. Were the policeman's actions unethical or did they constitute a crime? (For the instructor's information, this situation did happen in a large southern city in the fall of 1987, and the entire police department was put on probation for a three-month period, which curtailed police activities badly. While the action was not criminal, it was considered unethical.)

During this unit, the instructor should emphasize team work, oral presentation techniques, and good listening skills in addition to an examination of the ethical questions and situations. Group grades may be given for the group work, and a listening grade may be given to each individual.

The wise and resourceful instructor will provide training in this semester course on computerized testing. Should the instructor use the suggested writing techniques on the word processor, students need not be tested subjectively as the instructor will see samples of students' subjective work. There are many testing programs available in which the instructor keys in any number of multiple-choice questions. Students may be allowed to have a second try if the first answer is not correct, and the instructor may allow students to review the test if desired. Some programs allow for random questions, juggle the questions and answers, provide the student with the final grade, and record the final grade on the teacher's portion of the software program, which is accessed only by a password. Instead of taking the time to check each diskette for student grades, the teacher may record the grade as the student finishes the test. If students are paired on a computer, have them take some of the tests in pairs. This exposure to computerized testing will help students prepare to complete job application forms and take tests on computers, as many companies have gone to computerized testing and completion of job application forms.

FUTURE PROJECTIONS FOR PRESECONDARY COMPUTER LITERACY

Computer advances are not slow to reach the market. Even now a child beginning to talk can "reach out and see" his grandparents thousands of miles away with an electronic marvel that uses simple audio signals to send and receive photo-quality, black-and-white pictures over ordinary telephone lines. As more advances of this nature become affordable, as more user-friendly software programs become available, as more schools purchase computers for formal computer classes and for integrating computers into other classes, as more home computers become available for student use, as more keyboarding classes and computer-aided instruction are shifted down into the pre-elementary and elementary grades, and as society becomes more dependent on computers, students will become more computer literate before they enter the middle school grades. As a result of these advances and processes, computer literacy and computer education will become one of the four basic required areas of learning—reading, writing, computing, and mathematics. Indeed, it will be a continuing process throughout each student's educational career.

As the middle school students become more sophisticated in computer use, more will be accomplished at the middle school level, leaving the secondary and postsecondary schools free to offer specialized courses in computer applications, desktop publishing, telecommunications and networking, programming languages, and other undiscovered and unanticipated areas.

As computing becomes one of the four basic required areas of learning, business educators will be able to demand the respect now reserved for the academic areas; but business educators must become assertive in their leadership roles, must grasp all opportunities to stay abreast of new and emerging technology, and must spend untold hours in formal group training sessions and individual training sessions. They must be persistent. While the overwhelming changes and hours of training may seem formidable, the new and exciting areas of teaching opening to business educators will present challenges no other area of education can present. Business educators will never be bored again after typewriters are moved from the classrooms to accommodate sophisticated computing equipment that changes yearly.

SUMMARY

Computer literacy begins at the K level of instruction and continues through the postgraduate level. By the end of the present decade, few, if any, students will graduate from any educational institution without computer training. As computer literacy begins to shift down to the pre-elementary and elementary levels, secondary training will shift down to the middle school level. These movements, in turn, will cause a shift of postsecondary training down to the secondary level. At the postsecondary level, higher levels of training will be required as society depends more and more on computers and as career complexity raises the requirements for jobs.

At the present time, computer-aided instruction and keyboarding are already moving to the pre-elementary and elementary levels. At the middle school level, students must be trained in computer awareness and computer literacy in order to be prepared for secondary courses. Their training should consist of an orderly background of computers and how they fit into schools, society, and industry and a knowledge of computer hardware and software. In order to accomplish this in the middle school classes throughout the nation, business educators must assume an assertive leadership role to ensure that middle school students in all areas have access to computer literacy training. Business educators must also assume an assertive role to ensure that computing becomes one of the four basic required areas of learning, along with reading, writing, and mathematics.

CHAPTER 10
Economic Literacy at the Junior High Level

JOHN E. CLOW
State University of New York at Oneonta, Oneonta

The educational reform movement of the 1980's has promoted a considerable amount of hand wringing and distress on the part of the business education community. Few, if any, of the myriad of education reform documents provide much support for business education offerings in the schools. In fact, they have primarily brought about a de-emphasis of enrollment in business education courses. The increased number of required courses in the traditional areas of the curriculum, particularly at the secondary level, has prompted the crowding out syndrome whereby students do not have as much time to take business courses. Our professional literature and conference programming for the past few years are replete with ideas on what we must do to promote business education among our various constituencies in order to prosper.

The old adage that out of adversity comes strength can very well hold true for business education if the realities of the present educational climate are accepted and we in business education showcase what we have which will be of great value to students and will appeal to the educational community at this time. This concept of fitting our services to the present-day market is not new to business education. We have had to make such changes in the past and will undoubtedly have to do so in the future.

One major advantage of business education is our broad base of content. The proclaimed "turf" for business education in the school curriculum for decades has been to teach *about* and *for* business. This has been elucidated by many early and contemporary leaders in the field of business education as well as the Policies Commission for Business and Economic Education, a leading think tank in the profession. The "for business" includes the numerous courses in the occupational arena including keyboarding, marketing, word processing, and accounting. The "about business" includes those courses which tend to be more general education in nature, such as general business, business law, and economics.

A perusal of the educational trends of the last 30 to 40 years shows that American secondary education seems to swing from a heavy emphasis of prescribed general education courses to one with more freedom of choice as to the courses to be taken to earn a high school diploma. During the fifties, for example, the launching of Sputnik by the Russians surprised the American public. Concern was rampant that we were not keeping up technologically. Following that event, science and technology courses as well as more traditional general education courses were required in the secondary curriculum. During the sixties and seventies, there was a concern about relevance and freedom of choice in the secondary curriculum. Also, there was a concern about assisting young people to succeed in our economic system by providing them with employable skills. These trends along with the Vocational Education Act and Amendments of the 1960's in addition to the career education movement of that time provided the impetus for increased enrollments in occupational education classes. The "back to basics" movement of the 1980's emanated from a concern about maintaining our technological advantage as well as producing more culturally literate citizens. Thus, the focus is back to requiring more general education courses.

Since business education can be both vocational and general in nature, the field can conceivably maintain enrollments during the cycles which are an inevitable part of the American educational scene. If courses in occupational education are in vogue, business education will prosper because of the valuable vocational courses offered by the field. Similarly, if general education is the emphasis, enrollments in general education offerings of the field could well increase.

In reality, this somewhat automatic balancing of vocational and general offerings has not occurred. One major reason for this is that the general education component of business education has generally not been given as much attention as the favored member of the family, being the occupational group of courses. Thus, in periods of time such as the 1980's, business education suffers because the necessary spadework has not been done for demonstrating that the field can and should be a leader in an important area of general education.

A primary purpose of this chapter is to demonstrate how and why one particular area of business education, notably economic education at the junior high school level, is a fruitful field for development. The chapter will cover several aspects including what economic education is and why it is important at the junior high level, the nature of a proposed general education course at this level, strategies to use in encouraging its acceptance, general considerations to keep in mind when teaching a junior high economic education course, and the responsibility of teacher education institutions in helping to promote this facet of business education.

NATURE OF AND REASONS FOR ECONOMIC EDUCATION AT THE JUNIOR HIGH SCHOOL LEVEL

Anne Scott Daughtrey, a leader of economic education in business education, has defined economic education as

. . . comprising a large segment of general education. The purpose of economic education is to develop economic literacy which all citizens need in order to function effectively in their roles as consumers, workers, and citizens in American society. Economic education includes the knowledges, skills, abilities, and understandings everyone should have to (1) effectively carry out their personal day-to-day economic activities; (2) understand the nature, organization, and development of the American enterprise system; the sources, institutions, and values through which it compares with other systems, and (3) base their personal and society economic decisions on sound reasoning, through an analysis of alternatives and their implications for themselves as citizens and for the society in which they live.[1]

A primary reason economic education is so important in our society is our participatory economic system which means that individuals have the freedom to make choices of goods and services in the marketplace, to select jobs in the working world, to select different types of savings and investments, and to vote on different candidates and issues which focus on various economic positions. If individuals are not well educated as to economic knowledges, skills, and understanding, the individual and society will not be using their resources as efficiently as they could.

Economic education at the junior high level (grades 7-9) is important for at least three reasons. One is that there is a readiness level for learning about economic matters on the part of the students since many have part-time jobs, make independent decisions in purchasing goods and services in the marketplace, make saving and investment decisions, and are aware of various social institutions and issues. In other words, students at the junior high school age are actively involved in our economic world so economic education geared to their interest and experiential levels can be very effective.

A second reason is that junior high youths make a number of important decisions which will affect their lives for several or perhaps many years in the future. One of these is their tentative career choice. Their decision at this level will affect the courses and program they select at the high school level as well as the postsecondary level. Career decisions, just like consumer and citizenship decisions, have economic components which should be considered. A course focusing on economic concepts and an economic way of thinking can be very helpful to them.

A third reason is that a sizeable number of students will decide to drop out of school shortly after they leave the ninth grade. The junior high level may be the last formal economic education instruction that they will receive. Providing these school leavers with economic knowledges and understandings will assist them in making more informed decisions as consumers, wage earners, and citizens, which is important not only for them but also for the society.

GENERAL BUSINESS—AN IMPORTANT JUNIOR HIGH SCHOOL COURSE FOCUSING ON ECONOMIC LITERACY

A perusal of the common offerings of business education at the junior high level shows that the general business course is probably the "best" candidate for meeting the requirements of being a general education course with an economic education emphasis. Some schools entitle the course "Introduction to Business."

In the 1982 NBEA Yearbook, Thomas B. Duff described the course as developing economic literacy so that students can make relatively free

---

[1]Daughtrey, Anne Scott. *Methods of Basic Business and Economic Education.* Second edition. Cincinnati: South-Western Publishing Co., 1974. p. 41.

decisions (individual and group) in our economic system. He then delineated 10 major objectives of the course which are:
1. Identify and describe the major purpose of an economic system, determine the specific questions an economic system must answer, and compare and contrast the principal features of a market, centralized, and mixed economy.
2. Identify and describe the basic characteristics and functions of the private enterprise economy of the United States.
3. Describe the role of business, government, and human resources in our private enterprise economy and explain the interdependencies among the three sectors.
4. Describe and evaluate the ways an individual can contribute to our private enterprise economy in the roles of producer, consumer, and citizen.
5. Identify the reasons and develop a plan for efficient use of money resources by individuals, business firms, and units of government.
6. Identify the risks against which persons most commonly need protection and explain how risk sharing provides a means of protection.
7. Describe how banks, credit, and other financial institutions affect individuals, business firms, units of government, and economy as a whole.
8. Describe the role of savings and investments in our private enterprise economy and identify ways and places for saving and investing.
9. Identify the rights and responsibilities of consumers, and sources and uses of consumer information and protection.
10. Describe the need for a careful career choice, a general career area of interest as well as the preparation required for it, and the steps to be completed to find a job.[2]

A study of the articles in the Yearbook, *Revitalization of Basic Business Education at All Instructional Levels*, shows that many leaders in the field of business education agree with this approach to the general business course. A survey of current textbooks in the field reflects the emphasis indicated by Duff.

GENERAL BUSINESS—AN IMPORTANT GENERAL EDUCATION COURSE FOR ALL STUDENTS

Many schools already offer the general business course at the junior high school level. It is taken primarily by those interested in pursuing a business education sequence of courses at the high school level. Most schools, though, do not offer the course as a requirement for all students or as a course at the ninth-grade level in a traditional high school program that can be used to meet general education requirements for a high school diploma. Making the general business course a requirement can and should be pursued. The rationale and procedures for implementing this approach include the following.

Why can the general business course be considered general education? The focus of the general business course is to provide a general overview of our

---
[2]Duff, Thomas B. "The Role of General Business Education in Basic Business." *Revitalization of Basic Business Education at All Instructional Levels.* Twentieth Yearbook. Reston, Va.: National Business Education Association, 1982. Chapter 8, pp. 88-89.

economic system, the role and functions of business in our economy, and the skills and knowledges necessary for economic decision making as consumers, wage earners, and citizens. Certainly, this is general education. All students will be consumers, citizens, and earners of income regardless of ability level and socioeconomic background. All students ought to understand the role and purposes of business in our economy.

A suggested course outline for a one-year course in general business which reflects this focus on general education and is consistent with the objectives listed earlier is included at the end of this chapter. Obviously, a semester-length course pertaining to general business topics would include fewer topics.

A perusal of the course content indicates two aspects of economic education, both of which are important. The "how to" approach includes important things to consider and do when making purchases, using bank services, and using credit. These are integral parts of the course. A second focus of the course is on basic economic concepts which serve as organizing centers or reference points throughout the course—meaning that they are introduced and then reinforced throughout the course. The economic decision-making approach along with how markets operate and the interrelationships among various parties within the economy are some of the organizing centers which are apparent in the course outline.

How do you sell the idea? Several steps must be taken in order for general business to be a course for all students.

PROVE THAT BUSINESS EDUCATION IS MORE THAN VOCATIONAL EDUCATION. Many administrators do not understand that business education is more than occupational or vocational education. Among the reasons for this are the historical precedent of the field being primarily oriented towards vocational education and the reluctance of practitioners in the field to foster the general education aspects of business education.

A need exists for administrators to understand that the general business course is a type of course that deals with how an individual interacts and affects institutions—in this case the major focus being on the institution of business and our economic system. Even though it is a "social studies" type of course, the business teacher has a comparative advantage in teaching the course because of preparation in how businesses operate and how business interrelates with the individual and other economic institutions. Also, most business educators have a background in economics.

PROVE THAT CONTENT OF THE GENERAL BUSINESS COURSE IS IMPORTANT FOR ALL STUDENTS. Administrators need to first of all understand the need for developing economic literacy for all students. The general business course should then be shown as an important element in promoting economic literacy as a part of general education at the junior high school level. Supportive comments for both positions are given in earlier parts of this chapter. Certainly the suggested course outline has a general education orientation.

DETERMINE IF COURSE CONTENT OVERLAPS WITH THAT OF OTHER COURSES IN REQUIRED CURRICULUM. Obviously, if the content covered in the general business course is included elsewhere in the required curriculum, one will legitimately run into some resistance in having it embraced as a general education requirement.

If some other course is similar, look carefully at the way the content is covered. Perhaps the way in which the content is approached is different. The approach used in general business should be a blend of the "how to" and the application of economic theory for individual and group decision making. Similar courses offered by other discipline areas may focus on the "how to" approach with little or no emphasis on economic theory. Others may focus on economic theory with little emphasis on practical application. In these instances, point out that the general business course could serve as another option to fulfill the already existing requirement. As educational theorists tell us, one approach to covering content is generally not effective for all the learning styles and ability levels of students.

A related idea is to determine whether the general business course could meet the economic education mandate that your state may have. Between 25 and 30 states have such mandates. If your state has such a mandate, determine whether the general business course can meet the mandate. Perhaps some minor modifications could be made in the suggested course outline to meet the mandate.

SHOW HOW ROOM CAN BE MADE IN A CROWDED REQUIRED GENERAL EDUCATION CURRICULUM. The idea of adding another required course to the curriculum, especially at the ninth-grade or lower secondary level, may be difficult in some schools. One way to deal with this problem is to determine whether the course could be used as an option for meeting a general education requirement. For example, in some schools it might well be used as an option for meeting one of the several required courses in social studies. Such a precedent has been successful for other business education courses. Business Communications, for example, can be counted toward the English requirements in some schools. Similarly, Business Law has been counted towards the required social studies units in some states.

PROVE YOUR DEPARTMENT'S COMPETENCE AND COMMITMENT IN TEACHING THE COURSE. If your department is already teaching the course as an elective, find ways to demonstrate that your students are gaining some important learnings from the course. Familiarizing administrators with some innovative projects completed by the students is one way to do this. Showing innovative teaching strategies used by teachers of this course is another. It is also important to show that the course can be challenging to students of various ability levels if it is to be required for all students.

SHOW THAT COURSE IS CONSISTENT WITH EDUCATIONAL TRENDS. Theodore Sizer, in *A Study of High School*, one of the educational reform documents, feels that the curriculum, especially at the junior and senior high school levels, is too oriented toward individual disciplines with very little emphasis on showing the interrelationships of discipline areas. Life is not segmented according to different disciplinary areas. To understand various phenomenons in our lives, there must be an understanding of concepts from different disciplinary areas and how they interrelate with one another. The general business course is an excellent vehicle to show the interrelationships among the consumer, wage earner, and citizen since each is considered in the course and constant reference to these interrelationships is suggested throughout.

It is also important to demonstrate that the content of the course is not just memorization of facts and knowledges but the application of higher order thinking such as the application, synthesis, analysis, and evaluation of data. Many opportunities are available in general business for problem solving. Most educational reform documents of the 1980's have encouraged the schools to do more with these higher level abilities.

Another trend which is consistent with this course is the recommendations by several of the national education reform documents that an understanding of our economic system is important. Certainly, the general business course relates well to that recommendation.

GAIN THE SUPPORT OF LOCAL BUSINESS LEADERS. According to numerous studies, business leaders are concerned about students knowing how the economic system operates and how they can successfully fulfill their roles in the system. The general business course is a "natural" for fulfilling these objectives. Using local business leaders as guest speakers in the general business course is one good way to facilitate the familiarization process. Publicity in school newspapers and in the local paper regarding innovative projects completed by students is another. Such steps can be of assistance in gaining board of education approval, since many board members are business leaders in the community.

CHOOSE AN APPEALING TITLE FOR THE COURSE. As marketing people well understand, the name of a product or service can be very important in its sale. The same can certainly be true of a course. Perhaps, the selection of a title other than general business would be beneficial, especially if the content of the course is changed or the image of the course in your school is that of a dumping ground. "Introduction to Business," "Applied Economics," or "Our Economic World" are some examples of other possible titles.

OTHER OPTIONS FOR FOSTERING ECONOMIC EDUCATION AT THE JUNIOR HIGH LEVEL

Even though some districts have been able to initiate the general business course as a requirement for all students, there are situations where some schools will not make such an adaption. What, then, can be done to foster economic education at the junior high school?

1. Determine whether the course can be required of all occupational education students. In New York State, for example, a course entitled "Introduction to Occupations" is required of all students pursuing a sequence of courses in technology, health, agriculture, business, and home economics education. It is first offered at the ninth-grade level. The content does not duplicate the course outline for general business, but there are many similarities. Teachers from all occupational areas can teach the course. Business teachers, though, many times teach the modules dealing with personal resource management and our working world to all occupational students in the local schools.

2. Offer the general business course as a required course for all business majors. Set up elective minicourses or short courses for the nonbusiness

majors in the school focusing on various aspects of economic education such as starting one's own business, developing a savings and investment plan, managing personal resources (time and money), and knowing the nature of our working world including procedures for securing a job. Hopefully, in teaching these units, both the "how to" and applicable economic theory will be emphasized.

If these types of courses are perceived by the school administration as valuable and of a general education nature, they may well become part of the required curriculum for all students at a later time.

IMPORTANT CONSIDERATIONS IN TEACHING ECONOMIC EDUCATION TO JUNIOR HIGH YOUTH

There are many books and articles written on the effective teaching of the early adolescent. Many recommendations and suggestions can be made. Because of space limitations, three general recommendations as related to economic education are suggested.

1. Concrete applications of economic concepts are important. As the content outline shows, there are several rather abstract concepts which are a part of the instruction. If the learning of these concepts is to be optimized among this age group, concrete examples must be presented. For example, the concepts of scarcity, opportunity costs, and tradeoffs can and should be shown very concretely through the personal money management process as well as the process of making decisions by government in the utilization of our tax dollars. Showing how markets operate in the selling of fashionable clothing is another example.

2. Show people involved in the economy. An integral part of the general business course is to demonstrate how individual decision making and interrelationships are important in our economic system. Guest speakers and activities, such as case problems, focusing on business and personal decisions should be important components of the course.

3. Involve students actively in the learning process. Educational psychologists indicate that immediate or delayed recall of factual information is better when active involvement is the vehicle used to learn. Thus, the utilization of such teaching techniques as role-playing, discussion, and simulations is important.

Simulations, for example, can be not only a good way to cover some basic facts and knowledges but also a way to move toward more abstract concepts. One simulation used in classes relates to a bank where one person completes a check and gives it to another who endorses it at the bank; the bank then cashes it, and it moves through the check clearance process. This activity can lead to more abstract concepts, such as the functions of money and the definition of the primary money supply in this country (Ml). The concepts pursued would depend on the level of the student group with whom you are working.

Another simulation that can be very effective is the operation of a small business. To assist students in gaining the full scope of a business operation, it is best to simulate a firm that produces some type of item that they can sell. Paper flowers, school stationery that the students print themselves, or something similar should be selected. The three primary functions of a business should be represented in the business—production, marketing, and accounting; that is, some students should be in charge of production, some marketing, and some accounting. It is important, however, that all students be familiar with what each function is doing, an example of encouraging good communications within the firm.

WHAT IS THE ROLE OF BUSINESS TEACHER EDUCATION PROGRAMS?

Business teacher education programs have to place great importance on the economic education segment of our offerings. The responsibility of the business teacher education program is actually threefold. First of all, all preservice candidates should gain a good background in the content areas of business administration, accounting, and economics. A minimum of at least one course should be required in finance, marketing, management, and accounting for purposes of teaching the general business course. Obviously, more course work could be beneficial. Two courses in economics focusing on macro and microeconomics should also be required as well as a personal finance course which emphasizes the application of business and economic concepts to personal financial decisions.

A second responsibility is to provide sufficient methodology course work focusing on ways to teach economic education courses such as general business. Student teaching should include teaching economic education courses, with some experiences teaching students at the grade 7-9 levels. Also, each candidate should be exposed to the wealth of teaching materials available from such sources as the Joint Council on Economic Education, Junior Achievement, and the National Federation of Independent Business.

A third purpose is to provide inservice activities both of a credit and noncredit nature for teachers of general business. Many teachers find a general business course difficult to teach. They need assistance in finding new materials and keeping up with current business developments. They also need to be provided positive reinforcement that what they are teaching is important. The Joint Council on Economic Education with its 50 State Councils and over 250 Centers for Economic Education in college/university campuses can be very helpful in these inservice functions. Many State Councils and College/University Centers have periodic programs for teachers focusing on economic issues and materials. Business teacher education departments should work cooperatively with their State Council and/or Center in planning programs of benefit to their graduates or teachers in their service area.

SUMMARY

Business educators have for several decades had the objectives of education *for* and *about* business. Traditionally, the profession has focused primarily on educating students *for* business, equipping them with specific job skills. In this "back to basics" era where general education is important, business education should demonstrate more definitively how it can make an important contribution to general education. One significant way to do this is by developing more of an economic education presence at the junior high school level.

Suggested Outline for General Business Course
As General Education Offering
Junior High School Level

I. Overall Nature of Economic Systems
   A. Basic Scarcity Problem Which Prompts a Need for an Economic System
   B. Questions Which Must Be Answered by any Economic System
   C. Types of Economic Systems Including Analysis of Advantages and Disadvantages of Each System
      1. Traditional Economy
      2. Command Economy
      3. Market Economy
   D. Reasons Why an Economic System Is Generally a Mix of All Three Types of Systems

II. Characteristics of Our Modified Market System
   A. How a Market Operates
      1. Functions and Roles of Price in Our Economic System
      2. Law of Supply
      3. Law of Demand
      4. Determination of Equilibrium Price
      5. Reasons Why Prices Change
      6. Automatic Features Inherent in a Market
   B. Private Enterprise and Private Ownership
   C. Types of Competition—Degree of Control
      1. Pure Competition
      2. Monopolistic Competition
      3. Oligopolies
      4. Monopolies
   D. Role of Profits
   E. Reasons and Types of Government Intervention

III. How Decisions As Consumers, Wage Earners, and Citizens Affect Each Other and the Total Economy
   A. The Circular Flow of the Economy
   B. Analysis of How Individual (Consumers, Wage Earners, and Citizens) Decisions in the Aggregate Affect Our Total Economy

IV. Role of Business in Economy
   A. Reasons for Businesses in Our Economy
   B. Types of Business in Economy
      1. Service
      2. Goods
   C. Functions Found Within a Typical Business
      1. Production

        2. Marketing
        3. Accounting
    D. Businesses and Productivity
        1. What Is Productivity
        2. How To Increase Productivity
        3. Relationship of Worker Productivity to Standard of Living
    E. Effects of Computers in Business

V. The Consumer in the Economy
    A. Rights and Responsibilities of the Consumers
    B. Buying Goods and Services in the Economy
    C. Using Money in the Economy
        1. What Is Money
        2. Role of Banks in Our Economy
        3. Control of Money by the Federal Reserve System
        4. Types of Checking Accounts Including Electronic Funds Transfer
        5. Using a Checking Account
    D. Managing Your Money
        1. Importance of Budgeting to Individuals and Institutions
        2. Procedures To Use in Managing One's Money
    E. Saving and Investing
        1. Role of Savings and Investing in Your Economy
        2. Types of Savings and Investing Options
    F. Using Credit
        1. Role of Credit in Our Economy
        2. How Credit Is Generated in Our Economy
        3. Forms of Credit Available
        4. How To Use Credit Effectively
        5. Legislation Pertaining to Credit
    G. Insuring Against Loss
        1. Reasons for Insurance
        2. Probability and How It Relates to Insurance and the Setting of Rates
        3. Characteristics of Various Types of Insurance
            a. Automobile Insurance
            b. Health Insurance
            c. Real and Personal Property
        4. Role of Insurance Companies in Our Economy

VI. The Wage Earner in Our Economy
    A. Reasons Why Jobs Are Created and Deleted
    B. Types of Jobs Available in Our Economy
        1. White-Collar
        2. Blue-Collar
        3. Service Jobs
    C. Factors Affecting Wages
        1. Supply/Demand Considerations
        2. Value Society Places on Tasks Completed in Job
        3. Union/Non-Union Considerations
        4. Productivity of Work Force
    D. Choosing a Career Goal
        1. Interests
        2. Aptitudes

       3. Goals in Life
       4. Probable Openings in Future
       5. Advancement Opportunities
    E. Legislation Affecting the Wage Earner
    F. Unions and the Worker
       1. Purposes of Unions
       2. History of Unions Including Federal and State Legislation
       3. Effects of Unions on the Labor Marketplace
       4. How Unions Operate

VII. The Citizen in Our Economy
    A. How Consumer/Citizens Purchase Both Private and Public Goods and Services
    B. Governmental Taxation
       1. Differences Between Non-Tax and Tax Revenue
       2. Effect That Taxes Have on Economic Activity
       3. Different Types of Taxes
          a. Wealth
          b. Consumption
          c. Income
       4. Levels of Taxation
          a. Federal
          b. State
          c. Local
       5. Characteristics of a Good Tax
          a. Fairness According to Concepts of Progressive, Proportional, and Regressive Taxes
          b. Ease of Collection
          c. Acceptability
    C. How Government Affects Our Economy
       1. A Major Purchaser of Factors of Production
       2. Provider of Some Basic Public Goods and Services
          a. Education
          b. Legal and Penal System
          c. Transportation System
          d. Recreational Facilities
          e. Health Facilities
          f. National Defense
       3. Regulator and Police Person
          a. Legislation Focusing on Business
          b. Legislation Focusing on Consumer
          c. Legislation Focusing on Investor and Wage Earner
          d. Legislation Relating to Competition in the Marketplace
          e. Legislation Relating to Issues Affecting Entire Society, Such As Environmental
          f. Legislation Relating to Citizens
       4. Maintaining a Healthy Economy
          a. Fiscal Policy
          b. Monetary Policy
       5. Providing Aid to Specific Groups
          a. Transfer Payment to Indigent Retirees, etc.
          b. Subsidies to New Ventures Wanted by Society

CHAPTER 11
Job, Career, and Human Relations Skills

SUSAN J. VOGEL
Fort Madison High School, Fort Madison, Iowa

Teachers say that children have changed. Teaching is not what it used to be. Have children really altered their developmental patterns, or is society blind to the effects of its own attitudes?

So much of development is dependent upon attitudes. In human relations, it is still maintained that people tend to live up or live down to the expectations held of them by others. Junior high or middle school students are no exception to this rule. In fact, the presecondary student possesses behavior patterns not totally unlike that of a young springer spaniel—eager to please, energetic, and self-centered enough to have complete disregard for objects or people that get in his/her way. Capturing the attention span of the presecondary student requires harnessing this energy level with positive teacher expectations and combining high interest information, daily student participation, and yes, entertainment. Theatrical performance is without question a major tool in the art of teaching.

Adolescence. The junior high student is more receptive to learning by doing rather than by listening. Lecture material is ineffective and inappropriate unless student input is encouraged and teacher directed. To reach this age student with elective subject matter such as human relations or career awareness necessitates the use of many "fun type" learning experiences. Units of instruction for a human relations-career awareness curriculum must be fast paced and highly participative to be effective with this group. Strategic curriculum ideas, workshop plans, and an exploration course will be discussed further in the chapter.

Adolescence is a time of major change. Of particular interest is the change in the ways children think. The pedagogical implication is the move from concrete to abstract forms of thinking. Mental growth and sophistication can be readily observed in the adolescent. Also observable is a more questioning attitude towards beliefs held by figures of authority. Concepts of values and ideals give way to an insistence for fairness and justice. The conglomerate effect of these changes is the genesis for the independent self—the search for identity. What perfect timing for introducing the relatively new concept of career education.

Overview of career education. Job and career awareness information for today's youth should not be left to chance. Although the current increase in academic requirements has frequently made it difficult to schedule additional time for elective classes, departments like business and home economics have been astute in including this much needed information in their curriculums. With the increase of material available, adolescents should no longer defer consideration of their occupational futures until their senior year. Perhaps the reason the United States has one of the highest teen unemployment rates in the world is the failure to channel the necessary information and motivation at the opportune time—presecondary school.

Career development is actually a long-term process that lasts a lifetime. It means much more than preparing for a job. Career education means increasing student awareness and knowledge about the world of work. The world of work is changing so quickly that it is difficult to predict the specific jobs of the future. The growth of service occupations predominates in predictions for future trends based on the outlook for dual career families, demographic changes, and fast lane living. The computer has already brought vast changes to the managerial hierarchies, and massive business and corporate restructuring will follow. Providing the foundation of career education and utilizing intuitions and understanding can be key elements in preparing adolescents to find success in the world of work.

HUMAN RELATIONS

Before human relations can be taught at the junior high level, the formative nature of adolescent identity must be addressed. It is unlikely that adolescents will exhibit positive behaviors towards others when their own internal structures of self-confidence and self-esteem are floundering.

Personal perceptions. If adults want children to experience success in adolescence, they must help them develop positive, optimistic attitudes toward life, toward the future, and toward what they already can do successfully. Children's self-perceptions about their skills, degrees of acceptance, and responsibleness are measured externally. It is parents who shape the mold during this identity crisis period, but teachers, too, possess this power during the daily seven-hour period of surrogate parenting.

Facilitation of human relations skills at the junior high level can only come if educators first assist the adolescents in surviving the identity crisis and promote letting go of the self-centered past of earlier childhood. There are many qualitative ways teachers can expand and enhance the self-esteem and capacity for human relations instruction at this level.

Abstract thoughts are just beginning in adolescence. Coincidentally, interest levels in other significant beings, particularly those of the opposite sex, are also starting to bud. The adolescent is still childlike enough to be possessive about what is his/hers. This same adolescent is also sentimental enough to begin to value intangible qualities of the self and others. This is an ideal time for the creative teacher to compose a booklet of individualized student exercises for teaching human relations. Each page should have its own topic that requires personalized student input, discussion/sharing capabilities, and cartoon-like pictures that deliver the page topic. Typical page topics might include "Liking Myself," "What I Do Best," "Why I Get Angry," "People

Pleasers," "Uniquely Me," "Getting Along," etc. Allow space in the booklet for notes or thoughts. Also include simple poems or sayings to which young teens can relate. Students should exercise the freedom to compose, draw, color, or whatever they choose in their booklet. It is theirs to keep. It is a good idea to include a parent page at the end of the booklet. Any assistance in sparking understanding at this age level is a plus; use it.

Change and coping. A job can be the decentering point of selfhood. An adolescent, in a sense, becomes an adult when he or she takes a job. Changes take place as youth learn to put away childish things. A new era of coping with the adult world of work lurks ahead for young people. Human beings operate in a complex sociocultural and physical context. Both people and context change over time and are dynamically interactive. The career planning endeavor is a lifelong development because it extends across the entire lifespan and is influenced by the many changes characteristic of the passage of time.

Teachers can address change as an effort to change something that is already changing. Expose the adolescents to normative socialization of the work experience. Relate to historical events in the workplace and compare to current trends. Tie in nonnormative life events as well, such as death and prolonged illness. In other words, focus on the human development approach to career assessment. Utilize basic human needs as the driving force behind behavior and human relations. Adolescents can understand the meaning of fun, love, freedom, and self worth as being the instructional force behind what they do with their lives. They know, for example, when they are having fun or when they feel loved. What they do not comprehend is that the means of satisfying these needs change with time. They have difficulty coping. This is when the teacher exercises skill in timing, listening, understanding, and empathy.

Games. Junior high students love current games and competitions in the classroom. A game like "Wheel of Fortune" can be easily duplicated utilizing job titles and job-seeking terms. Students can draw for teams, rotate game host/hostess, and spin (classroom-made spinner) for prizes. Appropriate classroom prizes can be team or individual and include candy, money, points for fun days, pencils, special privileges, etc. Sheets of construction paper and tape can be used to conceal the hidden letters on the blackboard. Another workable game is "Career Trivial Pursuit." Job clusters and employment terms can be color coded to fit different categories on cards. Corresponding questions give clues leading to the answers. Each team has a blank pie shape with six categories and colored felt pieces to match the pie sections. One color is assigned for each section. A large die can be covered with matching felt colors to roll for categories of questions. The first team to answer all their questions correctly and fill their pie with all six colors wins the game. Again, prizes can be awarded; however, students usually are thrilled with the competition alone. In small groups, students enjoy the career version of "Pictionary," a game of charades on paper. The object is to guess the job title from drawings.

Students tend to be very industrious at creating these games. Allow them to contribute most of the work in assembling the game pieces. They will take much pride in their own efforts.

Child apprentice programs. A cooperative effort among school, community, and parents is the CHAPS program, or Child Apprentice Program. This threefold program includes the student spending a half day shadowing the job of an employer and gaining a supervised hands-on experience at various work stations at that job site. The student then proceeds to a business luncheon with the supervising employer. Lastly, the student has the opportunity to tour a selected industrial setting in the afternoon. Students follow up with a detailed report back to the class on their experience. This type of activity also draws great publicity from local media.

Career dress-up days. Students enjoy the opportunity to act out their fantasies by scheduling special career dress-up days. Students are required to investigate their chosen careers in advance and, if possible, interview someone in that capacity. They follow up by dressing in the role of the chosen career or profession. It may be necessary for them to borrow special uniforms from their career role model. An additional feature is to invite the career role models to the classroom. These guests can then supplement student reports to the class with pertinent information about that career. This is a real attention getter, good public relations, and an excellent exploration exercise.

Job description charades. The young adolescent is still very intent on utilizing attention-getting behaviors to establish social position among his/her peers. An entertaining, yet informative, means of tapping this behavioral pattern is to create a classroom game of job description charades. Students can be divided into teams, and each team member has the opportunity to draw a card that determines what job title or term must be acted out for the opposing team. The team members then work cooperatively to ascertain the appropriate clues for the role player to act out.

Formulating the game cards can be done in advance during a class activity. Allow students to brainstorm about job titles that fall into different occupational clusters. Code each of the different clusters with a distinctly colored felt marker on small pieces of poster board. Keep job title cards separated into clusters, and have the students design a spinner board containing the same colors as the job clusters. For added excitement, include a few "wild cards" to allow for open selections of a job title. You might insert a "pass" card which would allow the student to select again from any category and then name an opponent to act it out or lose a turn.

Job description charades is a fun exercise for the students, but it also reinforces a broader understanding of the duties involved in many careers. In addition to affording the opportunity for students to expand on what they already do well—namely, show off—the activity involves group cooperation in achieving a common goal. This has been more recently labeled as cooperative learning, a dynamic new method of student motivation.

Cooperative learning groups. Cooperative learning is a newly researched area of interest that seems to be gaining popularity in the Midwest. The premise for the theory is that students may learn better and take more interest in learning if they are more directly involved in the process. Cooperative learning breaks students into small work groups. The groups are presented with problems or exercises. Each student is responsible for a given set of materials and must then teach those materials to the other members of the group. The interdependency that is created in the group forms a bond, and each of the students strives to see that all members of the group are benefiting. An evaluation procedure must be utilized to measure the degree of learning that has taken place.

Cooperative learning requires much advance planning for the teacher. Activities must be carefully selected, and groups must be assigned with scrutiny. The positive results in addition to textbook learning are the advancement of human relations skills and the development of time management techniques.

MODEL CAREER INSTRUCTION PLANS

Parental involvement. Parents can play an important role in the future of job awareness programs by encouraging schools to provide career education for middle schools and junior high students. Career development is a long term process. Since the continuum lasts a lifetime, it is imperative that parents support an aggressive approach to instilling work-related ethics and attitudes in the eager minds of our youth.

Career guidance for middle school and junior high should be a joint effort of schools, community, and family. Parents can become actively involved in many of the strategic elements previously mentioned in this article. It is they who are most likely to participate in the dress-up days or child apprentice programs by sharing their expertise. Parents also contribute to the publicity aspect of career awareness by involving media contacts and local advertising.

Exploration course in career awareness. Ages 9 to 13 are crucial years for students to be involved in career education. One solution for addressing this curriculum void is to offer a semester course or a minicourse on careers. An approach that works well is to treat the students in the course as trainees and offer them job descriptions with a list of competencies that must be met in order to retain their jobs. As they work their way through the course, they not only learn about the specific career of their choice, they also gain knowledge about themselves and the world of work.

This type of course can be conducted much like a real job with the trainees earning a minimum wage based on a classroom currency. Real job regulations such as tardiness rules, sick leave, abuse of work time, and vacations can be included in a handbook. Students can even apply for promotions in their classroom jobs which require additional responsibilities (extra credit) and earn extra pay.

Each class of students can form a worker organization and elect officers, establish bylaws, and promote work-related publicity and activities. This is an excellent means of building schoolwide interest in the business curriculum.

The purpose of a course of this nature is to provide formal opportunity for students to experience work life outside of the classroom walls. Bringing features of the working world into the classroom enables students to see the relevance of advance planning and preparation in striving for their career goals. The working world is much more meaningful when experienced rather than merely discussed.

A career awareness curriculum needs to cover life skills as well as the basic job-seeking skills. At the presecondary level, attitudes, interests, and abilities are just beginning to bloom. Students are able to see where their strong points lie and can be directed to match their ambitions with realistic career goals. However, because goals of adolescents change with great frequency, it should be highlighted that self-understanding is a key factor to seeking permanent future plans. In other words, flexibility must be addressed while investigating the knowledge of specific jobs in making occupational decisions.

The middle school youth has already succumbed to the temptations of money as a means of acquiring wants. To make a career course lifelike, students can be required to utilize time cards to determine payroll and calculate deductions to arrive at a net pay. Leftover figures can then be expended for typical life budgets such as rent, utilities, food, car payments, insurance, etc. Meeting the budget and having spending money left is exciting to the student. One suggestion to make the money aspect meaningful is to conduct financial fitness projects. Some areas of interest to build projects around might be earning money, spending priorities, shopping for best buys, reaching long-term goals, or handling adult responsibilities. Each of these areas can be supported by providing the students with good financial and consumer information. This is also an appropriate time to begin teaching a planning process for achieving goals. This way students can apply the process to their project objectives and view the process in motion as the projects take shape.

The activities of career-oriented classes can gain attention from student peers, fellow teachers, administrators, and the public. Though students reap their own pleasure from participation in such programs, teachers should not disregard the need for recognition of the students for their efforts. Of all people, teachers are aware of the need for pats on the back and positive reinforcement in the workplace.

Workshops for career development in children. Holding the attention of a child frequently requires recreation or entertainment activities. Sound familiar? Educators also enjoy an entertaining learning experience. The difference is that teacher workshops are generally a requirement whereas workshops for children can be offered as options or on an elective basis.

The objective of offering a career-oriented workshop for children is to develop an increased awareness of the process of career decision making and to promote the use of this process. Children ages 9 to 13 are very receptive to new ideas. Many of the biases of the adult world have not become permanently embedded in young minds. Myths about appropriate career selections can be introduced at this time and received openly. The prejudices both for and against nontraditional careers can be examined without preformed judgments interfering with comprehension. Motivation to explore new dimensions in occupations can inspire eager youth.

To maintain an interest level requires generating many career options in cluster areas. The students must have direct participation in the career experience. The most important feature for success of the workshop is to relate the careers to the values of youth. For example, using catchy themes for job clusters such as the "Business of Sports" for the business world and "Pepsi Generation" for the sales cluster allows students to relate what they already see as being valuable to real career opportunities. "Things That Make Noise" relates to the industrial world, and "Who You Gonna Call?" depicts the service occupations. With a little imagination, there is no limit to gearing most occupational cluster areas down to the interest level of children. What's more, the unanticipated outcome is—it's fun!

When a recreational aspect is attached as a motivating factor, positive results can occur. Activities must enable the children to see and use equipment. Furthermore, physical activity is necessary in order to wear down some of the unbounded energy level present in most children of this age group.

A successful workshop provides the opportunity for children to share their own experiences. Self-expression and cooperation are vital tools in the workshop process. Intended outcomes of youth-oriented programs of this nature are increased knowledge of career clusters, improved self-awareness, and increased ability to work with others. Because these activities are fun and positive, constructive behaviors are fringe benefits of the workshop.

CONCLUSIONS

As 1990 approaches and promoters of excellence in education push for traditional academic offerings in the public schools, the vocational educators can relax in knowing the pendulum must eventually return. Business educators are ready. Just as keyboarding and computers have found their way into the elementary and junior high classrooms, so have the subjective areas of self-awareness and goal setting. Excellence in education does not call for stoic presentations of lecture materials accompanied by student regurgitation of facts. True excellence in education means showing the student how to utilize those facts for a productive life. It means saying to the student, "Here it is, and this is what you do with it." Preparation to meet the future and cope with the realities of the world is a major objective in education. Vocational educators have always recognized the value of this goal. The rest of the world is finally realizing what we have known to be true for a long time.

A senior student (vocational/academic) recently commented on the subject of human relations skills, "All the math and science in the world won't do me any good if I do not first know me and have the ability to work beside the other people of the world."

The bottom line is obvious. The future is imminent. Business educators must strive to reach young adolescents with tools that will continue to build a life-time process of career development and human relations skills. The time is now.

Part IV
ASSERTING AND REASSERTING BUSINESS EDUCATION AT THE SECONDARY LEVEL

CHAPTER 12
Basic Skills and Core Competencies

BLANCHE ETTINGER
Bronx Community College, Bronx, New York

Education must be a forecast of what individuals need to know so that their learning serves them in the future. Since every person is in some way dependent on the world of business, business educators are in a unique position to offer those individuals who seek it the general and occupational knowledge and skills that will provide them with the tools for lifelong learning. Therefore, it is incumbent upon business educators at the secondary level to "assert and reassert the role of business education."

The U.S. economy is expected to generate more than 21 million additional jobs between 1986 and 2000.[1] The data also reflects that individuals change jobs approximately seven times during a lifespan. How does this impact programs? Simply stated, goals must be established that are broader than just training for specific jobs. The focus must be on careers, and individuals must have access to programs that will provide them with the key ingredients to enable them to grow into responsible positions and to adapt to changes as they occur in the workplace.

Structurally and developmentally, all things start with a foundation, which is the main support of future growth. A strong foundation is the mainstay of education and the quality of life. Mastering the basic skills will provide this foundation and will give individuals the power to understand, to draw inferences, to give meaning to new situations, to adjust to a changing environment, to transfer learning, to perform at higher levels, and to continue the learning process.

Benchmarks of learning. A person who is well grounded in the basic skills or reading, writing, speaking, listening, and computing and who has mastered the skills of information processing, personal and attitudinal development, economic literacy, and consumerism has developed a framework for learning. These are the very skills and knowledge that are valued by business and industry and lead to an upgraded, thinking work force wherein innovation and creativity flourish. Thus, an appropriate formula for enhancing students' employability would be basic skills plus core competencies plus vocational aptitude.

---

[1] Kutscher, Ronald E. "Overview and Implications of the Projections to 2000." *Monthly Labor Review* 110:4; September 1987.

Business education fulfills personal, social, economic, and vocational goals for noncollege and college-bound students. All students, regardless of their career goals, need to be prepared for "life's transitions and for the world of work and for future education and training."[2]

This chapter has the following objectives: (1) to present an overview of the workplace and to identify the needs of the work force as projected into the twenty-first century; (2) to define the opportunities and problems that business, industry, and the professions are encountering; and (3) to suggest instructional strategies and activities that incorporate the basic skills and the core competencies in business education programs.

OVERVIEW OF THE WORKPLACE

The fast pace of technological innovation, the information-intensive economy, and the growth trends in white-collar workers resulting from a transition in our country's economic base from manufacturing to service-producing industries have led to substantial changes in the workplace. How have employment, personnel qualifications, and education and training been impacted?

Employment trends. A number of factors will affect the composition of the work force by the year 2000: (1) Nearly all of the projected growth will be in the service-producing industries. (2) There is an expected increase in the 36-54 maturing age group in the labor force and a decrease in entry-level workers aged 16-34. (3) One out of five new labor force entrants will be a minority youth. (4) Immigrants will represent the largest portion of the work force since World War I. (5) Women, minorities, and immigrants will account for more than 80 percent of net additions to the labor force. (6) The number of women working will continue to rise through the next decade, representing 47 percent of the work force.[3] The latter factor has impacted positions at the managerial level, since women are competing now with their male counterparts. As this segment of the labor force seeks higher-level positions, a shortage of applicants will exist to fill those entry-level jobs that historically were filled by women.

Occupational and educational implications. Business educators will be confronted with the problem of integrating a non-English-speaking group of immigrants, Asians, and Latin Americans into the work force and elevating the economically disadvantaged through an educational plan that will ease their entry into the job market. With such a large percentage of individuals from such multicultural backgrounds, the educational plan will have to incorporate an understanding of the employer-employee responsibilities in the American economic system and the American social structure. Equally important will be the development of proper attitudes, good work habits, and interpersonal relationships that will lead to successful job experiences.

---

[2]Finn, Chester E., Jr. "A Fresh Option for the Non-College-Bound." *Phi Delta Kappan* 68:237; November 1986.

[3]U.S. Department of Labor, Employment and Training Administration. *Work Force 2000.* Washington, DC: U.S. Government Printing Office, 1987. pp. 1-2.

Recently, there has been severe criticism of the inability in our educational system to prepare students adequately for the workplace. Studies reflect that more employees than ever are deficient in the basic skills that are required on the job. In inner cities nationwide, approximately half of the youth score below the ninth-grade level in reading and math skills. Employers who were asked to identify the most serious skill deficiencies of their employees, according to a survey by the New York-based Center for Public Resources, named speaking, math, problem solving, listening, comprehension of verbal instructions, and communication of ideas.[4]

High school graduates have the same deficiencies as those students who never complete high school. They are graduating with fifth- and sixth-grade reading and math skills. In an urban school district with a high minority enrollment in Oakland, California, the average senior scored at the ninth-grade level in math and English, three years below the national average.[5]

In a *Wall Street Journal* article, results of a test administered by the New York Telephone Company revealed that of the 21,000 entry-level job applicants who were tested, only 16 percent passed a basic reading and reasoning test. Of the 3,600 people from 21 to 25 years who were tested in a study conducted by the National Assessment of Educational Progress, only one-third could calculate a restaurant bill tip and only 20 percent could interpret a bus schedule.[6] What is industry looking for in our high school graduates?

The challenge. Business educators must prepare high school youth with the skills needed for entry-level jobs as well as for advancement to better positions. To do so effectively, educators must be aware of the changing society and accordingly be willing to update, innovate, propose new curriculums, and use teaching strategies that relate school learning to the world of work. The economy is moving in the direction of knowledge-oriented jobs which will require individuals who can think and make decisions, are able to conceptualize, can analyze and resolve problems, are capable of implementing new ideas, and use good communication skills. Also, because individuals will experience so many different career changes during a lifetime, they need to be educated and trained to be flexible and able to adjust to changing employers and environments. Employers want high school graduates who can read, write, calculate, follow instructions, be punctual, maintain regular attendance, and do a hard day's work.[7] According to an article in the *Wall Street Journal* of May 27, 1987, "Most new jobs in the large urban areas, where so many of these 'at risk' people live, will demand far higher literacy, work skills, and work habits than many possess." A cashier or a sales clerk must know how to read, write, and do basic math. Employees in retail stores, hospitals, restaurants, and hotels need a modicum of social grace and interpersonal skill as well as an ability to speak English.

---

[4]Feuer, Dale. "The Skill Gap." *Training* 24:30; December 1987.

[5]Bernick, Michael. "Illiteracy and Inner-City Unemployment." *Phi Delta Kappan* 67:365; January 1986.

[6]"The Wrong Stuff." *Data Training* 7:4; December 1987.

[7]Hamilton, Stephen F. "Excellence and the Transition from School to Work." *Phi Delta Kappan* 68:240, November 1986.

Employers prefer a curriculum that stresses literacy, mathematical skills, and problem-solving skills. They believe that the most important task of public education is to insure that "all school children are grounded in basic academic skills, behavioral patterns, and positive work habits."[8] The ability and willingness to learn throughout a working lifetime is also perceived as a most desirable quality for employees to possess.[9]

A balanced approach. In a society that is technology-intensive, business educators must take heed of learning directions taken. Just teaching for technical skills is unacceptable. Business educators must be wary of concentrating solely on equipment and software packages. Yes, to know how to operate equipment is frequently required; yet, more important is the ability to understand the capabilities and logic of technology, how each task contributes to total productivity, and how each employee is a vital part of the organization. Equipment and software constantly change. How do employees cope when jobs are eliminated?

Business educators must take a broad perspective and use a balanced approach that integrates a general education with occupational preparation. A dichotomy cannot exist between general education and technology. They must be unified and balanced.

Role of business educator. Business educators must redefine their role and restructure courses and curriculums to fit into the educational plan which emphasizes the basics and core competencies that are critical to successful careers of high school students. Concurrent with curriculum planning, courses should be made exciting, content should be relevant, and students should be shareholders in and developers of the learning process. At the outset of the course, rather than using a strictly teacher-designed format for the semester, a good approach would be to have class discussions that culminate in an oral contractual agreement concerning grading and expected outcomes of the course. Periodically during the semester, time should be allowed for self-assessment and achievement of course goals. Teachers should assume the role of facilitator of learning.

This is a small investment to make considering the impact students who benefit from this kind of instruction have on student enrollment in business education courses. Now is the time to reaffirm our commitment to business education and to the maintenance of viable high school programs that are keeping pace with a changing society.

A GENERIC APPROACH TO TEACHING BASIC SKILLS AND CORE COMPETENCIES

Language provides the direction, the means, and the vehicle for reading, writing, reflecting, speaking, thinking, and computing—the specific elements of information skills. A proficiency in these areas ultimately leads to the higher-level skills of analysis (breaking the whole into parts), interpretation,

---

[8] Finn, *loc. cit.*

[9] Finn, *op. cit.*, p. 236.

reasoning, decision making, problem solving, synthesis (creating a new "whole"), and evaluation (judging against a standard). These competencies should be the very minimum standard of learning and should be an integral part of all subject areas of the curriculum. Initially, each information competency will be discussed separately and then integrated into the other core competencies of personal development, economics, consumerism, and technology.

Reading. In business, students need to comprehend what they read, must understand business terminology, be able to follow directions, and be capable of interpreting written materials, such as information that appears in office manuals and reference books. Employees in administrative support positions must be able to code and file incoming correspondence correctly, interpret work orders, read directions for using newly adopted software packages such as word processing and database management, and summarize information from reports, articles, and speeches.

Business educators cannot take for granted that students' reading levels are adequate for employment, not to mention for instruction. A consistent, systematic approach must be used to reinforce reading in all courses. Casual references and reading assignments will not necessarily raise student reading levels. An emphasis on vocabulary and word pronunciation will contribute to improved reading skills.[10] Noteworthy is that 60 percent of comprehension or word meaning is accounted for by vocabulary and that subject area word knowledge correlates highly with overall knowledge, success, and grades in the course.[11]

The following procedures may be used to develop reading skills:

- Search through reading assignments for "stumbling blocks" and specialized words. Preview them with students.
- Analyze prefixes, suffixes, and roots of words as used in context for clues to help students unlock meanings of words.
- Develop understanding of words at the three levels: specific (what is apparent), functional (usage), and conceptual (generalization).
- Use vocabulary in a variety of contexts and student experiences.
- Summarize main and subsidiary ideas.
- Be cognizant of facts and inconsistencies.
- Interpret graphs, charts, and tables.
- Survey required course textbook and note main headings, sideheadings, chapters, and index. Help students visualize the book as a whole.
- Turn headings into questions and recite answer after reading appropriate section of text.

In addition to reading assignments from course textbooks, use case studies, articles from professional and technical journals, advertisements, newspaper columns, classified ads, and current best sellers in the area of business, such

---

[10]Thomas, Ellen Lamar, and Robinson, H. Alan. *Improving Reading in Every Class.* Boston: Allyn and Bacon, 1972. p. 11.

[11]Forgan, Harry W., and Mangrum, Charles T. *Teaching Content Area Reading Skills.* Columbus: Charles E. Merrill Publishing Co., 1976. p. 136.

as *Megatrends*. The content from each source should be used as topics for discussion, for drawing inferences, for analysis, for reasoning, and for application to business situations. In consumer classes, students might also be asked, for example, to read an advertisement critically and to excerpt words that would prompt them to buy the advertised product. Include oral reading for detection of mispronunciation.

To better prepare the nation's high school graduates for business, Schmidt identified office documents that could be used as the basis for preparing reading materials.[12] She found that such materials do help students attain improved reading skills in verifying and comprehending office detail. Whenever possible, gather realistic documents from diversified local businesses and integrate materials such as financial reports, statistical tables, account statements, invoices, and legal documents into economics and consumer courses as well as keyboarding and information processing.

In mathematics courses, understanding the vocabulary is vital. Students must have the experience of reading problems, equations, tables, graphs, symbols, and abbreviations. Again, vocabulary should be studied in context, and students should be taught to see relationships between parts of a problem. After comprehending the problem, students are ready to devise an equation that states the problem.[13]

Writing. According to Albert Joseph, most large companies have ongoing training programs to teach professional men and women how to write. Although national reports criticize schools for failing to teach basic language skills, the situation, he comments, is more critical. The fault lies with the teachers who cannot teach writing.[14] This is a serious accusation, for writing is a skill that is in universal demand in business, regardless of specialization. Assigning writing exercises without instruction demonstrates a weakness on the part of the teacher. Writing must be taught as a process, and instructors must create realistic opportunities that provide the stimulus and model for written communications. Writing is a "way of thinking on paper, clarifying, refining, displaying ideas, feelings, and facts. Thus, it is as useful and important in science, math, and history as it is in American lit."[15]

Effective writing must be easily read, and the message must be clearly and precisely understood. The process must include the purpose for the written communication, the audience addressed, the information to be conveyed, the method of arranging and organizing the data into a logical and coherent manner, and the development of the ideas into meaningful sentences and paragraphs. Concomitantly, as business students are taught to write, so must the rules of correct English usage, punctuation, and spelling be taught. Particular attention must be given to subject/verb agreement, pronoun usage, and use of correct verb tenses, particularly with the influx of such a large

---

[12] Schmidt, B. June. "Preparing Business Students To Read Office Documents." *Delta Pi Epsilon Journal* 29:111; Fall 1987.

[13] Walters, George Lewis. *Development and Refinement of Reading Skills in Business Education*. Monograph 128. Cincinnati: South-Western Publishing Co., 1975.

[14] Joseph, Albert. "You Pay the High Cost of Poor Writing." *Training* 24:106, March 1987.

[15] Davidson, Wilma. "Letters to the Editor." *Training* 24:21, May 1987.

number of students from multicultural backgrounds. Revising and editing work becomes an integral part of the writing process. Use action verbs in all questions, such as identify, create, compare, and defend so that students have to use reasoning and problem-solving techniques in their responses. Activities in an office procedures class might include an employee-evaluation task and a team project, such as planning a seminar. The latter assignment involves letters of invitation, reservations, confirmations, and publicity as well as posters and news releases. The benefits from such a project include not only the development of writing techniques but also interpersonal, leadership, organizational, and decision-making skills. In an advanced keyboarding or career orientation class, students may be asked to compose a letter of application for a specific job taken from a newspaper ad which is then evaluated and edited by a classmate. The classmate then writes a critique of the application letter, stating whether the applicant merits an interview.

In an economics class or a business concepts class, develop questions on thought-provoking topics, such as "the effect of foreign competition on the American worker." Other types of realistic materials to use to broaden students' analytical, decision-making, and writing experiences are financial statements, annual business reports, and stock market quotations. Discussion groups may precede the process.

In a keyboarding class, teach composition at the typewriter or computer. Begin with simple word responses to teacher's questions about students' feelings about themselves or about a lesson, followed by word, sentence, and paragraph responses. Pictures of office landscapes and graphics used for advertisements are good motivational devices for student composition.

Writing improves with frequent practice. Well-structured writing assignments should be an outgrowth of class reading, discussion groups, and other projects. Prompt feedback and evaluation from teachers are important steps in the development of students' writing skills.

Speaking and listening. Speaking, listening, and reading are connectors in the learning process. Research reflects that the better an individual is in using spoken language, then the more apt he is to be competent in reading the written language. Similarly, individuals who listen well can generally repeat what they heard.

Individuals employed in business need to be able to communicate orally information, knowledge, feelings, and directions to those employees and customers with whom they are in contact. No longer are the telephone or on-site meetings the primary means of conversing. Developments in office technology have changed the ways in which information is communicated. There has been an upsurge in voice messaging, voice recognition, and increased usage of recorded dictation. Therefore, the ability to give meaningful, accurate messages, to give clear instructions, to clarify and verify information questioned, to persuade clients, to participate in staff meetings and conferences, to make presentations, and to participate in small, informal discussion groups, whether in person or over telephone wires, is essential for successful employment.

Listening is the most frequently used communication skill; yet, it is the least taught. Raymond Dumont and John Lannon define listening as a "complex and selective process of receiving, focusing, deciphering, accepting, and storing what we hear."[16] Listening is an active process and consists of three sequential stages: hearing, attentiveness, and understanding. The latter implies the ability to get the meaning of the intended message as well as the basic context. Being a good listener is one of the most crucial skills necessary in the office. An acronym suggested by Dave Lewis that has worked successfully in teaching listening is C-H-E-E-R. C is for concentration, active listening, appropriate mind set; H is for hearing, listening critically, and interpreting spoken as well as unspoken words (gestures and inflections); E is for empathy, the key to handling problems; E is for eliciting information through skillful questioning; and R is for remembering, which comes from paraphrasing, summarizing, and visualizing.[17]

Listening can be taught in skill as well as in nonskill courses. Give directions once—and only once. Prepare a set of questions, preliminary to discussion, on a topic in concept courses such as economics, money management, and business analysis. Review the questions, conduct the lesson, and end with student responses to each question. Clarify facts, discuss opinions, and evaluate responses.

Computing. Individuals need math skills for personal and business use. As consumers, individuals use math skills to carry out daily activities such as in making out personal budgets, marketing for groceries, paying installments on household purchases, and balancing checkbooks. In business, many office tasks require employees to perform the basic arithmetical functions of addition, subtraction, multiplication, and division as well as to work with fractions, calculate time and cost factors, compute simple interest, maintain petty cash accounts, keep a record of travel expenses, verify invoices, and send end-of-month statements. Knowing how to compute is an essential part of a good business education program because students learn to think logically, to break down the whole into parts, to analyze and to make estimates. A small business entrepreneur, frequently a position which appeals to a high school student, would need this knowledge. Although computers and calculators are useful as an educational tool for solving problems, a theoretical understanding of computing is also necessary. As technology continues to impact society, workers with a better knowledge of computing may qualify for more jobs.

Personal development. President John F. Kennedy said, "Human resources and natural resources are inexorably intertwined, and tomorrow's children, if they are to manage this land well, will need the precision of scientifically attuned minds, coupled with a sensitivity to their fellow men (and fellow women) and creatures."

Personal development should be an essential component of a high school business education curriculum. One of the most important, yet most difficult,

---

[16]Dumont, Raymond A., and Lannon, John M. *Business Communications.* Second edition. Boston: Little Brown and Co., 1987. p. 526.

[17]Lewis, Dave. "Listening: The Forgotten Skill." *BNAC Communicator* 47:15, 18; Winter 1987.

skills to develop involves relationships with other people. Individuals need to understand the psychology of people, must have insight into behaviors and motives, must be assertive and maintain a sense of values, must know how to handle stress and criticism, and must be able to communicate and function both within groups and on a one-to-one basis. Also, the inability to communicate orally with friends and family may cause serious problems of misunderstanding and tolerance.

Students who have the right mental attitudes, a proper code of ethics, positive feelings about oneself, appropriate grooming habits, and career goals generally are academically successful. A meaningful activity is to have students evaluate their strengths and weaknesses and to establish a plan and time frame for improvement of traits which displease them. The instructor should create an environment in the classroom which accentuates positive attitudes and builds self-confidence. The instructor, now more than ever before, should be a role model.

Other attributes needed by students are self-management techniques where students learn to budget money and time wisely, to handle personal affairs with confidence, to set realistic goals, and to follow a plan for physical fitness and emotional well-being. Projects that require students to assume responsibility for performing and implementing tasks build leadership qualities. Another aspect of personal development is career awareness. High school students generally have a diversity of work experiences performed while still in school. Some may plan to find full-time employment immediately after graduation while others may go on to college. No matter what the decision, students must learn about the opportunities available to them, their likes and dislikes, and how to conduct a job search that involves letter writing, development of a resume, and preparing for an interview. What makes a good application letter that gets results? How do employers read an applicant's resume? What kinds of questions are appropriate to ask in an interview? These are just some of the topics that should be taught to help students attain their first jobs. However, students must also learn that education doesn't stop here. It is an ongoing process.

Many demands are made on young people today because of this complex society. A challenge they must face is to develop their critical thinking and decision-making skills, so crucial to coping with change, so that they can function effectively as citizens at home, in society, and in business. Students must be taught how to process knowledge and how to make judgments about that knowledge. They must be able to plan, organize, and make decisions. In effect, people must learn to deal successfully with their various environments. Problems and case studies are excellent learning strategies when taken from students' own experiences. The most important steps in finding solutions are to define the problem so that it is understood and to examine contingencies and consequences before making a decision. Alternative problems on the same topic should be developed for study so that students learn to see a situation from different perspectives, for example, an employee's point of view versus an employer's or the effect of a corporate decision on both employees and consumers.

Economic, consumer, and business concept skills. As consumers of services and products and as employees of part-time and summer jobs, high school students need to understand how the American economy functions, the types of business ownership, the roles and contributions of employers/employees to business enterprises, and the impact of special interest groups on the economy. Young people also need to understand the concepts of supply and demand, the pricing of products, the competitive market, inflation, fluctuation in interest rates, and the role of industry in making jobs available and in raising the standard of living.

A creative unit on the stock market can be a valuable learning experience. Terminology, evaluating and graphing stock activity, calculating gain and loss on purchases and sales of stock, and developing job descriptions of the various positions on the floor of the stock exchange are a few teaching ideas. Discussions and debates on some of the philosophies of the economists do capture students' interests.

Money management. Every individual needs to know how to manage money. Many young people have access to credit cards, they buy cars on the installment plan, and they take out loans. Therefore, they need to be able to calculate interest charges and know how to budget. How do you open a checking account, write a check, balance the end-of-month statement? Develop a teaching unit on trends in services of banks and financial institutions.

Business and its environment. In a school environment, business concepts can be learned from the school store. Students may be involved in fund raising for capital, selling campaigns, staffing, computerized inventory control, and oral and written communications.

Technology skills. To properly prepare business education high school students for successful and productive professional and personal lives, teachers must ensure that students are computer literate and have a thorough understanding of office technology. Since keyboarding proficiency will be a requirement in practically all occupational areas—particularly because it is the most widely used input device for computers—it has become increasingly important for all students to learn keyboarding.

The content of an introductory course on computers should include the following topics: historical development of the computer, component parts and computer applications, booting up a computer, system and applications software, security, and the impact of computers on business and everyday living.

In keyboarding classes, incorporate the basic language skills of communication. Develop English usage, punctuation, and capitalization exercises for students to complete which require reformatting and rekeying of the exercises into a listing, using either Arabic or Roman numerals. To develop math skills, students may be assigned text that includes a combination of figures that need to be added, averaged, or checked for accuracy. In advanced classes, incorporate proofreading exercises of text that contain intentional errors in English, punctuation, subject-verb agreement, and consistency of information.

Computer literacy can be improved by requiring keyboarding of composing and editing assignments on the microcomputer. Production of correspondence and reports to be keyed on a computer and stored on a disk would enhance students' abilities to use software effectively. Directions for all exercises should be written so that students receive constant practice in following instructions.

Innovative programs. Several business education programs that impact enrollment and retention rates as well as provide an excellent quality of education are enumerated below. Each program has broad general and vocational educational components that prepare students for careers.

Washington Irving High School in New York City has become a center for international studies. A six-month International Secretarial Program was instituted for seniors, beginning February 1988. Basic English and predetermined reading grades are prerequisites for acceptance. Topics are taught from a global perspective, and students are required to learn and apply specialized vocabulary in their studies. The shorthand system used for the dictation and transcription of correspondence is speedwriting.

Another inner-city honor business program that is special is the Business Career Center at George Washington High School in New York City. What makes it unique is its support structure. A coordinator, special counselor, and special official class teacher from the business education department remain with designated students for their entire school experience. The focus is on ninth-grade students who are interested in a business career and who have on-grade math and reading scores as well as excellent attendance and punctuality records. Entering students may opt for a business concentration in accounting/computing, secretarial studies/word processing, or marketing. Even though students have six major subjects instead of the usual five subjects each term, student applications for admission far exceed available seats. Keyboarding is the first-semester requirement. A significant factor is that this program boasts a 90 percent attendance record of the students in 14 official classes and a passing grade in all or most of the subjects taken by students each semester.

Another approach to uphold excellence in education is evident in the Minimum Competency Program of Westside Community Schools in Omaha, Nebraska. This program was mandated by the K-12 school district. Before graduation, high school students must demonstrate a minimum competency in math, reading, writing, oral communications, consumerism, problem solving, and the democratic process. The program has been very successful and exemplifies the abilities and body of knowledge that every high school graduate should possess in meeting the challenges of the future.

SUMMARY

All students, both academic and vocational, can benefit from business education programs. Business education at the high school level does not provide sterile learning; it is an avenue through which individuals learn how to function in society and business and how to compete in the labor force.

Instructors should make a renewed effort to reinforce the basic skills and core competencies of reading, writing, computing, personal development, economic literacy, and consumer awareness in *all courses*. The use of integrated activities in all subjects provides the vehicle for aggregate learning. The focus of teaching should be on understanding and application. Through creative programs, business education students will gain the general and technical skills needed to grow, to change behaviorally, and to continually learn throughout life.

The time has come to "assert and reassert the role of business education" at the secondary level.

CHAPTER 13
Processing Data

EVELYN A. SCHEMMEL
Cannon's Business College, Honolulu, Hawaii

Methods for input, output, and manipulation of data have always been an integral part of the business education curriculum. Data has been processed by one method or another since the beginning of time. However, the technology of the past decade has revolutionized the processing of data more than any other period in history. It leaves many challenges for the business education curriculum, and it provides many opportunities for business education to attract the attention of students as well as the business community.

Computers have made their impact in every aspect of society, but the business and personal applications which are best taught in the business education curriculum provide important opportunities to attract students. Technological advances have allowed students to see the computer as an instructional aid or medium as well as a tool for business and personal activities. In the business education curriculum computers can be used to provide a variety of learning opportunities. Various learning styles can be accommodated, decision-making skills can be developed, and real-world experiences can be simulated through the use of appropriate software.

The challenge for business education is to provide an instructional delivery system that prepares students with marketable skills for a world of constantly changing technology. A close working relationship with the business community will allow the business education curriculum to remain competitive and in tune with technological change. Producing graduates that meet the entry-level competencies of the local employers identifies the business education program as an important community resource and attracts students to the business classes.

CLASSROOM ACTIVITIES TO DEVELOP STUDENT COMPETENCIES

Technology has had a tremendous impact on the speed and efficiency with which data is processed, but the base of knowledge that provides the foundation for identifying and interpreting the data has not changed significantly. The focus in many of the business education courses must continue to address the basic competencies for entry-level skills that will meet the needs of employers.

The following classroom activities suggest the basics to be reinforced. While technological advances may draw students to the classroom, the entry-level skills for employment will ultimately assure student success in the business world. The content and delivery system in the business education curriculum must not lose sight of the basic needs of employers.

Recordkeeping and accounting. Recordkeeping is often a course which orients students to the business education program and the business world. It becomes the stepping-stone to accounting for many students. To produce the entry-level skills needed by students entering the business world, recordkeeping and accounting courses must emphasize the use of source documents and records that are actually used in business. The processing of data cannot occur without appropriate input. Student activities that deal with practice sets and include source document tests provide preparation for the real world. What better way for the student to become accustomed to the world of work than through "in-basket" activities for recordkeeping and accounting.

Business forms are a good example of basics that have not changed significantly for many years. The checks, invoices, credit memos, purchase orders, etc. should not only be identifiable, but the function of each should be general knowledge of the potential worker. The method of manipulating the data will be different depending on the company, but the initial processing involves basic knowledge that has been a part of the business education curriculum since the beginning.

The transition from manual to automated accounting is an important area to be addressed in the business education curriculum. Again, the impact of technology has allowed the routine and repetitious tasks to be handled by the computer. This provides the increased productivity that is important to the business world; but the reality for the student is that the manual system must also be learned well to understand what the computer is doing.

A valuable exercise for the beginning accounting class is to complete a manual practice set and then, using the same or similar data, computerize the practice set. There is a greater appreciation of the basics as well as an appreciation of the types of tasks that computers can perform more cost effectively.

Electronic calculator. The computer keyboard has reinforced the need for the most popular skill in the business education curriculum—keyboarding. Add to that the touch operation of the 10-key pad, and the two skills stand out as the foundation for efficiency in data entry. The electronic calculator provides the means for gaining speed and accuracy on the 10-key pad. The best place to develop this skill is not in the business machines classroom of the past, but rather in an accounting classroom where the skill can be applied to the problems in accounting. The portable, hand-held calculator has become the tool of many students, but it is not realistic in the business environment.

Ten-key proficiency with required levels of competency for speed and accuracy should be included in all accounting courses. This can be accomplished on the calculator or the computer, and it is a skill that employers expect.

Mathematics. Basic computational skills are essential to the success of the entry-level employee. The issues and concerns of business mathematics with or without the electronic calculator have met with mixed opinion. If the calculator can be used to spur interest in mathematics, then the focus changes regarding the basic skills to be addressed. Once students become equipment dependent for answers, there are new considerations. For example, the ability to accurately estimate answers is very important for the student who relies on the calculator or computer for computations. Appropriate classroom activities to reinforce skill in estimating will enhance student employability.

Microcomputer and minicomputer operations. The microcomputer has had the greatest impact on the processing of data, and business education has accepted the challenge to help students learn how computers process data. Yet, the ability of users to fully understand the hardware and software they are using continues to be a major concern in the business environment. Vendor support has not met the needs of the business community, and students with a solid foundation in the basics of operating systems as well as programming languages and applications have the competitive edge in the job market.

For example, an essential element in processing data is creating backup files; yet without proper training, many businesses have learned about this topic the hard way. Volumes of data can be lost instantly and for a variety of reasons. The new technology that allows us to store data so economically can cause serious problems as well. The success with which we use the technology depends on the effectiveness and completeness of the initial training. Incorporating sufficient training in such areas will meet the needs of the business community.

Computer applications. Second only to word processing applications, the spreadsheet is widely used for business and personal use. The basic ability to use formulas and to understand the common sense or reasonableness of data that has been manipulated is a very important skill for the real world. Learning how spreadsheets are used as tools for decision making and analysis is another area to be addressed. Also, in recognizing the needs of business, it is often more important to know *what* a computer program can produce than *how* the program works. We must be assertive with business in reminding managers that maintaining a database of important financial records is best handled by a trained accounting clerk or bookkeeper. Business education trains the skilled workers who will use the applications to improve productivity while supplying essential data. The ability to use spreadsheet software enhances general computer knowledge and builds confidence in dealing with the changing technology.

BUSINESS AND INDUSTRY INVOLVEMENT

The ability to focus on the marketable skills that meet the needs of entry-level workers in the local community is an advantage of the business education curriculum. To maintain this focus greater involvement is required with business and industry.

Advisory committees. The use of advisory committees has provided a major step in the right direction. The involvement of business provides opportunities for teachers to gain "real world" exposure and provides opportunities for students such as bringing equipment demonstrations to the classroom, field trips to various businesses, internships, and communication with successful business people.

Input from advisory committees regarding appropriate job titles, job descriptions, and skill competencies is very important to an effective curriculum. When program names relate to job competencies, it is easier for business to relate to the training provided. For example, a program entitled "Bookkeeper" should meet the entry-level skill requirement of business to perform the bookkeeping tasks.

The use of advisory committees also gives the business education classes the chance to impress the business community with the caliber of students and the comprehensiveness of curriculum. The best advertisement for the business education program is a well-prepared graduate who becomes a productive employee and a contributing member of society.

MOCK INTERVIEWS. An activity that provides mutual benefit to students and employers is to have mock interviews conducted by the advisory committee members from the business community. Students seem more receptive to the comments and suggestions made by the business representatives, and the business representatives are given an advance opportunity to screen potential employees. If they don't like what they see, the business representatives have the opportunity to contribute toward making the product better in the future.

In technical fields such as computer programming, and operations, data entry, and accounting, the knowledge of the people working in the field can be particularly valuable in providing a realistic interview for the students. Relating to the personalities of individuals who work in the field also provides insight for the students.

INTERNSHIPS. Advisory committee members can be instrumental in coordinating internship programs that provide still another opportunity for students to gain practical experience. With the technological demands placed on the classroom and the budget, it is always difficult to expose students to the latest in equipment and procedures. Extending the classroom to the workplace is an effective way to gain experience with the most modern methods of processing data. It also provides the potential for on-the-job training that leads to permanent employment.

RETRAINING. Encouraging business to consider the classroom as an extension of its personnel and training department can help meet the needs of the business community. Companies must be reminded that the classroom is not only a source of entry-level workers. It can provide refresher courses and retraining through the postsecondary and adult education programs. The impact of technology has made the business community increasingly aware of the continuing need for retraining in the workplace.

Advisory committees are an important link to the local business community, and the key to a successful committee is involvement. Active involvement provides the opportunity for the committee members to influence the product of the program—their future employees.

A partnership in learning. The remainder of this chapter will describe a program currently offered in Hawaii which has been nominated for the

Secretary's Award in Secondary Vocational Education. The Award is offered through the U.S. Department of Education, Office of Vocational and Adult Education, to recognize 10 outstanding programs. The criteria on which the programs are judged include relevancy of curriculum, servicing of special needs, articulation with postsecondary education, integration of basic skills, and development of business skills. The criteria emphasize specific areas where business education has an opportunity to develop assertiveness.

The assertiveness of Waipahu High School's administration and faculty in working with the local business community to develop this program is commendable. The cooperation of Jean Miyahira, director of the Business and Computer Technology Learning Center at Waipahu High School, in providing the program content below is graciously acknowledged.

ONE-SEMESTER EXPLORATORY PROGRAM

Program description. The one-semester exploratory program at Waipahu High School, Leeward District, Oahu, Hawaii, provides students with technological concepts and problem-solving, life-survival skills for on-the-job training with careful career planning. The Business and Computer Technology Learning Center is a unique approach which provides students who normally do not have the opportunity to enroll in business/marketing education elective courses with hands-on laboratory experiences in all of the advanced levels. It also provides an opportunity for generating further interest in business courses among students in such courses as general business. The learning center students receive training in seven different courses during the one-semester exploratory program: Introduction to Business and Career Planning, Keyboarding, Computer Literacy/Programming, Speedwriting, Office Management, Accounting, and Interview Techniques.

Program objectives.
1. Develop and incorporate basic skills in reading, writing, and mathematics as they apply to career and technological changes.
2. Develop a positive self-concept necessary for successful career planning.
3. Develop decision-making and problem-solving skills.
4. Develop an awareness of career opportunities and career ladders based on career clusters.
5. Develop an appreciation of computer terminology and utilization, keyboarding and word processing and business machines operations, speedwriting development, employment forms, and income tax preparation.
6. Develop vocational and educational proficiency in job skills and the application for employment.
7. Develop an understanding and appreciation of technology and the desire for self-improvement.

Program activities. Two Introduction to Business classes per semester were the target group for the 1987-88 initial learning center. The classes included students from grades nine through twelve. Students were programmed into these classes based on prior interest indicated in the elective course.

Students enrolled in Beginning and Advanced Shorthand, Accounting, Data Processing/Computer Programming, Business Machines, Office Procedures, Advanced Typing, Advertising/Merchandising, and Marketing and Distribution participate in the learning center programs. They assist in the instruction of the rotational cycle and utilize the office equipment in a simulated business office.

An additional after-school strand is available for students identified as college and career planning applicants. This group meets after the school day to receive guidance in career planning and college and scholarship applications. Students are identified through their discipline classes and are recommended for participation in the activities. The guidance department and the learning center director are involved with this group.

Careful curriculum and career planning by the high school student will promote the participation in the Early Admit/Advance Placement Program with Leeward Community College. The high school student will be able to enroll and receive college credit while continuing in high school.

Program schedule. The plan for the 18-week exploratory program is provided below. It is organized according to its objectives.

1. Identify career clusters and personal goals.
   General Business (2 weeks)
   —Career exploration.
   —Classified ad, qualified occupation for simulation.
   —Career Kokua (a computerized career information bank).
   —Application form.
   —Compose a letter of application.
   —Compose a resume.
2. Demonstrate the proper keyboarding techniques.
   Keyboarding (2 weeks)
   —Learn the keyboard of the electronic memory typewriter and personal computer.
   —Type a sample of a letter of application for students who have had typewriting.
3. Identify the concepts of computer literacy.
   Data Processing/Computer Programming (2 weeks)
   —Introduction of terminology, components, programming, proper usage of diskette.
   —Hands-on programming, spreadsheet, business evaluation.
4. Demonstrate the business machines/word processing techniques in a rotation cycle.
   Office Management (3 weeks)
   a. Office procedures
      (1) Learn the operation of a personal computer.
      (2) Type, edit, print resume for reference.
   b. Business machines
      (1) Learn the proper fingering procedures of an electronic calculator.
      (2) Operate the electronic calculator by touch.
      (3) Add numerical columns by touch.

  (4) Participate in reprographics of materials utilizing scanner, duplicator, mimeograph, and copying machines.
 c. Electronic memory typewriter
  (1) Edit letter of application.
  (2) Type and print letter utilizing memory functions.
5. Demonstrate speedwriting techniques.
Speedwriting (2 weeks)
—Learn the brief forms, phrases, and sentences of career and job interview terminologies.
—Write sentences utilizing words in conversation and notetaking.

HOME BASE (1 week)—An opportunity to catch up as well as an opportunity for guidance counseling by teachers.

6. Identify and complete proper forms required for jobs.
Accounting (1 week)
Completion of: a. W-4 Form
      b. Social Security Application
      c. State and Federal Tax Exemption Forms
      d. 1040 EZ, 1040 A
7. Demonstrate proper job interview techniques.
Marketing and Distribution (3 weeks)
—Discuss proper attire for interviewing.
—Review a request for an application form.
—Complete and discuss interview questions and conversation.
—Videotaping of mock interview.
8. Understand equal opportunity laws.
General Business (2 weeks)
Advisory committee member presentations:
 a. Explanation and discussion of equal opportunity laws.
 b. Discussion on sexual harassment and viewing of film.

Program evaluation. Each teacher in the cycle evaluates the curriculum with the students for program improvement. During the first day of the learning center program, students are provided with an evaluation form to assess attitude, personal goals, and interest. On the last day of the learning center program, students also complete an evaluation form.

Advisory committee. The members of the advisory committee for the learning center provide representation from the following areas: business, district and state department of education, local legislators, parents, students, graduates, secondary teachers outside the business education field, and community college teachers. There are 14 current members and several members represent more than one area. For example, a teacher at Waipahu High School from outside the business education area is also a parent. Interestingly, a graduate of Waipahu High School who serves on the advisory committee is pursuing a business education major at the University of Hawaii. The advisory committee meets quarterly, and many of the members are more frequently involved in other support activities.

Instructional staff. The success of the program is dependent on the compatibility of instructors. Flexible instructors who are skilled in teaching a variety of business subjects share classes in the regular curriculum and the learning center. Seven instructors, including the director, are currently involved. The program has provided an excellent opportunity to rejuvenate the entire business education department staff.

TELECOMMUNICATIONS COURSE

As a second phase of the Business and Computer Technology Learning Center, a course in telecommunications has been designed. The unique aspect of this course is that it involves a direct link with a local Waipahu business, Charley's General Tire/Auto Parts/KIS Photo. The president of the company is a graduate of Waipahu High School and currently serves on the advisory committee for the learning center. The company has been involved with DECA students for many years.

Through the medium of telecommunications, the class will perform actual business tasks for the company. A variety of learning experiences will be incorporated to accomplish the tasks and satisfy the course objectives. All data will be transferred by use of facsimile communication between the classroom and the business.

To reinforce spreadsheet, database, and graphics concepts, daily sales activity information will be collected and transmitted from the company to the classroom. The appropriate spreadsheets, graphs, and charts will be prepared by the students and transmitted back to the company. Letters to customers and reports in rough draft form will be transmitted to the classroom, and students will use word processing equipment to complete final copy and transmit it back to the company. The electronic calculator skill will be reinforced by students totalling daily receipts which will be transmitted by the company for calculation. Learning experiences will also include reprographics and desktop publishing to produce company fliers and announcements. Bulletins for business in Waipahu as well as for parents of the students participating in the learning center program will be prepared to share the activities and achievements of the students. Electronic mail will be used to communicate with other schools and organizations, and a personal computer with modem will provide access to the Career Kokua computerized career information center.

Career shadowing will be accomplished without leaving the classroom by use of the Luma Phone. The director will visit five individuals per day at their places of employment, and the students will remain in the classroom to observe and ask questions via the phone. This will allow approximately 15 career-shadowing opportunities in three days, an obvious impossibility if the students were to be transported to the employment locations.

The learning experiences provided in this course will emphasize the technology of the local business environment. Through the advisory committee and the cooperating business, the learning center will receive guidance and input as to the needs of employers. The practical applications will reinforce the latest methods of processing data as well as other important aspects of business such as business ethics and confidentiality of materials. Using actual business data will create a greater sense of accountability and responsibility.

Students from high schools other than Waipahu will also be offered the opportunity to participate in this program. They will use their high school as home base and attend Waipahu High School for an afternoon session, or they will be permitted to register at Waipahu High School. This provides a much broader base from which to build enthusiasm for business education.

The Business and Computer Technology Learning Center is an excellent example of an innovative effort to build enrollment in the business education curriculum. It provides a unique opportunity to "turn students on" to business and "turn business on" to the importance of business education. It is the result of hard work, good planning, and excellent cooperation between the educational and business communities.

The Waipahu High School principal, Milton Shishido, was responsible for the concept of the learning center. The public relations efforts with the other departments of the high school, the business community, and state legislators as well as the project writing and applications for funding are the responsibility of the director of the Learning Center, Jean Miyahira. The approval of the program by the district and state has led to plans to extend the program to adult education classes in the evening. Parents have become so enthusiastic that they want to take the courses, too!

The business community has also become very enthusiastic about the program. Many companies are demonstrating support by contributing equipment and supplies as well as personnel to serve on the advisory committee. Other businesses are now waiting in line for the opportunity to participate in the same manner as Charley's.

Prior to the development of the learning center, Charley's had hired many DECA students and had offered many scholarships. The company continues to offer scholarships in lieu of salaries for the students. To qualify, students must prepare a resume and autobiography. Winners have the funds applied directly to the institutions where they register for postsecondary education. All winners to date have pursued business programs!

CONCLUSION

Business education has the opportunity to demonstrate assertiveness when it joins forces with the business community to address the basic competencies required for entry-level employment. It can incorporate learning experiences that explore technological concepts, problem-solving skills, job training, and career guidance to attract new students to the business education classroom.

A creative and productive partnership between business and education can keep pace with the changing technology of a competitive business world. It can also develop unique strategies to attract more students to the business education curriculum.

CHAPTER 14
Owning and Managing a Business

COLLEEN VAWDREY
Utah Valley Community College, Orem

What child has not at some time set out to "seek his fortune" by means of a lemonade stand or cookie sale? Even though the venture may have lasted only an afternoon and the tangible rewards may have seemed meager to an outside viewer, the "entrepreneur" deemed it a success, and seeds may have been planted for the future. The seeds can be nourished and grown in today's high school programs. In this article, the who, why, where, what, when, and how of entrepreneurship education will be discussed.

THE WHO OF ENTREPRENEURSHIP

Entrepreneurship is defined by most people as an enterprise owned and managed by an individual for the purpose of making a profit. These entrepreneurs bring their own creativity and ingenuity to the business and assume responsibility for the success or failure of it.

Owning and operating a small business has been and continues to be "big business" for many Americans. Statistics by the National Federation of Independent Business show that almost four million small enterprises exist in the United States and over 16.5 million people are engaged in some type of independent business. The U.S. Small Business Administration reports that more than 1,600 new enterprises are launched every day! What a testimonial to free enterprise! Will the trend continue? The prediction is that it will and that by 2000, self-employment will grow even more rapidly than it has been and small firms will produce about 40 percent of U.S. output.

If these predictions come true, business educators have a tremendous responsibility and opportunity to be involved in this explosion of business ventures. Along with traditional business subjects, students have a need and a right to know what is involved before they must find out through the hardest teacher of all—experience!

THE WHY OF ENTREPRENEURSHIP

NBEA recognizes this potential for growth and assesses it as an area of focus in the NBEA curriculum guide, *Database of Competencies for Business Curriculum Development, K-14*. Business educators cannot afford to pass up this exciting opportunity to give students a more complete picture of life outside the classroom. Teachers also have a responsibility to students to help them see realistically what is involved. In this time of educational change where students are pulled in many directions in their educational pursuits and where business education is struggling to keep enrollments, a solution to the problem seems to be making sure courses are relevant to students' needs. What better way to meet this relevance issue than with a course which could offer so much to students, particularly those who may lack the desire or ability to gain a college degree. These students need a chance to develop their potential and be made aware of the opportunities which can exist for them.

With the current increase in entrepreneurial ventures also comes an increase in business failures. Dun and Bradstreet estimates that about two of every three new firms close their doors within four years. Why do businesses fail? One of the most common reasons seems to be the entrepreneur's lack of management skill and understanding of the system. These potential entrepreneurs need to know the risks involved early so they can be prepared to avoid some of the pitfalls which could require dissolving the business.

THE WHERE OF ENTREPRENEURSHIP

Most teachers will agree with the concept, but many believe this education should be reserved for the elect few students who really know at the outset what they want to do and take those courses in a college setting which will give them that training. This approach is simply not enough. Many high school students are more aware of and involved in free enterprise activities than most adults realize. Through encouragement and education, these students and others can be encouraged to be part of this team of "good guys" doing "good things" for a "good purpose."

Utah has become aware of this untapped resource of youthful enthusiasm and has begun to reward the business ventures through the means of a Young Entrepreneur Contest for high school students. Sponsored by the governor, the event gives recognition to students who are currently managing their own business during an annual Student Entrepreneur Conference. Since its beginning in 1987, hundreds of high school entrepreneurs have been identified and have competed for honors. The top award is $10,000, donated by a local entrepreneur who believes these young people are the key to the future of free enterprise. In 1988 second and third prizes of $3,000 and $2,000 were also added. The finalists are all given recognition through a television program where they can "show off" their businesses. The senior student who won first place in 1987 owns a window-washing business and employs six other people in the operation—two of them full-time employees to work during the day while he was in school. The 1988 winner has three thriving enterprises going at the same time: making and selling woodcrafts, complete yard care, and snow removal. He hires different employees for each of the businesses while he keeps the books and manages them. Other finalists have similar stories; all are involved in thriving, competitive businesses.

Since the program is sponsored by Utah's governor, it receives much support. Directors of the program believe Utah is a leader in the nation in recognizing these achievements. Many have been amazed that students so young have accomplished so much. Along with having business licenses, company goals, employees, and accounting systems, they know all about profit and investing in the future. The advocates of the program believe high school education should work toward a balanced effort between academics and practical use to make the system work.

Learning to take risks and organize activities is not innate; it must be learned. Where should students gain the knowledge and skill necessary to achieve success? The logical answer seems to be school, and the sooner the better. An article in a recent issue of *The Association of Private Enterprise Education Newsletter* told of a project in Mt. Vernon, Indiana, where elementary students were taught about economics and entrepreneurship by experiencing it. They were given opportunities to earn play money by doing classroom jobs, running their own businesses, and meeting certain behavior standards. They paid taxes, bought and sold property, rented out games and other toys, and made investments. They were not learning about free enterprise; they were experiencing it! Think how much more prepared these students will be to receive advanced instruction in high school settings, not to mention those who may elect to go on to higher education.

THE WHAT OF ENTREPRENEURSHIP

A closer look at the areas in which students should become competent reveals at least seven curriculum categories. For those teachers who are convinced that seven new courses could not possibly be added to an already overloaded teacher preparation schedule, think about the possibility of combining these concepts into already existing courses. A unit of study can be included in many different areas. However, how the situation is approached is not as important as seeing that it is done!

Characteristics of successful entrepreneurs. Initially, students need an opportunity to assess their strengths and then to see how well they fit with accepted characteristics of successful entrepreneurs. Although many people think entrepreneurs are born, not made, studies of company founders suggest that a variety of experiences helped these self-motivated people succeed. One influence is the family. Children from families where parents have owned a business are more likely to want to venture into their own companies.

Helping students see the importance of self-confidence and goal setting in achieving success is essential. People who start companies seem to believe that they can control their own destinies; and though their activities seem an enormous risk to uninvolved observers, the entrepreneur believes the risks are actually moderate and can be minimized. Those who are innovative, hardworking, and dependable have a better chance of success in entrepreneurial activities. Whether students plan to own their own businesses or choose to become involved in more traditional careers, all teachers can agree that these attitudes are important in achieving success yet they are most often overlooked in the traditional curriculum.

Once the students are aware of their strengths, introduce them to some successful entrepreneurs. Stories of Henry Ford, Colonel Sanders, and Ray

Kroc will be fascinating for the students since they are acquainted with the products, but don't forget contemporary entrepreneurs like Debbie Fields and her cookies or Steven Jobs and Steven Wozniak and their Apple computers. Such stories as these can inspire students and help increase their own self-confidence.

Planning the business. Students can easily see that they would never begin a trip without organizing a schedule, collecting the necessary materials, and consulting a map for directions. The same plan is necessary before beginning a business. Some people may "fall into success," but that is definitely the exception rather than the rule. Planning ahead and knowing what to anticipate will significantly decrease the chance of being one of those failure statistics.

Make the planning process more realistic by letting students choose a business of their interest and assume they are starting it. Then have them talk with entrepreneurs in that field and find out what steps are really involved in planning and organizing the venture. Students could then use this assignment as a springboard for future assignments in the management area. Consider having students choose different businesses. A culminating process then could be the interaction of this "business community" where students could share their expertise with other students and increase all students' learning.

Economic principles. All students—regardless of their career plans—must have a basic understanding of how our free enterprise system works. Asking students questions about fundamental economics quickly reveals the fact that most of them are ignorant of the facts. When more high school students know about Karl Marx and communism than about Adam Smith and capitalism, economic education definitely needs additional emphasis! If students don't understand how supply and demand works in the marketplace, they cannot be expected to function successfully in any phase of the business world.

Students are given a distorted view of some economic elements, for example, government involvement or labor unions. Most of the comments students hear are very one-sided. Hearing both sides of the issues and having a chance to determine their own value system when they have all the facts will lead the students to become more responsible members of society, whatever their future plans include.

Along with the importance of this curriculum area is the fact that economics lends itself to much teacher creativity, which will increase students' enthusiasm and retention of the principles. A practical approach whenever possible is a great way to keep students actively involved in the learning process. Many personal-use principles should also be included here. Such ideas as balancing a checkbook, buying insurance, figuring taxes, and becoming an educated consumer are important concepts for students to understand. If these topics are not covered in high school, when can students expect to find out about the business world around them?

Managing the business. Students may have the mistaken belief that starting the business is the hardest part and once it is going, the business will just "run itself." Students need to be introduced to the myriad of tasks under the umbrella term "management." Decision making is an abstract concept for most students, yet a most important skill for entrepreneurs to have. They must realize there is much more to making decisions than just saying "yes" or "no." A systems approach to decision making where students are required to analyze a variety of concerns may be a most effective way of helping them see the many factors which must be considered before a final decision can be made. Knowing that the consequences of those decisions rest squarely on the shoulders of the entrepreneur makes the decision making a much more serious process. Use current "failure and success" stories to illustrate.

Other important challenges are the management of other employees, the pros and cons of a proprietorship and a partnership, the financial planning involved, and the paperwork from all sides. Through some creative simulated activities, teachers should be able to make these challenges live for their students and give them some experience with management. Chances are the future entrepreneurs will discover management has more varied responsibilities than they ever thought possible. This awareness will probably be much different from the perception given on television that the manager or entrepreneur is the boss and can decide to work or not according to his or her whim.

Business law. Understanding legal terminology and being able to follow legal documents is an important concept for personal use as well as business ownership. Use the students' natural curiosity about law. Here is an excellent opportunity for field trips to court and/or visits from judges, attorneys, or others involved in daily law practices. Care must be taken to ensure that students are learning business law, not criminal law, since this area at first may appear to be the most flashy and intriguing part for the students. Many concepts from current events can be used to teach students the legal implications of their behavior and decisions. Keeping in mind the goal of practical use, let the students participate in the legal process through mock trials. They will enjoy "trying" some of the principles learned and determining how these rules are integrated into the business world.

Finance. No business is successful until the matter of money is solved. Few would-be entrepreneurs, young or old, have enough money to begin the venture without help. Students must understand sources of both internal and external credit. Such other financial concepts as savings, investments, and stock and commodity markets will be interesting and useful to all students. Once the business is operating, financial reports are necessary, too. A basic understanding of accounting principles is important as well.

Marketing. Understanding competition and its effect in the marketplace will better equip students to become part of the system. Students need to understand that consumers do not buy products for the sake of buying, but they buy to solve problems for themselves. Marketing products or services which are not popular with the public accounts for another common reason businesses fail. An entrepreneur who begins a business of selling "widgets" because those products intrigue him or her may be disappointed to learn that "widgets" are not problem solvers for consumers.

Even those businesses involved with popular products are not exempt from marketing problems. Determining prices is a complicated process not within most students' understanding. Here is another opportunity for teachers to increase understanding of new concepts. Why are prices increased or decreased? Most students will be surprised to find out that it is not just because the entrepreneur decides he or she needs more money.

Knowing something about emotional appeals and how advertising uses them to its benefit will be fascinating to students. They can analyze current advertisements to help bring these concepts to life. Analyzing other similar businesses will also help them see what strengths can be implemented and how weaknesses and problems can be avoided. Using the same business that students analyzed earlier can provide continuity to the project.

THE WHEN OF ENTREPRENEURSHIP

The only answer to this question is now! The general consensus is that change is all around. Values are changing, society is changing, the economy is changing, and education must change in order to keep up. Any article or book about future trends will point out the importance of adding these skills to the repertoire of the business education curriculum. The bottom line, of course, is giving students the best possible education.

THE HOW OF ENTREPRENEURSHIP

Being committed to the principles, however, doesn't necessarily mean that educators feel qualified to teach these concepts. The majority of business teachers have an expertise in skill and technological areas and feel somewhat less than prepared for the nonskill part of the curriculum.

They need not feel that they are alone. Many sources of help are available to teachers. Such organizations as the Small Business Administration, National Federation of Independent Business, and Joint Council on Economic Education have a strong commitment to these entrepreneurial concepts. They have a variety of up-to-date materials and are very willing to share them with teachers. Other sources of support for teachers and students are such organizations as Junior Achievement and FBLA. Giving students an opportunity to try simulated hands-on experiences will be a great learning experience for both them and their teachers. Local chambers of commerce will be happy to become involved with those teachers who are trying to bring this type of realistic education to their students. State offices of education should be approached about providing seminars for additional inservice training for teachers interested in these important areas. Teachers don't need to believe they must be experts in the field or have had experience in operating their own business before they can be qualified to help students understand these concepts. The important thing is to become as committed to free enterprise and entrepreneurial education as to other long-time "traditional" business education curriculum areas. Helping students learn about "making jobs" is just as important as about "taking jobs." Not only students but education as a whole cannot afford to be without it. Who knows, it may be the means of survival for business education!

CHAPTER 15

Marketing and Distribution

STEPHEN P. SPOFFORD
Kennett High School, Conway, New Hampshire

Marketing programs, if run successfully, are similar to real business plans. It is important that marketing educators approach their subject area as if it were an actual business, using all the marketing skills that they will ultimately teach.

Most educators are natural marketers by necessity, their skills being perfected by study and work experiences. In business, as well as in education, it is important that a marketing plan be created and utilized before a successful educational program can even be implemented. Once the plan is created and utilized, it then becomes necessary for every marketing program to recognize and change in response to changes in our society and our economy. In this chapter, the elements of the marketing plan and the curriculum responses needed to assert ourselves in marketing will be discussed.

THE FOUR P'S

The Four P's of a marketing plan set the stage for the proper educational mix. These four elements are not unique to the business world; they are commonly used in marketing education and include price, promotion, place, and product.

Price in a marketing program is the reward, or value that a student attaches to the program. Some students are motivated by price only and are readily willing to invest in your program, while others require a "hard sell" each day. Educators negotiate a sale each day with their students. As a facilitator of knowledge, this sale will eventually result in an equitable reward earned by a student. Some students get a minimum price, while others go beyond our expectations.

In essence, price fixing abounds in many marketing programs today, because mastery learning is an expectation of business education. As businesses require their employees to have demonstrable skills, so too will the knowledgeable classroom manager. Students are often allowed to repeat exams in order to gain mastery in core competency areas. Students are also given pretests to determine if their background has given them skills in these areas before the new unit is covered. If competency is met, another unit will be selected for the student. Certainly, with the diverse and varied background of many of today's youth, this system will allow and promote greater academic growth and marketing potential. Academic success has a price; it builds self-esteem, which spills over into many other areas.

Promotion is the educational style one uses to present the product, which in marketing education is the course of studies. Good teachers are strong promoters. Promotion can be "flash and sizzle," or a sense of deep caring used to influence the market (student). Educators refer to this as teaching style, but in marketing, this is the method used to reach the public. What makes successful promotion? Marketers have been making successful promotions for years. Certainly, educators who are successful marketers for many more years have held the edge and had the opportunity to be more effective promoters than most of our competitors. Marketing, in most schools, is not a requirement for graduation. But all classes are successfully competing for their market share of students.

Public educators have the advantage of a captive audience, and there is no doubt that today's marketing classes represent a diverse and challenging population. The very nature of the marketing program, usually an elective, requires that marketing educators have flexible teaching style. Marketers are survivalists, using a plethora of teaching techniques to create an atmosphere of excitement. This enriching environment allows students to develop and surpass their potential.

Place refers to the learning environment used by the marketing instructor. What an array of opportunities marketing teachers have at their disposal. Most of the competition (contemporaries) use the traditional classroom as their exclusive delivery system. Some educators actually believe that effective learning can only occur in such a classroom.

Marketers who are adept in advertising realize the importance of using different media to convey a message, and their use of many learning environments reflects this capacity to be creative. Certainly, the classroom is a valuable resource, but not the only resource. Cooperative education allows actual on-the-job learning and experiences to allow the student to grow. Few, if any, controlled laboratory school environments can duplicate the actual work world. In-school stores or marketing laboratories create a marketing learning environment where factors can be controlled and manipulated to create simulated working conditions. Job site visitations allow students to visit and experience businesses firsthand. What an opportunity students have when they see, firsthand, the excitement of entrepreneurs as they describe a business venture. Enthusiasm is an important concept in successful marketing, and the community's business members are usually more than willing to share theirs. Work study allows many students the opportunity to experience the world of work, as they explore new career interests. Marketing, a subject area that encompasses the eight business functions, allows students to explore a diverse selection of job clusters. Our marketing programs have an ecology of content which touches all disciplines.

Product, the last component of any successful marketing plan, refers to the areas that marketers (teachers) communicate through their content. Marketing is a constantly changing and evolving product. Curriculum, like all products' life cycles, is no exception. There must be utility and a need for this service. Many educational products delivered in today's high schools are outdated. Marketing requires that curriculum be responsive to today's students. Competition in the educational marketplace requires that marketing educators remarket, reposition, and revise the curricular product being sold. The vocational advisory committee, or craft committee, serves as an up-to-date economic indicator of many marketing programs. Their professional input dictates the direction of a good marketing program. Marketing strategy, however, is the domain of the instructor. What techniques will be used to shape and direct your public?

RESPONDING TO CHANGING TRENDS

Marketing trends of the eighties and the nineties will require that students and curriculum be responsive to the dramatic changes that are emerging today.

As our economy changes from an industrial society to an informational one, prepared students will be those who are computer literate and who possess effective communication skills. Marketing students will have an advantage in this area because many of today's marketing programs require computer knowledge and information processing. Communication skills such as public speaking, personal selling, parliamentary procedure, and written competitive events will prepare students for the challenges ahead.

Human relations activities found in competency-based curriculum will be another focal point of the eighties and nineties. Human interaction is essential for successful development of human relations. Marketing students should have as many opportunities as possible to interact with people in a positive way. Through state and local meetings, competitive events, national conferences, local civic-consciousness projects, and leadership roles at the high school level, marketing students have the chance to foster strong human interaction skills. Some marketing students who have had academic difficulties can learn to channel and develop strong human relation skills and achieve great success in our programs. This success allows increased academic confidence and a more well-rounded student.

As our economy changes from a national economy to a world economy, fundamental and difficult economic concepts must be understood by all of society's members. Students in marketing courses should have an awareness of world economies and be taught the necessities and realities of the free enterprise system. Students in marketing courses that allow store operations or cooperative work experiences have had opportunities to see and experience business trends firsthand and be able to forecast new business cycles. This understanding, although in microcosm, allows marketing students to see cause-and-effect relationships and to make farsighted observations. Certainly, America's economic problems will require problem solving that is farsighted and generated by an economically literate society.

Marketing activities focus on real business problems and real business decision making. Critical thinking is a necessary component of the student's thought process. Students who are taught to think and seek out information in the informational age of the eighties and nineties will possess survival skills and achieve success in their vocational choices. Marketing requires that information reflect the changing values and customs of our evolving society; students must be accurate and capable information seekers.

Exchanging information horizontally, instead of from top to bottom, is called "networking." Marketing students involved with the DECA marketing club have an opportunity to meet and learn from their peers. This learning process is the goal of many classroom teachers and an essential component of later professional growth. The introduction of "networking" on the high school level allows many students the advantage of meeting and interacting with new people who have similar or varied backgrounds.

Due to the diversity of the marketing curriculum, students will have multiple career options and acquire a greater knowledge base in order to make important future career choices. Many of today's workers will be making three and possibly four different career choices within their lifetimes. Vocational flexibility will allow the marketing student to have greater self-confidence and entrepreneurial spirit.

Leadership is created and developed in the marketing classroom environment. Today's marketing students are encouraged to pursue leadership roles via the local and state DECA organization, store management, school functions, and community service projects. Leadership promotes self-help and self-confidence. Today's high school students are placed in a demanding and challenging world. Decision-making skills require leadership through one's actions and the self-confidence to make the right choices.

CONCLUSION

In most educational programs it is difficult to extrapolate success and to predict the future of our students, but marketing is a subject that will prepare and promote individual achievement and a willingness to be innovative. Marketing education is a field in which we have yet to assert ourselves to a potential that well serves our students and our programs.

Part V
ASSERTING AND REASSERTING BUSINESS EDUCATION AT THE POSTSECONDARY LEVEL

CHAPTER 16

Basic Skills and Core Competencies

ALICE A. TAYLOR
Northern Virginia Community College, Woodbridge

All business teachers know that business education has something to offer all students; but are both business and nonbusiness majors aware of business offerings and what benefits students may derive from taking business courses? There are four core competencies and basic skills areas that should be taught at the secondary and postsecondary levels to help every citizen succeed in society and earn a living according to the NBEA Database of Competencies: information skills—reading, writing, speaking/listening, and computing; personal development skills—self-management, interpersonal relations, decision making and critical thinking, leadership, and career awareness/goal setting; economic, consumer, and business concepts skills—American economic system, money management, and business and its environment; and technology skills—computer literacy and keyboarding.[1]

Important skills necessary to succeed in everyday life activities are taught in business courses. More specifically, in business courses such skills as human relations and personal and professional development are taught. Communication skills, keyboarding, economic literacy, career education, business concepts, and basic skills are other examples of areas included in business courses where the development of many of the skills necessary to survive in a rapidly changing, technologically sophisticated society are taught.

It is not enough that business educators know that business courses have something to offer everyone; the profession must disseminate information to apprise everyone—students and potential students—of business courses and their benefits to society. Many teachers would appreciate some help in identifying courses along with their concomitant advantages to students. With this in mind, this chapter presents examples of business courses that can be offered and their usefulness to all students enrolled at the two- and four-year college level and in private business schools. Suggestions and strategies that may be employed to promote business courses are also discussed.

SKILLS NEEDED TO SUCCEED IN SOCIETY

Whether one's role is that of mother, father, doctor, teacher, lawyer,

---
[1]*Database of Competencies for Business Curriculum Development, K-14.* Reston, Va.: National Business Education Association, 1987. pp. 4.5-4.48.

housekeeper, manager of a fast food store or of a large corporation, scientist, bus driver, or engineer, there are skills that are needed to perform as a citizen and productive member of society in America. Very few will argue against the fact that a husband and wife need to behave in such a manner that unnecessary conflict is avoided, nor against the fact that employers seek employees who can work together without disrupting the work flow. These and other human relations skills are taught in business courses that are discussed below. Also, other skills and concepts included in business courses that are of use to the general public are related in the following sections.

Human relations skills. To be successful in today's society, human relations skills which will aid individuals in achieving their occupational and social goals must be learned. For example, through formal business courses students may be made aware of and helped to acquire skills, attitudes, and attributes such as getting along with others; cooperativeness; pleasing personality; professionalism; coping; meeting and greeting others; working with peers, supervisors, and subordinates; and making conversation.

Also knowing how to approach others in a friendly and nonthreatening manner can be invaluable to those who seek to become supervisors and managers. A look at employment recommendation forms will reveal that quite often the person who is recommending another for employment is asked to indicate whether a prospective employee is personable, dependable, reliable, industrious, of good character, and has a good attendance record. Business faculty teach these and other human relations skills. Knowing that many employers feel that students need to be taught "the work ethic," business faculty strive to develop student attitudes that reflect that students are willing to do "a day's work for a day's pay." Business instructors and professors are well equipped to teach human relations skills not only because of the subject matter they teach but because of their professional background and their work experiences.

Personal Development, Professional Development, Office Systems and Procedures, and Office Management are titles of courses in which some two- and four-year college instructors and professors teach human relations skills. Some colleges offer a special course such as Human Relations in Business.

Career education and personal and professional development skills. Career education skills are developed in students by providing them with information on various careers, vocational opportunities, job expectations, and technical aspects of jobs and vocations so that they are able to select the career for which they are most suited. Students are provided information which shows them that a job and a career or vocation may be quite different.

Personal development skills concentrate on imparting information and techniques which allow and even encourage students to develop their individual attitudes and behaviors in a socially acceptable manner. Students learn how to improve themselves as individuals and how to enhance their personal image. Students are taught to expect, accept, and appreciate change. Good grooming, dressing appropriately, giving a firm handshake, and smiling warmly and sincerely are among the skills students are taught to cultivate.

These skills and knowledge are needed to help individuals in planning their vocations and making career choices.

Though career education, personal development, and professional development knowledge and skills overlap somewhat, professional development focuses on helping students to acquire the skills necessary to succeed and advance in a chosen vocation or profession. In many professional development and personal development courses students are taught how to fill out job applications, how to write resumes, how to write letters of application, how to perform job searches, how to listen effectively, how to behave during a job interview, and how to keep abreast of the changes in their jobs or professions. These skills can be most helpful to individuals entering the job market or contemplating a career change. Many of these skills are taught in office systems and procedures/office management, office automation/word processing, business English/business communications, and keyboarding courses.

Communication skills. Communication—the ability to write, speak, listen, and transmit information effectively—is an essential skill which can serve all individuals well, whether in a purely social setting or in a work environment. In order to convey thoughts, ideas, feelings, attitudes, and instructions, communcation must take place even if it is nonverbal. Effective communication skills help to assure that the desired response is forthcoming. Communication takes many forms—sales letters, letters of applications, reports (oral and written), and electronic and telecommunicated correspondence, speeches, and reports. At two- and four-year colleges, courses in business English, business communications, and shorthand all help students learn to be effective communicators.

Keyboarding. As businesses, government agencies, and individual members of society purchase and use more and more computers, the importance of keyboarding skills increases. Keyboarding skills are no longer used just to type words and information on an electronic or an electric typewriter, or even on a word processor, or at a data entry terminal. Keyboarding skills are needed and are being used to input data efficiently, to enter commands, to retrieve and transmit information, to run application programs on large and small computer systems, to interact with information services such as CompuServe and Dow Jones, and to perform other telecommunications tasks. Business faculty are uniquely qualified by their experience and their expertise to teach keyboarding/typewriting skills. Many two- and four-year colleges offer keyboarding and typewriting courses under a variety of names.

Computer literacy. To be considered computer literate, citizens have to know what a computer system is, how to operate a computer, computer applications, how to use some software packages, and basic computer terminology. The impact that computers have had and are having on American society behooves all persons to become computer literate in order to function effectively in a rapidly changing, technology-oriented society. Business faculty contribute to the development of computer literacy skills by including computer concepts and applications in their keyboarding/typewriting, word processing, filing and records management, accounting/

recordkeeping, personal finance, and office management/office systems and procedures courses.

Economic literacy. American consumers are constantly besieged by new and "better" products advertised by businesses in newspapers, television, magazines, flyers, and other media. To be wise consumers or to get the most for their money, citizens must develop an appreciation for the American economic system, its principles and functions in a democratic society. In other words, the economics literate person is able to make intelligent personal and social economic choices daily in the American free enterprise system. Introduction to business, business law, and office management/office systems and procedures are examples of courses taught by business faculty which contribute significantly to the development of economic literacy skills.

Business concepts. Business concepts and consumer and economic concepts are interrelated. If individuals are to become literate in economics they have to understand business as an economic institution and its role in the American enterprise system. In addition to the courses mentioned above, courses in introduction to business, business law, and office management/office systems and procedures, business communications, and business English can contribute to the development of business concepts by including business concepts topics in assignments given to students.

Basic skills. Reading, writing, speaking/listening, and computing are the basic skills that all citizens should know. Most business courses contribute to the development of students' ability to read, write, and speak or their ability to communicate effectively; however, by the nature of their content business English and business communications courses specifically develop most of these basic skills. Computing skills involve developing the ability of individuals to solve arithmetic problems requiring addition, subtraction, multiplication, and division that confront ordinary citizens in their homes, the marketplace, their jobs, and other aspects of their daily lives. Public education has been criticized in recent years for failing to equip students with satisfactory computing and other basic skills. Business faculty help to develop students' computing skills in courses such as business mathematics, personal finance, and accounting/office recordkeeping.

BUSINESS COURSES OFFERED AT TWO- AND FOUR-YEAR COLLEGES THAT HELP TO DEVELOP SKILLS NECESSARY TO SUCCEED IN SOCIETY AND TO EARN A LIVING

Two- and four-year college business courses with general appeal to nonbusiness majors and business majors are listed and described in the following sections. Some of the benefits students may derive from enrolling in the courses are discussed, as well as the contributions of the courses to developing the core competencies and basic skills.

For clarity, brevity, and convenience, discussions of the courses below either include course descriptions excerpted from Northern Virginia Community College catalogs[2] or from Virginia Community College System

---

[2]*NOVA 1987-88 Catalog* and *NOVA 1988-89 Catalog*. Annandale, Va.: Northern Virginia Community College, 1987 and 1988.

Curriculum Guides.[3] (Any other two- or four-year college catalogs could have been used.) In planning for the promotion of business courses, business faculty could use their own college's catalog along with their departmental course content summaries and faculty course outlines to highlight the salient points of business courses.

Introduction to Business.

BUS 100 Introduction to Business—Presents a broad introduction to the functioning of business enterprise within the U.S. economic framework. Introduces economic systems, essential elements of business organization, finance, marketing, production, and risk and human resources management.

The advantages of taking this course lie in its significant contributions to the development of economic, consumer, and business concepts skills; in its contributions to the development of the information skills of reading, writing, and speaking/listening; and in its contributions to the development of the personal development skill of career awareness/goal setting. This information could and should be disseminated to all members of the college community and to prospective college students so that possible enrollees are made aware of how they can benefit from having taken Introduction to Business.

Business Mathematics.

BUS 121 Business Mathematics—Teaches mathematics relating to business processes and problems such as checkbook records and bank reconciliation, simple interest notes, present value, bank discount notes, wage and payroll computations, depreciation, sales and property taxes, commercial discounts, markup and markdown, and inventory turnovers and valuation.

The benefits of Business Mathematics to the general college population are that it develops and advances that basic skill of computing and it contributes to the development of the economic, consumer, and business concepts skill of money management.

Business English. Although this course is not always taught by business faculty, business faculty cover similar content while emphasizing transcription skills in courses similar to the one that follows.

OFT 107 Editing/Proofreading Skills—Develops skills essential to creating and editing business documents. Covers spelling, diction, punctuation, word division, capitalization, and sentence structure.

Other titles may be used for similar courses. Obviously, however, the benefits gained by all students from such courses are that the information skills of reading and writing are improved. A corollary benefit is that nonbusiness majors are made aware of some business terminology and practices.

Business Communications. The content of this course is often the same as Business English for all practical purposes except that it specifically adds oral communication.

---

[3]"Instructional Programs Section." *Virginia Community College System Curriculum Guide.* Richmond: Virginia Community College System, 1987 and 1988.

OFT 205 Business Communications—Teaches techniques of oral and written communications. Emphasizes writing and presenting business related materials.

All students who enroll in this course are benefited by increasing their ability to read, write, speak, listen, and communicate nonverbally.

Personal Finance.

BUAD 116 Personal Finance—A course designed to build a framework of money management concepts. Content includes establishing values and goals, earning income, managing income, developing consumer buying ability, using credit, understanding savings, insurance, and responsibilities as a consumer.

The economic, consumer, and business concepts skills as well as the computing skills taught in this course are advantageous to all citizens. Obviously such a course can help students manage their income and expenses, pay their bills, and save for the future.

Professional/Personal Development. This course may be entitled Personal Development or Professional Development.

OFT 206 Professional Development—Develops professional awareness in handling business and social situations. Emphasizes . . . goal setting and decision making.

This course is of value to business and nonbusiness majors in enhancing their personal development, professional development, and career awareness skills as formerly discussed.

Keyboarding/Typewriting.

OFT 111 Keyboarding/Typewriting—Introduces the keyboard with emphasis on good techniques, machine mastery, letter formats and styles, tabulations, centering, and reports.

The benefit business majors and nonbusiness majors receive from taking keyboarding is principally that the technology skill of efficient touch keyboarding is developed. If students are taught keyboarding/typewriting on microcomputers, computer literacy skills may also be enhanced. Another benefit is that the information skills of reading, writing, and computing may be indirectly improved.

Shorthand.

OFT 121 Shorthand I—Focuses on shorthand theory reading and writing skills, development of general business vocabularies, word usage, and general business dictation.

A lot of time and effort is necessary to become proficient in shorthand; therefore, its main benefit is to the business major. However, nonbusiness majors may benefit from the course's development of reading, writing, and listening skills as well as its development of the ability to take notes quickly.

Business Law.

BUS 241 Business Law I—Presents a broad introduction to legal environment of U.S. business. Develops a basic understanding of contract law and agency and government regulation.

All students can gain benefit from Business Law's contribution to the development of economic, consumer, and business concepts skills as well as gain an awareness of and an appreciation for the laws that govern business transactions that affect their lives.

Filing and Records Management.

OFT 137 Filing and Records Management—Introduces indexing principles, filing procedures, and systems, including electronics and micrographics. Teaches selection of equipment and supplies and solving records management problems.

Although its primary benefit is to majors, Filing and Records Management can help nonbusiness majors use filing procedures to store and retrieve their personal records such as names, addresses, telephone numbers, recipes, bills, receipts, deeds, and warranties and help to develop their computer literacy skills by teaching them to use electronic databases or other computer software.

Accounting/Office Recordkeeping.

OFT 136 Office Recordkeeping—Introduces types of recordkeeping duties performed in the office, such as financial, tax, payroll, and inventory. Utilizes specialized software where applicable.

There is a more comprehensive accounting course entitled Principles of Accounting which may be offered. Spreadsheets and other software packages may be incorporated in teaching these courses. Both of these courses certainly develop computing, money management, and computer literacy skills that can be beneficial to all students. Accounting procedures are useful to individuals in managing their earnings, bills, household and business expenses, and their taxes.

Word Processing.

OFT 216 Word Processing Procedures—Teaches use and operation of word/information processing equipment. Incorporates specific advanced applications.

Business and nonbusiness majors can profit greatly from taking a word processing course since it develops computer literacy and the basic skills of reading and writing. Students may use these skills in preparing reports and correspondence for their other classes and day-to-day activities.

Office Procedures/Office Management.

OFT 251 Office Systems and Procedures—Teaches office protocol, solutions to office problems, managerial functions, and other topics associated with office technology.

Office Systems and Procedures or an office management course can be invaluable to business majors and nonbusiness majors who wish to learn how to plan, organize, direct, and control activities. The skills and knowledge learned in such courses have practical, everyday applications; the skills can be used to organize social or charitable groups, to organize household affairs, to plan for future employment, to plan a daughter's wedding, and numerous other activities.

WAYS TEACHERS CAN PROMOTE BUSINESS EDUCATION

Now that some business courses have been identified, their content described, and the usefulness of the courses to business majors and non-business majors in carrying on their daily activities has been pointed out, some of the ways that two- and four-year college faculty can promote and sell business courses and programs will be discussed.

Open houses, parties, teas. One way to attract new students to business courses is to invite special groups in to visit the campus. The special groups can represent high school students, new college students, members of the local chamber of commerce, church leaders, businesses, government agencies, or whatever group is identified. Business faculty can plan an open house whereby visitors tour the business department, listen to brief talks about certain courses or programs by selected faculty members, receive literature concerning courses offered, and participate in demonstrations of new technology by students or faculty. Refreshments may be served; games may be played and prizes made available to the winners. A register of guests should be kept for follow-up purposes.

An afternoon tea or a party on or off campus may be planned to which special groups are invited. Business faculty and business majors currently enrolled in business courses may be asked to mingle with guests and chat with them about courses or aspects of the program students found particularly interesting or useful.

A theme party where each guest is given a numbered slip of paper on which the name of a business course is written may be used to promote particular business courses. Discussions on descriptions, usefulness, and purposes of the courses led by faculty will enlighten guests. Interest can be maintained by awarding prizes based on predetermined numbers.

Tours. If time is of the essence, special tours of classes, office technology and other labs, and faculty offices may be planned for legislators for politicians so that they can be made aware of the college's needs and its offerings. During the tour, program briefings or course highlights may be given. Other groups and individuals such as high school guidance counselors as well as the college guidance counselors and prospective employers of graduates may also be given tours of business program facilities to keep them abreast of current offerings. It is important that business courses and programs are exposed to as many people as possible who may take business courses or who may influence others to take courses. Tours can be a quick way to brief others on course and program offerings.

Speeches. Informal talks and chats at meetings of campus organizations about some topic of interest to members followed by a discussion of business courses which would be beneficial to members may spark the interest of some campus groups. Briefings and talks to government agencies and other municipal groups on course and program offerings may be successful in increasing business course enrollments also.

Formal speeches delivered during Vocational Education Month (February) on a topic such as "Vocational Opportunities in the Nineties" to grouped or individual high school classes or to Future Business Leaders of America meetings and other large audiences help to apprise high school students and others of business courses. After the speech, literature may be distributed and questions concerning business courses may be answered. This serves to inform the audience that business faculty teach business courses of use to prospective students. Also individual faculty members could invite prospective students to visit the office or to sit in on a class of interest.

Flyers. Computer-designed flyers and brochures may be created easily and inexpensively. Whether they are done "in-house" or professionally, the flyers may be used to highlight a particular course, a group of courses, or a specific program. The flyers should contain such information as course number, name, and description; course meeting times and dates; instructor name; contact person name and telephone number; enrollment period; and special features of course. A file of a variety of flyers and brochures to distribute at speaking engagements and to mail to special groups could be maintained. Flyers and brochures could be disseminated at local meetings, local conferences, or anywhere there is contact with the public and such dissemination is not inappropriate.

Educational television and radio appearances. Business education faculty members can make contact through their public relations person or directly contact the television studio or radio station. Some colleges have their own television and radio stations so a phone call may be all that it will take to appear on a show. The appearance could take the form of an interview or a more elaborate program. Regardless of the situation, some information of interest to the general public should be shared with the audience; then program specifics and courses could be highlighted.

Public service announcements and programs concerning business course offerings could also be presented on local community cable television stations. Business faculty could design an exhibit on business programs which could be presented and explained on community television or set up and manned in local malls as part of a collegewide marketing effort as another way to promulgate business courses.

Information exchanges. Business faculty could network by establishing state or regional computer bulletin boards to exchange information on the latest successful recruiting efforts for business programs, implications of the newest technology for business courses, or other information of common interest to business faculty.

Local information exchange meetings with faculty in other disciplines could be held to discuss courses that are especially useful to all students. Keyboarding could be presented by business faculty; other disciplines would describe courses they deemed appropriate.

Student and local newspapers. Business faculty could work with the campus student newspaper staff to offer assistance in publishing the newspaper. Or, business faculty could write feature articles highlighting some new trend or technology that will affect students and show how one or more business courses can help students cope with the innovations. Business faculty could seek to be interviewed by student and local newspapers. Advertisements of business courses in local and school newspapers could be written and encouraged by business faculty. One way to fund advertisements in local newspapers is to highlight recent successful graduates working in the area. Obtain a specified donation from each graduate's employer, and include the name of the company of each graduate, the graduate's name, picture, and major along with information about the program in the advertisement.

Workshops and seminars. To appeal to individuals who are full-time employees, who are homemakers with children who are about to go away to college, who are not quite sure what they want to do, or who are contemplating reentering the job market after retiring or for other reasons, workshops and seminars ranging from a couple of hours to several days may be very helpful. The workshops and seminars should concern timely information which will update students' knowledge and skills. Often students impressed by the information to which they were exposed, realize that they need more information and instruction in the subject. Consequently, they sign up for a semester course or enroll in a business program to get the knowledge and training they need to be promoted or gain employment. Seminars and workshops can be powerful tools depending on the subject matter and how well they are advertised. They can be very simple and inexpensive; they can be very elaborate; they can be offered for credit or not offered for credit.

Short courses and weekend courses. Regular business courses that have been condensed to two, three, or four weeks or that are only offered on Saturdays or Sundays may appeal to those who cannot attend day or evening classes during the week. Other special shortened courses that have been formulated from regular courses may be offered for one or two credit hours. For example, a three-semester hour microcomputer applications course could be shortened to one credit hour and include instruction on the use and operation of *Framework II*. The course could be taught on two or three successive Saturdays. Or, a course a month could be taught by scheduling Saturday and Sunday all-day sessions each weekend during the semester. A student could take approximately three courses per semester on weekends.

Meetings with guidance counselors. Business faculty could participate in meetings to which high school vocational and guidance counselors as well as college counselors are invited. These could take the form of luncheon or dinner meetings at which business faculty are given the opportunity to highlight their courses and programs. The administration would probably be financially supportive of such meetings if faculty from other disciplines were also invited to participate in the meetings. The luncheon or dinner meetings could he held on campus or at local hotels. Two- and four-year college business faculty could meet with high school business faculty and college and high school counselors to discuss existing articulation agreements or development of articulation agreements between college and high school business courses and programs so that instruction is not unnecessarily duplicated at the two- and four-year college level and so that high school faculty and students are made intimately aware of two-year and four-year college business program offerings.

Courses designed for a specific company or other organization. Often businesses and other institutions have special training needs. Business faculty can boost their enrollments by designing and teaching courses tailored to the special needs of specific companies. The courses could be offered under special course numbers and titles that may be repeated for credit such as "OFT 235 Specialized Software Applications" or "OFT 299 Supervised Study." For example, a company with recently purchased microcomputers and software might need to have all their secretaries trained. The secretaries could be enrolled in OFT 235 or OFT 299 at a special day and time set aside for them to learn to use the software. The instruction could be provided on the company's site if it had the facilities. Instruction on records management, office procedures and management, and other word processor, database, or spreadsheet software packages used in offices may also be offered upon request as special courses. Business faculty will need to make sure business and industry are aware of their ability to take care of their special needs through mailings, flyers, brochures, newspapers, and other advertisements.

CONCLUSION

The discussions on the courses, the advantages of taking them, and the strategies for promoting business courses are not intended to be exhaustive. It is hoped that they have shown you there are ways that you can help educate the public.

Business faculty offer courses that contain content that is beneficial to all productive members of American society. Some of the basic skills and understandings needed to succeed as citizens and as workers are included in the content of business courses and were reviewed.

Individual business faculty members can make sure that they are well versed on the content that they teach and the contributions, advantages, and benefits of that content to the larger society. In the third section of the chapter, specific business courses along with the course content often associated with such courses were identified. Quoted course descriptions were included to summarize explicitly the content and some of the benefits of each course discussed.

If prospective students are informed of the nature of business courses, they may be more likely to enroll in one or more business courses. The fourth section of the chapter related ways that business faculty at two- and four-year colleges can promote business courses and their content. Open houses, tours, speeches, flyers, briefings, television and radio shows, newspapers, workshops and seminars, short courses, weekend courses, meetings, and special courses were among the ways suggested to recruit students.

Decreasing enrollments in business courses may suggest that business faculty need to make sure that all potential students are made aware of the advantages and benefits of taking business courses. If this is true, individual faculty members must take active roles in heralding business education's trumpet; they cannot sit back and wait for others to do it! Business educators must assert their role in educating all college-level students in basic skills and core competencies.

CHAPTER 17
Administrative Support Systems

MICHAEL BRONNER and BRIDGET N. O'CONNOR
New York University, New York

What was once called secretarial education at the two-year postsecondary level has evolved to include courses ensuring that students acquire hands-on skills in using new technologies. These new technologies were originally considered only substitutes for traditional tools. However, these technologies are *more* than just substitutes; they are changing the entire office and have resulted in new organizational structures, new work procedures, and a new definition of the role of the office worker.

A change in title from secretary to administrative support specialist or administrative secretary does not do justice to the changing role of today's— let alone tomorrow's—office worker. How can this problem be put into perspective for office educators and what are postsecondary schools doing to fulfill their mission of providing well-trained individuals for office careers?

The purpose of this chapter is to address these questions. The first section helps identify the problem. The second section offers models of office education contrasting the traditional of the past with the transitional of the present, offering curriculum models from two community colleges and one professional organization. The chapter concludes with strategies postsecondary educators can use to make curricular changes.

UNCLEAR DEMAND, NEW SKILLS

The U.S. Department of Labor, in recent forecasts, suggests that the outlook for clerical office positions will continue to keep pace with, or even surpass, other job categories. However, the Office of Technology Assessment (OTA), Washington, D.C., predicted that office automation would result in slow growth for office employment over the next decade. In fact, the OTA has reported that office employment would actually begin to decline by the year 2000. No matter which of these two predictions is accurate, the office has and will continue to change—and include a wider range of positions than ever before.

Besides clerical personnel, many office-based professional-level workers such as accountants, lawyers, and consultants, will be affected by office automation. Professional-level workers are differentiated from clerical office workers in that professionals perform cognitive tasks requiring specialized knowledge. Their specialized knowledge is typically gained through education and training, and often includes special certification or licensing. No one is predicting an increase or decline in these occupations. However, these information-intensive professionals will be more affected by the impact of office automation than individuals in other professions. With the advent of expert systems and relational databases, many of the professional's duties may be accomplished by a *para*professional with far fewer credentials than the professional but decidedly more skills than the traditional secretary.

For the professional worker, new office technologies are accused of "de-skilling" work. De-skilling implies that new technologies result in fewer skill requirements. Accountants, for example, armed with the appropriate software, can complete even complex tax returns very rapidly. More tax returns completed equals more productivity; however, the accountant's job shifts from data analyses to one of data input or computer operations. The accountant's job, thus, may be de-skilled.

The office worker is faced with the same problem; like the accountant whose productivity is measured in output (in this case, tax returns), office output also can be expected to multiply, given the same technology, and with similar results. However, the output of the professional—memos, reports, letters—is often the same as the office worker. Therefore, if the professional can now accomplish the office worker's job, what will the office worker do? Thus, office workers are not being de-skilled; they are being re-skilled. The change in job requirements means learning new ways to do work and a variety of new tasks and responsibilities.

As automation reduces the need for office personnel to perform repetitive tasks, potentially fewer clerical office positions coupled with higher expectations will combine to force traditional office educators to reexamine their current curricular offerings. New skills must be integrated into the curriculum.

Office educators, likewise, face difficult times. With fewer 18-year-old women planning careers as secretaries coupled with new pressures to update existing curriculums, postsecondary secretarial educators find themselves at a crossroad—whether to hold onto the traditional curriculum or to move into the realm of technology education. The purpose of the following section is to describe traditional offerings and offer "transition models"—real examples of how two community colleges and one professional organization are bridging the gap between traditional and future curriculums.

MODELS FOR OFFICE EDUCATION

Traditional office education. Traditional office education emphasized keyboarding speed and accuracy, shorthand speed, and the ability to transcribe shorthand notes into mailable documents. Courses such as those listed here made up the typical secretarial curriculum of the seventies.

Beginning Typewriting	Beginning Shorthand
Intermediate Typewriting	Intermediate Shorthand
Advanced Typewriting	Advanced Shorthand
Business Machines	Office Procedures
Records Management	Business English
Office Management	

With many hands-on activities and extensive skill building, such courses addressed the psychomotor abilities required of a clerical worker. Moreover, the tools of the trade were mechanical—bearing only minor resemblance to the tools found in the electronic office.

Transitional office education. The term transitional is used in this chapter to describe curriculums which are moving away from traditional courses, offering courses in the use of office automation technologies and including human relations skills. Two institutions have been selected as models of transitional office education efforts: LaGuardia Community College in New York City and Saddleback Community College in Southern California.

FIORELLO H. LAGUARDIA COMMUNITY COLLEGE. Fiorello H. LaGuardia Community College, part of the City University of New York (CUNY), offers a certificate program in word processing (34 credits) and five associate degree programs (66 credits). Four of these associate degree programs are traditional in nature: administrative office assistant; legal secretarial/pre-court reporting; executive option; and bilingual secretary. Its office technology program, on the other hand, may be classified as transitional.

Office technology includes 21 credits of liberal arts courses (English, mathematics, humanities, and social sciences). It also includes eight credits of management, accounting, and computer information systems which are offered in another department. The office technology series of courses retains six credits of typewriting and four credits of word processing. In addition, however, separate courses in microcomputer-based word processing, spreadsheets, and databases are required, for a total of seven credits. This series of courses also includes administration of information processing, business communication, electronic office procedures, for a total of nine credits, and two unrestricted electives.

To LaGuardia's credit, the introduction of new courses and curriculum has always been coupled with appropriate faculty retraining. The instructor enters any new course with appropriate skills and competencies.

In short, LaGuardia Community College has developed a program bridging its traditional curriculum with one that no longer includes shorthand classes. Emphasis, instead, is on being able to use the wide variety of technologies available to the modern office worker. The curriculum develops a support specialist—but not within an identified industry. This specialty covers all forms of office-related information processing.

While LaGuardia's curriculum reflects a transitional design, two important features of this two-year college are (1) that academic terms are based on a ten-week quarter system, and (2) that all students enrolled in this program are required to spend three quarters in outside cooperative business internship experiences. This close link with metropolitan New York businesses provides LaGuardia students with practical applications for specialized coursework and is an important and integral foundation of the college's mission.

SADDLEBACK COMMUNITY COLLEGE. On the West Coast, Saddleback Community College in Mission Viejo, California, illustrates another approach to a transitional curriculum for the preparation of office administration personnel.

Located in a new building completed in 1987 and designed for innovative change, the business science division includes departments of office information systems and computer information management, in addition to the more traditional departments of accounting and management, legal assistant, and banking and finance, among others.

A unique feature of Saddleback's new home is its information center, which allows for personal computer access to five class sites with large monitors and projection equipment serving each room. Over 100 personal computers are networked in the department, linked through three interconnected systems including a state-of-the-art network server, which stores software available for student downloading to their individual units.

Because the faculty and administration felt that a strong curriculum was required to keep pace with the forward-looking physical plant, major curriculum revisions were incorporated for the office information systems department. These curriculums, consisting of 25-30 units within each of six subject areas—general office, legal secretarial, general secretarial, administrative assistant, certified professional secretary, and word processing—all lead to certificates; none are degree-bearing curriculums.

Some of the innovative curriculum offerings include two eight-week modules on keyboarding—basic and advanced—that allow for easy-entry, easy-exit. Saddleback emphasizes microcomputer application technology for the word processing certificate. For this certificate program, three units are allocated to each of the courses in business English, business communications, and introduction to word and information processing. One and one-half units are allocated to office skills, electronic desk management, DOS (or UNIX), spreadsheets, database, graphics, communications, and desktop publishing. Four and one-half units are uniquely spread in the word processing area with a three-tier (level) approach to seven different word processing packages. Each level extends and builds on previous experiences. A course in word processing applications and a one-point internship is also part of the word processing certificate program.

In addition to the foregoing school-specific models, professional associations have also impacted curriculum with their suggestions and recommendations. The Data Processing Management Association (DPMA) developed a four-year model curriculum for programming careers. The Office Systems Research Association (OSRA) developed a four-year model curriculum for office systems careers. Professional Secretaries International (PSI) has begun development of a two-year model curriculum for secretarial education.

PSI MODEL CURRICULUM. This model for secretarial education can also be labelled as transitional office education. Recognizing the need for more relevant secretarial education as well as the need for "professionalizing" the secretarial position, PSI has developed a model based on the student's need/want to enter and exit the program at various stages. Each semester of study has identifiable job skills. Students can enter the curriculum at their own skill level and stay for a semester or long enough to complete an associate's degree. The model thus caters to traditional populations as well as the returning student.

Following is an overview of the curriculum (1988); specific course outlines are available in *PSI Postsecondary Model Curriculum for Office Careers*, available from South-Western Publishing Company.

Semester 1:
Document Formatting*
Administrative Support Systems and Procedures
Fundamentals of Business Communications
Information Processing Concepts and Applications
2 Electives

*Prerequisite: Keyboarding

Semester 2:
Document Production/Word Processing
Professional Development
Applied Business Communications
    Choose one:
Advanced Word Processing Applications
                or
Advanced Information Processing Applications
1 Elective

Semester 3:
2 Specialization*
Principles of Accounting I
Office Supervision
Office Systems and Technology Management
1 Elective

*Specialization: information processing, desktop publishing, office systems, legal, or medical

Semester 4:
Behavioral Science in Business/Applied Psychology
Business Law
Principles of Economics
Principles of Management
Principles of Accounting II
Elective

While the curriculum "teaches" to the Certified Professional Secretaries' (CPS) examination, the certification process also, by definition, raises the secretarial position to that of professional. The PSI model, developed by educators and professional secretaries, should also lead to more relevant associate degrees.

Earlier sections of this chapter have described traditional office education, selected transitional curriculums, and the PSI model curriculum. For those postsecondary schools wrestling with the problems involved in moving from the traditional to the transitional, the ground has already been broken. One has but to look at recent issues of the *AACJC Journal* and a number of recent ERIC documents concerning innovation at this level to find other imaginative programs.

However, what does the future hold for those schools already into the transitional realm or for those institutions wanting to make the quantum jump into a curriculum for the year 2000? Here are a few suggestions and considerations.

GUIDELINES FOR CURRICULUM CHANGE

The guidelines presented here are based on the perceived trends and needs of the office of the (near) future, as well as exemplary practices gleaned from the three model curriculums discussed in this chapter. In no particular order, they are:

1. Emphasize self-learning. Stress the development of competencies which can be transferred. Throughout their work lives, office workers will need to adapt to new technologies. For example, one word processing program could be taught traditionally, and then students would be required to learn two or three others on their own, but demonstrate competence at some culminating point.

2. Include stress management strategies. Ergonomics-related information, including workstation arrangement, appropriate seating, safe and comfortable use of video display terminals, and lighting needs, should be integral to any technology application course. Also include individual stress management techniques—desk-based exercises, the need for frequent breaks, and the like.

3. Include project management techniques. Students will need to be able to handle projects from beginning to end with only a modicum of supervision. Project management techniques such as Pert or Gantt charts should be applied in case projects which require new hardware/software acquisitions.

4. Prepare students for the integration of technologies. This suggests using word processing, spreadsheets, database, graphics, telecommunications, and like applications in conjunction under a single course or project umbrella.

5. Teamwork should be an essential part of any course. Group activities should be established to provide experiences involving a number of students to accomplish a project. Special attention should be paid to integrating a wide variety of personality types into this project setting.

6. Establish an advisory council. An advisory council, composed of executives from a cross section of companies in your locale are in an excellent position to help you develop curriculum and courses appropriate for your students.

7. Meet the needs of the returning student. Allow students easy exit and reentry as in the PSI model. Certificate programs may be more appropriate in many cases than degree programs. Always make provision for advanced placement opportunities. Such an approach allows the program to attract returning students.

8. Require internships. Preferably, periodic internships or extensive field experiences should be spread throughout the academic experience. Any culminating internship should be a paid experience because by the time students are ready for the internship, they have developed employable skills. A well-paid internship can encourage the completion of the degree or certificate program.

9. Develop courses which promote workplace literacy. The office professional needs to understand how organizations operate and how one can best advance to higher level positions. Keeping a job, moreover, requires more interpersonal skills than technical skills. See that students understand the history and future prospects for women (male students need this information as well as female students) in organizations and their implications. Discuss career ladders and career paths and encourage students to view themselves more as a paraprofessional than as a clerical worker.

10. Establish minimum basic prerequisites. Office courses should not consist of remedial English or remedial math. Students should be screened carefully to establish minimum competencies in these two areas. Instruction, then, may be concentrated in the mastery of subject matter rather than the acquisition of basic skills.

11. Cross-list courses. Work with other departments to cross-list or co-offer courses which may affect the other's turf. An entire business school, for example, could benefit from applications courses offered by the office technologies department. Likewise, when applications are taught in another department, they too should be cross-listed.

12. Call the program what it is! Consider changing the name of the program or department to describe the technology-based course offerings. A change in program title could draw students from throughout the school; nearly everyone entering the workplace will need information processing skills.

13. Encourage faculty internships. Supporting faculty for internships in local businesses in which they could appy their skills and experience organizational behavior firsthand can be a rewarding experience. Faculty as well as their students benefit.

14. Prepare faculty for new teaching assignments. Encourage faculty enthusiasm for teaching new courses by ensuring that they receive substantial training for any new course offered. Reduced teaching loads are suggested for the duration of the training.

CONCLUSION

This chapter has attempted not only to establish the need to reevaluate office/administrative support curriculums but to offer illustrations of this curriculum evolution from the traditional to the transitional. Not any given model will fit a given environment. Be this as it may, bear in mind that the office has changed and will continue to change—sometimes in a revolutionary fashion. Office educators must keep abreast of these changes and update office-oriented curriculums accordingly. Make sure students are agents of change—not victims of it!

CHAPTER 18

Information Systems

THOMAS B. DUFF
University of Minnesota, Duluth

A quick review of the popular business periodicals, the professional business education journals, and the postsecondary business education textbooks published in the past five years indicates that the term "information systems" and the concepts related to it are among the most popular business buzzwords of the day. Even though there are still many different definitions for the term and it has been used broadly less than 10 years, the frequency of its mention and discussion in the popular literature provides sufficient evidence to indicate that there is a broad-based and intense interest in information systems (IS). This interest is present among practitioners in the business world as well as among business educators in the postsecondary institutions of the United States and the world.

Based on the amount of attention currently being given to the general concept of IS and its terminology, it appears that the preparation of the business employees, managers, and leaders who will assume their roles in the 1990's must include IS education. The general purpose of this chapter is to discuss the role which business education can play in the IS education provided for prospective employees and managers by postsecondary educators. Specifically, the chapter will describe what an organizational information system is, identify what education is needed by IS workers and users, and suggest how business education can contribute to this component of the postsecondary business curriculum.

WHAT IS AN ORGANIZATIONAL INFORMATION SYSTEM?

There are probably as many different definitions or descriptions of an information system as there are textbooks written on the topic. Some people prefer to use a very short, simple definition; others insist on a longer definition laced with technological jargon. For any definition to be meaningful, it is necessary to know what is meant by the terms "information" and "system" as they are being used in the business context.

Information. As the nineties approach, almost everyone has heard or read about things like the information explosion or living and doing business in an information society. What is meant by such statements? What is information?

As it is used by IS professionals, information is described very simply as meaningful data. Data is basic facts or figures. Data can be one symbol or groups of symbols combined in some way. The words, sentences, and paragraphs on this page consist of data. They are made up of alphabetic symbols (data) combined to create words (which might also be data), sentences, and paragraphs.

In order to get information from data, the data must be processed in some way and presented in a way which a user finds meaningful. The foundation of any information system is data processing. Hopefully, the combinations of letters and words in this chapter have been processed and presented in such a way that the reader can take them in, process them, and derive useful information from them. The mental processing techniques used by the reader are much more complicated than those used by the most sophisticated computers available today. However, the goal of the reader's processing activities and those of the computer are the same; both are trying to make the data meaningful or create information from it.

Like alphabetic characters, individual or groups of numerals are data until they are processed or combined in some way so that they are meaningful. When a person buys something with a charge card at a department store, for example, several data items represented by numerals are collected. The credit card or account number, an identification number for the article, the article's price, the amount of tax, and the total amount of the charge are recorded. Each of these is a meaningless data item individually. When they are combined in a particular manner and recorded together, they become information about a business transaction.

Although most business data processing is done by computers today, it is important to keep in mind that it is possible, and in some cases necessary, to do manual data processing. Manual data processing was being done with pencils and paper for many years before the arrival of adding machines, calculators, typewriters, and computers. Computers are used for routine data processing activities because they do them much faster and with greater accuracy than humans. In addition to the role they have played in creating large amounts of information and, thus, the information society, computers have also been instrumental in the development of business systems.

Systems. In simple terms, a system is a set of related parts that work together in an organized way to achieve some stated purpose or purposes. The parts are often called components, and their relationship is described as being interdependent or dynamically linked. Each component affects and is affected by the other components in the system.

People live and work in a variety of systems. For example, there are legal, economic, and political systems in our society. Business firms and other organizations have systems that are less abstract and more familiar to those who work in them each day. Accounting, inventory, or payroll systems are smaller, less complex systems than an economic system, for example; and people deal with them more directly.

All organizational systems have a long-term purpose (or purposes) and shorter-term goals or objectives. There are inputs to the systems such as labor, energy, material, capital and the like; and people, machines, buildings and so on (the components) process or transform the inputs into outputs. There are, of course, interactions and interrelations between and among the components. Each system has boundaries which define what is included within the system and separate it from what is outside the system—the environment in which it exists. Finally, there are usually several subsystems within a system. The process of system analysis consists of breaking down systems into their subsystems and studying their components and the nature of their interrelationships until the smallest subsystems are identified.

Information systems. Assuming there is understanding of and general agreement on the descriptions given for the terms information and system, it should be possible to define the term information system. One definition is a set of procedures developed and used to systematically collect, process, and store data and to disseminate information in an organization.

Knowing *how* to define or describe an information system is important. It is equally important to know *why* it has been developed and *how* it is used in an organization. The ultimate objective of an organizational information system is to provide accurate, timely, and appropriate information to all decision makers in the organization. Depending upon the size of the organization, there may be few or many humans who have decision-making responsibility. They may range from operations level personnel to chief executive officer or board of directors level, and they make decisions related to all the functional areas of a business—production, operations, marketing, finance, and so on. Some of the decisions are very structured because they can be defined and analyzed quantitatively; others are very unstructured because they involve more qualitative factors and are made on the basis of intuition, trial-and-error, or common sense.

To achieve its objective, the IS must provide as much information as decision makers desire in the form they desire. The decision makers will judge the performance of the information system on the basis of how well it provides them with information they feel they need. Having the information they need should allow decision makers at all levels to make the best possible decisions related to the purposes or long-range goals of the organization. Providing decision makers with the right information at the right time in the right form will not guarantee that the right decision will always be made. However, one of the criterions by which an organizational information system is judged is whether it significantly increases the probability that the outcomes of decisions will support the goals, objectives, and long-range purposes of the organization involved.

WHAT EDUCATION IS NEEDED BY INFORMATION SYSTEM WORKERS AND USERS?

As discussed above, even though information systems have been around for years, they are receiving much more attention currently than in the past. Much of this attention is due to the fact that the computer has become an integral part of the information system in almost all organizations. In fact, the computer has become so much a part of them that it is impossible to discuss any aspect of an information system without addressing computer-related items as well. Therefore, the discussion of what education is needed by IS workers and users quickly turns to the topic of computer literacy and other computer-related areas.

Many business education leaders have made reference to education *for* and *about* business over the years. It seems reasonable and logical to view the education requirements for IS workers and users in the same way. Although there is overlap, there are also significant differences in the education postsecondary institutions can and should provide to prepare persons to be knowledgeable users of information systems in their various occupations and that required to prepare persons to work directly in IS occupations. Thus, postsecondary institutions should review their programs and decide what education is needed *about* the purpose and use of information systems in organizations, education needed by all employees as the 21st century begins, and what education is needed *for* employment in IS occupations.

Education *about* the purpose and use of information systems in organizations. Because of the pervasiveness of the current interest in and emphasis on information systems and their computer-based components, all prospective employees need a certain level of education in this area. Basically, all employees in the 1990's and beyond will need to be familiar with the vocabulary and purposes, appreciate the important role they play in the success of an organization, and know how and when to use some of the computer-based tools to help them be productive employees whatever their occupation.

Employees at almost all levels and in every occupation need to be familiar with some of the basic vocabulary. They do not need to know technical definitions. However, they do need to know the difference between data and information, input and output, software and hardware, and manual and computer-based processing systems. Most postsecondary institutions are helping business, accounting, and other students achieve this basic level of IS literacy by offering an introductory course to be completed during the first year of study. The introductory course has various names, and there are currently over 50 textbooks published for use with such a course. Therefore, some of the content varies depending upon the length of the course, the textbook being used, and the instructor. However, the core content and objectives are generally the same in all of these offerings. They are designed to help students become familiar with the vocabulary of data processing, information systems and computers as well as general concepts related to data processing operations, data storage and handling, input and output devices, programming languages, software packages, communications and distributed data processing, management information systems, databases, and systems analysis and design. The course may or may not require students to learn some BASIC programming, but it is almost certain to require them to complete activities using a microcomputer or a terminal connected to a mainframe computer system.

While such a course may be considered a computer literacy course by some, its focus is broader than most of the popular computer literacy courses.

Traditionally, such courses have been offered to help persons learn how to operate a microcomputer with little or no attention paid to how this tool fits into the bigger IS picture. If it is to contribute to the general business background needed by all employees, the introductory course described here must include a discussion and illustrations of the important role information systems play in contemporary organizations. Students must leave this course with an understanding of and appreciation for the basic points made in the earlier section on information systems.

Possibilities for illustrating the components, functions, and importance of information systems abound within any postsecondary institution. Systems which directly affect or relate to students usually serve as the best examples for explanation and study. Student records, class registration, and financial aid are three which immediately come to mind. Such systems can be studied to determine the data elements, how data is input and stored, how data is processed, what information is output, and how the output is used by decision makers within the institution or by persons from outside the institution. After reviewing the purposes and importance of the information provided by these and other systems which affect them at their postsecondary institutions, students will have a better understanding of and appreciation for the importance of information systems.

In addition to knowing the basic vocabulary and appreciating the IS role in an organization, the most productive employees of the future will be those who know how to use some of the basic computer-based tools. As noted above, students can become familiar with basic computer operation—the components, how to turn them on and load software; and how to complete simple input, storage, retrieval, and output activities—in an introductory course. As every business educator knows and as almost all computer technicians have now come to realize, it is also necessary for one to possess some basic level of keyboarding proficiency in order to use the computer productively. In order to earn an appropriate return on the investment in equipment and other resources needed to provide an employee computer access, the employee must possess keyboarding skill and be able to perform basic input, storage, retrieval, and output activities before the investment is made.

Along with this preparation for using the basic IS tool, the computer, it is crucial that all postsecondary business students possess knowledge of and ability to apply the most frequently used types of business software packages. All business and accounting graduates should be familiar with the basic concepts involved and be able to use the computer as an aid to completing electronic mail, word processing, electronic spreadsheet, database management, and graphics activities. There are many different software packages being marketed and used in each of these application areas. Therefore, educators have to make a decision regarding which specific package to teach in each application area. The most important point to be made here is that students need to understand the general principles of each type of application and be able to use at least one software package in each of the areas; which specific package is not the most important issue. Students who are familiar with and able to use one package of software as a tool in an applications area will be able to learn how to use a different package very quickly. The basic concepts are the same; only the format and structure of the commands and some of the advanced applications differ. The transfer of learning is highly positive in this case.

Postsecondary business and accounting graduates seeking employment in any of the functional areas of business will need to have the general preparation described above. Whether working in an accounting, finance, human resources, marketing, operations, production, or general management occupation, one will be affected by and involved in using the information system and computer in an organization in the years ahead.

Education for employment in IS occupations. Persons wishing to obtain employment directly in IS occupations must possess the knowledge, understanding, and appreciation of information systems and the computer skills described as necessary for all business employees. In addition, they must complete computer science or other programs which include a variety of more technical courses. Exactly what additional knowledge, understanding, and skills are needed by these employees will depend on the specific occupational area involved. Because of the central role of the computer, however, all IS occupations require a heavy dose of technical know-how.

There are many ways to categorize and describe IS or computer information systems occupations or careers. One way is to categorize the occupations into three general areas—application and development support, computer center operations, and technical support. The application and development support occupations include those usually referred to as programmer, programmer/analyst, systems analyst, and the like. An individual obtaining entry-level employment directly in information systems in a large organization will usually do so as a programmer. Programmers prepare detailed design and write code in a procedural language, such as COBOL or Pascal, for processing modules specified by more senior programmers or analysts. Therefore, they must complete courses in one or more programming languages as well as other technical courses on the operation of the computer, data storage and manipulation, input and output devices, and other peripheral equipment.

After working as a programmer for a period of time in a large organization or perhaps at the entry-level in smaller organizations, an applications and development person may be involved in analysis as well as programming. The programmer/analyst does analysis work directly with users to identify what applications they wish to have developed. Depending on the specific situation, the programmer/analyst is then completely or at least partially responsible for designing and writing the computer program to carry out the requested application. The systems analyst, on the other hand, will work with users and then work with a programmer or programming group through the design stage. Systems analysts are not as directly involved in doing the actual program coding. In addition to the technical skills needed by programmers, analysts need to have good interpersonal and written communication skills. These skills enable analysts to accurately identify what users want in an application program, to prepare a design description which can be understood by users and programmers, and to ensure that documentation is written so it can be understood by future users.

While the applications and development occupations are related to both information systems and the computer, occupations in the areas of computer center operations and technical computer support are primarily computer-related. Because the computer is so pervasive, persons working in these occupations are indirectly involved in information systems. However, those in computer center operations are employed in production positions connected with the actual operation of an organization's computer facilities. Similarly, those employed in technical support occupations are directly involved in configuring computer hardware, installing new or updated versions of operating systems, and installing or maintaining systems software in general. Preparing students for employment in either of these two technical areas is not part of the mission of most postsecondary business education programs. However, as discussed below, business education programs can contribute a great deal to the other areas of IS and computer education.

HOW CAN BUSINESS EDUCATION CONTRIBUTE TO INFORMATION SYSTEMS EDUCATION?

Business educators who have read to this point in this chapter are aware that business education has contributed to IS education in the past and continues to do so today. The typewriting or keyboarding courses offered at all educational levels, including postsecondary, are usually offered through the business education program. General courses related to the use of the computer in business and instruction related to the use of word processing and electronic spreadsheet applications are a part of many if not all of today's postsecondary business education programs. In addition, programming and other technical courses are part of the business education programs offered in some technical institutes, two-year colleges, and the associate degree programs at four-year colleges.

Given this situation, it is clear that business education is currently contributing to IS education. To emphasize this contribution and make other academic areas, prospective employers, and the public in general more aware of its role, business educators at the postsecondary level need to take two steps. First, they must change some of the emphasis and terminology in their present offerings to bring them up to date. Second, they need to carefully review the curriculum to determine what new knowledge and skills they may be best able to include to better prepare business and accounting graduates for employment in the 1990's.

Changes in emphasis and terminology in present offerings. The changes in emphasis and terminology are subtle but important ones. A review of the general education needed by all business and accounting students, as identified in the section above related to education *about* information systems, indicates that postsecondary business educators have the best preparation to provide this component of a student's postsecondary program. All that is needed is for business educators to communicate with their business, accounting, and computer science colleagues to let them know that the emphasis of their courses is more than skill development. One of the major problems for business educators has been the fact that they have not been able to convince others that they teach more than skill development.

The perception that business education programs focus primarily on skill development is a carryover from the days when typewriting and shorthand dominated them. To be accepted as a full partner in IS education and to be given the role of providing the general IS education, business educators must make others aware that they are willing and able to do more than simply teach keyboarding and word processing. And, of course, they must mean it when they say it. As noted previously, all postsecondary business and accounting students need general IS education. Business educators at these institutions are prepared and poised to meet this need, but they must convince others by making some changes in the courses they teach.

Those teaching the general introductory courses must include coverage in the core areas included in the most popular texts provided for that course. They must become familiar with the most current IS and computer vocabulary and concepts and help students to do the same. Similarly, those teaching word processing must emphasize the role it plays in the overall IS and communications activities of an organization. It is not enough to teach students how to use the software packages and general concepts of word processing. This is especially true for those who will use word processing software as a support tool rather than being employed in a word processing occupation where providing administrative support is the primary task. And in office administration, office information systems, accounting, and other courses where other applications software is used, business educators must emphasize why the software and computer are being used. Again, it is not enough to teach students how to use the software. They must think of the software and computer as a package of tools which are available to aid them and other decision makers. They must become aware of how these tools fit into the overall IS of an organization.

There are many other examples of how business educators can gain a more complete part in providing general IS education for postsecondary students. However, it is not the intent of this chapter to identify a long list of such examples. Business educators simply must remember to emphasize how the various topic areas they teach in their courses relate to, support, and are a part of organizational information systems. In addition, they must prepare students to understand current computer and IS vocabulary and make them aware that they will need to continually learn new jargon as it changes. A change in emphasis and terminology will enhance the image of postsecondary business education programs. However, business educators at this level must also think about new knowledge and skills which they can include in their curriculum.

New knowledge and skills for the 1990's curriculum. In order to continue or expand their role as contributors to IS education, postsecondary business educators must change with the times. Although it will take some study and work to prepare to teach them, there are some current and emerging areas of IS education that business educators are well prepared to teach. As is true for production in any organization, it would seem that postsecondary institutions should be concerned with improving productivity by using the principle of comparative advantage. Therefore, if they are willing to expand the curriculum, business educators should be able to convince colleagues and administrators that they can teach in some areas not always considered to be part of the business education program.

For example, they could have a comparative advantage in teaching various application software packages other than word processing—electronic spreadsheet, database, graphics, desktop publishing, or integrated packages. The discussion of the various forms of electronic messaging and other forms of data communication is a natural for business communications courses. Further, almost all those currently involved in information systems recognize that employees in the 1990's will need better oral and written communication skills than their predecessors. Business educators can take the lead in conducting research to determine what types of communication skills are needed to be successful in an IS environment and can then design and offer business communication courses to meet those needs. Most of the skills and knowledge needed by systems analysts in any area are the same as those needed by those who design office systems. Those teaching in the office systems area are well qualified to teach a general systems analysis and design course. They simply need to broaden their scope and develop a willingness to teach a more general course.

Again, these are simply some suggested areas in which postsecondary business educators may look to expand their offerings. There are many others depending upon the unique preparation of instructors and the environment in which the programs are offered.

CONCLUSION

Business educators at the postsecondary level have been contributing to information systems education and continue to do so. They must work to communicate more accurately what they are capable of doing to overcome the perception that they simply provide skill development education. By changing the emphasis of some of their traditional courses and convincing colleagues and administrators that there is a comparative advantage to having them teach in some other areas, postsecondary business educators can become an integral part of the team providing the overall information systems education needed by all business and accounting employees in the 1990's.

CHAPTER 19
Marketing/Distribution Systems

ROGER W. HUTT
Arizona State University, Tempe

This chapter examines the role that postsecondary marketing plays in the overall business education program. First, the early years of marketing education are reviewed. Second, the background of marketing at the postsecondary level is examined. Third, the structure for postsecondary marketing is described and includes community colleges, proprietary schools, and four-year colleges and universities. Fourth, various trends in postsecondary marketing, such as specialized programs and articulation programs, are identified and discussed. Fifth, the application of marketing principles to marketing education is considered.

MARKETING EDUCATION—THE EARLY YEARS

Marketing education at the prebaccalaureate, occupationally oriented level came into existence in the early 1900's when some high schools and postsecondary proprietary schools began preparing their students for jobs in retailing. Marketing courses were introduced into four-year colleges and universities during this same time period. Junior and community colleges trace the roots of their marketing education programs to the thirties.

The George-Dean Act of 1936 placed increased emphasis on high school programs in what was then called distributive education. The name distributive education was replaced with marketing education some years later in the high schools. The original purpose was to provide education for those already employed in distributive occupations. It was the midst of the Depression and jobs were scarce. Congress believed that training dollars should be spent on those currently in the labor force, not on students preparing for employment. Distributive education, therefore, became a program comprised of persons who were half-time students and half-time employees. Students who were not already working at least 15 hours a week (i.e., one-half of a week's 30 hours of class time) could not enroll. Distributive education was one of the first educational programs to make widespread use of the cooperative plan of instruction at the secondary level. The cooperative plan is a pattern of instruction involving regularly scheduled part-time employment to provide students with an opportunity to practice on an actual job what they learn in the classroom. The purpose is to help students obtain the knowledge, skills, and attitudes required for a specific occupation by receiving job training that is correlated with classroom instruction. Until the mid-sixties, cooperative education was the primary instructional method used. When marketing education was introduced by junior and community colleges, the cooperative method became a popular instructional method at that level as well.

MARKETING AT THE POSTSECONDARY LEVEL

A person reading the literature of business education, especially when it covers the last two to three decades, will probably find different, and perhaps conflicting, definitions of the term postsecondary. To some people, the term includes levels of education beyond the secondary level that are of a prebaccalaureate nature. In other words, education leading to a four-year college degree is not included in this definition. To other people, the term is broader in scope and refers to all levels of education beyond the secondary level and, therefore, includes programs offered by four-year colleges and universities. It appears that the broader definition dates back to the Education Amendments of 1972 when there was a desire to clarify that not all education beyond high school means a four-year academic program leading to a baccalaureate degree. Based on this definition, this chapter deals with marketing education in the following postsecondary schools and colleges:

1. Community and junior colleges
2. Area vocational-technical schools and technical colleges
3. Proprietary schools
4. Four-year colleges and universities.

Community colleges are a major institutional factor in providing marketing education. Reports indicate that such colleges can be found in every region of the country. These educational institutions were at one time called junior colleges. While some public and private institutions have retained the junior college name, the majority of the public-supported institutions are now designated as community colleges. This name identifies the colleges' mission as being that of serving the wide-ranging needs of the residents of the community and not being limited to providing a college education at the freshman and sophomore levels. In some instances, institutions have dropped both the junior and community designations and call themselves colleges, for example, Phoenix College in Phoenix, Arizona.

Community colleges in several areas of the country began offering general business courses, including those in marketing, as early as the 1930's. These offerings were often labeled as mid-management programs in marketing or merchandising and were typically included by institutions in their associate degree programs. Samson identified the objectives of these postsecondary programs as:

1. To offer curriculums in marketing and distribution for persons who have completed or left high school and who are available for full-time study in preparation for entering a distributive occupation
2. To prepare persons for distributive occupations in manufacturing, wholesaling,

retailing, and service businesses which may include mid-management and management careers
3. To prepare persons who may eventually own and/or operate their own distributive businesses
4. To continue the general education of the individual to enable him to make a better contribution to his society.[1]

Some states provide their residents with postsecondary area vocational-technical schools and technical colleges. In Wisconsin, for example, there is the Vocational, Technical, and Adult Education (VTAE) System, and in Minnesota there are the Area Vocational Technical Institutes (AVTI). In some instances, states or local areas have established vocational-technical schools rather than community colleges. In other cases, both community college systems and vocational-technical school systems are established by the state. Marketing programs in these institutions are eligible to establish junior collegiate chapters of Distributive Education Clubs of America for their students.

Proprietary schools have had a long association with marketing education, dating back to the early part of this century when they conducted training programs for prospective employees in retail stores. These private schools have continued to provide marketing education, particularly in such specialized areas as fashion merchandising. Examples of private schools providing marketing education are the Bradford School in Pittsburgh, the Fashion Institute of Technology in Los Angeles, and the International Academy of Merchandising and Design, Ltd., in Chicago.

During the time period from approximately the beginning of this century to World War I, marketing courses were added to the curriculum in four-year colleges and universities. However, it is believed that relatively few such courses were offered until after the war years. Today, many four-year colleges have departments of marketing, offering a wide array of related courses at the bachelor's, master's, and doctoral degree levels.

THE STRUCTURE OF POSTSECONDARY MARKETING

A review of the literature indicates that many people believe postsecondary marketing education programs came into existence to fill a gap in the educational continuum. At one end of the continuum are the high schools preparing students for entry-level jobs. At the other end are the four-year colleges and universities providing education for executive and professional management positions. Thus, a gap is created in middle level management and supervisory training. The term mid-management became the appropriate label for courses at this level. In the *Instructor-Coordinator's Handbook for Postsecondary Distribution and Marketing Programs*, Holder describes the purposes of mid-management programs as follows:

1. To help students enter or advance in a management career

---

[1] Samson, Harland E. "The Basis and Emergent of Postsecondary Distributive Education." *Current Perspectives in Distributive Education*. (Edited by Mary K. Klaurens and Gail Trapnell.) Dubuque, Iowa: Kendall/Hunt Publishing Co., 1974. p. 60.

2. To provide an avenue for supervisors to gain the knowledge they need to upgrade their performance so that they can be promoted
3. To provide occupational courses which students need to enter specific fields of business such as real estate, fashion merchandising, banking and finance, and others
4. To serve the community's needs for management personnel.[2]

Historically speaking, marketing education at the community college level has several characteristics which distinguish it from programs offered at other educational levels. These characteristics, as defined by Samson, are that marketing education at the postsecondary level:

1. Provides both intensive and extensive instruction in a marketing function, product area, or business
2. Provides instruction which leads to specialization in a marketing function, product area, or business category
3. Serves a student population from a large geographic area
4. Provides curriculums oriented to local, state, regional, or national occupational needs
5. Follows a collegiate schedule of classes with special flexibility to permit appropriate applications of learning
6. Has standards and quality leading to supervisory and management competencies
7. Utilizes businessmen from a wide range of business interests and from a wide geographic area for advisory and resource purposes.[3]

Marketing occupational specialty areas. Marketing occupations include many different types and levels of jobs. Many people are aware of the numerous jobs found in the marketing of consumer products and services. However, this is only a part of marketing employment. Marketing jobs are also found in a wide range of production, manufacturing, and business services firms as well.

As a way of clarifying what is included in marketing, the National Center for Education Statistics has identified and classified the various marketing specialty areas as follows:

Apparel and Accessories in Marketing

Business and Personal Services Marketing

Financial Services Marketing

Floristry, Farm, and Garden Supplies Marketing

Food Marketing

General Merchandise Retailing

Home and Office Products Marketing

Hospitality Marketing

---

[2]Holder, Doyle. *Instructor-Coordinator's Handbook for Postsecondary Distribution and Marketing Programs.* U.S., Educational Resources Information Center, ERIC Document ED 234 189, June 1981.

[3]Samson, Harland E. *Postsecondary Distributive Education.* Washington, D.C.: U.S. Government Printing Office, 1969. pp. 5-6.

Insurance Marketing
Real Estate Marketing
Transportation and Travel Marketing
Vehicle and Petroleum Marketing[4]

Principles of marketing course. The principles of marketing course is the cornerstone of the postsecondary marketing program. A review of course outlines indicates that the following is a representative outline of topics for principles of marketing:

1. Overview of the Marketing Process
2. The Environment for Marketing Decisions
3. Marketing Strategies and Tactics
4. Segmentation of Consumer Markets
5. Segmentation of Industrial Markets
6. Consumer Behavior
7. Industrial Marketing
8. International Marketing
9. Product Planning
10. Pricing
11. Physical Distribution
12. Channels of Distribution
13. Retailing
14. Elements of Promotion
15. Advertising
16. Personal Selling
17. Marketing Research
18. Societal Issues
19. Nonprofit Applications

Community college marketing courses. Community colleges typically offer one- and two-year curriculums at grade levels 13 and 14 for persons who have completed the secondary school. Students are usually enrolled in one or more related courses leading to a one-year certificate or to an associate or other two-year degree. The programs are designed to accommodate either full-time or part-time students, including those who are employed and seeking occupational mobility. The courses are responsive to students' occupational interests and to the needs of businesses in the various marketing specialty areas.

In a review of selected community college marketing offerings, these courses were identified and are presented here in no particular order for illustrative purposes:

Principles of Marketing

---

[4]National Center for Education Statistics. *A Classification of Instructional Programs.* Washington, D.C.: U.S. Government Printing Office, 1983. pp. 56-62.

Human Relations
Principles of Salesmanship
Principles of Retailing
Fashion Merchandising
Fashion Buying
Marketing Management
Sales Management
Small Business Management
Public Relations
Advertising Principles
Advanced Advertising
Merchandising

Four-year college and university marketing courses. Marketing courses in four-year colleges and universities are taught at the junior and senior level. Students planning to take their first two years of college work at a community college are typically advised to take only those courses in business and economics that the four-year colleges and universities offer at the freshman and sophomore levels. The principles of marketing course is designed to give students their first look at the field of marketing. The course is a component of the business core curriculum which all students majoring in business are required to complete successfully. In addition, the principles course is a popular elective for students who are not majoring in a field of business. A major field in marketing often comprises approximately 18 semester credit hours in addition to the principles of marketing course. The titles of these courses are similar to those listed above for community colleges.

The dynamic nature of marketing requires educators to be alert to new content to be included in the curriculum as well as to alternative teaching methods. Through a review of publications designed for marketing educators, some topics of current interest to the field have been identified. The list of topics includes providing internships for students, enhancing retail marketing education, including experiential learning in marketing courses, and adding courses in nonprofit marketing and direct marketing to the curriculum.

TRENDS IN POSTSECONDARY MARKETING

Marketing education is constantly being challenged to meet the changing needs of the nation's dynamic marketing sector. Two ways community colleges have found to meet these needs are specialized marketing programs and articulation agreements with other educational institutions.

In addition to the business management area of concentration leading to the Associate in Applied Science degree at John Tyler Community College in Chester, Virginia, students may enroll in a specialized program in beverage marketing. This program, consisting of 97 quarter hours of credit, is designed for individuals seeking one of these careers in the beverage industry: branch manager, account manager, bulk sales manager, or vending operations manager. Some of the specialized courses included in this program are introduction to beverage management, softdrink production and utilization, and warehouse management. During their final term, students enroll in a coordinated internship.

Lakewood Community College in White Bear Lake, Minnesota, in cooperation with District 916 Area Vocational Technical Institute, offers specialized programs in such marketing-related areas as apparel services and fashion merchandising. Using the "career ladder" concept, students who received specialized training in high schools, private trade schools, vocational schools, or from certain other sources, may receive advanced placement for some of their work toward the associate degree. In addition to their course work, students take part in 100 hours of professional development activities, including a New York study tour and state and national Distributive Education Clubs of America competitions. According to Erickson:

> Consistent with 916 AVTIs goals for competency-based education—fully articulated programs, year-round use of facilities, open entry programs and part-time, full-time and limited objective student enrollment—the fashion merchandising program provides instruction based on the student's needs and schedule.[5]

As another example of specialized postsecondary instruction in marketing, Penn Valley Community College in Kansas City, Missouri, offers these programs: cooperative food and beverage management, food service management, and lodging management.

Two articulation plans were initiated in Wisconsin in 1986-87 between Vocational, Technical, and Adult Education (VTAE) System institutions and high schools in their areas. One plan involves the Appleton Area School District, Neenah Joint School District, and Fox Valley Technical Institute. Under this arrangement, students who complete equivalent marketing course work in high school may receive postsecondary course credit which is applicable toward an associate degree. According to a description of the plan:

> Articulation planners agreed upon specific competencies for both courses and made them available to program area staff. In addition to receiving three credits of advanced standing based on the course waiver, students from each school could test out of another postsecondary course which was not waived.[6]

Participants in the second plan are the Milwaukee Public Schools, Greendale Public Schools, Brown Deer Public Schools, and Milwaukee Area Technical College. This plan, called the Metro Milwaukee Employment Curriculum Articulation Project, is designed for students in fashion merchandising, retail management, and marketing and includes students from 12 Milwaukee high schools and two suburban high schools. Steps are being taken to expand both plans to include on-site, dual-credit arrangements.

THE MARKETING OF MARKETING EDUCATION

The "marketing of marketing education" is another way of saying

---

[5]Erickson, Lea. "Competency-Based Instruction in Fashion Merchandising." VocEd 56:30c; May 1981.

[6]*A Guide to Curriculum Planning in Marketing Education.* Madison: Wisconsin Department of Public Instruction, 1987. p. 154.

"recruiting students." Whatever it is called, postsecondary marketing instructors and program administrators have found effective, and sometimes unique, ways to reach their target populations.

Elizabeth R. Strenkowski, director of retail management at Pittsburgh's Bradford School, believes marketing educators should make employers in the industry aware that the marketing program will provide the type of employees they need. She suggests:

> Why not approach them with your program to train their employees? With the exception of "Executive Training Program" and some dollars still being allocated for on-campus interviewing, training programs as we knew them five years ago at retail operations no longer exist. Where will the future department managers, group managers, floor supervisors, and assistant store managers come from . . . ? From your program, that's where![7]

The key to Strenkowski's plan is to convince top management to accept the postsecondary marketing program as an alternative to an in-house training program. This requires marketing educators to sell their programs, something they, as marketing people, should feel comfortable doing.

In his discussion of student recruitment, Jose Duvall suggests that marketing research must be conducted to determine the image prospective students have of the college.[8] He also mentions the need to direct recruiting efforts at adults who would enroll on a part-time basis and to others, such as the following, who may not have been previously targeted as potential students:

- Women who have preschool children, provided day care is an incentive
- Reentry homemakers who wish to complete their formal education and/or occupational training
- Males changing careers
- Senior citizens
- Unemployed and underemployed
- Welfare recipients
- Adults in need of updated or new occupational licensing requirements.[9]

Based on her analysis of the marketing of continuing education programs by the public-supported community, Barbara Ash suggested that some of the more important marketing strategies include:

- Working with business and industry to provide upgrading and retraining for blue-collar workers by negotiating day-release time for educational purposes
- For older adults and those of lower socioeconomic status, teaching courses in a variety of instructional modes
- Involving adults in the program planning, organization, and implementation of the curriculum

---

[7]Strenkowski, Elizabeth R. "Nontraditional Recruiting for Postsecondary Education." *Business Education Forum* 36:15; May 1982.

[8]Duvall, Jose. *Recruitment of Students at the Community College.* U.S., Educational Resources Information Center, ERIC Document ED 284 604, May 1987.

[9]*Ibid.*

- Utilizing personal contact as a means of getting information on programs to low-income workers; utilizing media for the recruitment of white-collar workers.[10]

SUMMARY

Having been added to the curriculum in proprietary schools and four-year colleges prior to World War I and to the two-year colleges during the 1930's, marketing has become a well-established program in postsecondary educational institutions. Marketing education is constantly being challenged to meet the changing needs of the nation's dynamic marketing sector. Two ways community colleges have found to meet these needs are specialized marketing programs and articulation agreements with other educational institutions.

Through a review of publications designed for marketing educators at both the two-year and four-year levels, some topics of current interest to the field have been identified. Some topics deal with content to be included in the curriculum as well as to alternative teaching methods. The list of topics includes providing internships for students, enhancing retail marketing education, including experiential learning in marketing courses, and adding courses in nonprofit marketing and direct marketing to the curriculum.

Through the application of marketing principles, marketing educators have identified various methods to use in promoting their programs. The starting point of these efforts is to gain an understanding of the needs and wants of students and marketing businesses. Marketing education is a growth area today, one in which we continue to assert and reassert ourselves. It is a field that holds promise for a bright future.

---

[10] Ash, Barbara F. *Marketing Continuing Education Programs in the Public-Supported Community College.* U.S., Educational Resources Information Center, ERIC Document ED 270 143, 1986.

CHAPTER 20

Accounting Systems

ROBERT L. DANSBY
Columbus Technical Institute, Columbus, Georgia

C. DAVID STRUPECK
Bradley University, Peoria, Illinois

This chapter includes a brief description of the history of accounting education in the United States and the status of accounting education in the eighties. A more detailed presentation of the current state of accounting education, especially the impact of computers, will follow. The remainder of the chapter is devoted to the emerging trends in accounting education, including a discussion of the status of five-year accounting curriculums, impending changes in the content of the CPA examination, and a summary of the American Accounting Association's Futures Committee Report.

ACCOUNTING—AN OVERVIEW

Historically, accounting education at all levels has focused on a procedural, or "how-to-do-it," approach. A procedural approach emphasizes *how* accounting techniques are performed but often neglects the theoretical foundation underlying *why* certain practices are followed.

Early definitions of accounting tended to focus on the traditional record-keeping functions of the accountant. For example, in 1941, the American Institute of Certified Public Accountants (AICPA) defined accounting as "the art of recording, classifying, and summarizing, in a significant manner and in terms of money, transactions and events which are, in part at least, of financial character, and interpreting the results thereof." In this definition there are references to the *how* of accounting: recording, classifying, and summarizing.

A more recent description of accounting, provided in 1970 by the Accounting Principles Board (APB) of the AICPA, states that:

> Accounting is a service activity. Its function is to provide quantitative information, primarily financial in nature, about economic entities that is intended to be useful in making reasoned choices among alternative courses of action.[1]

According to Woelfel, the APB definition of accounting is more descriptive of the true role of accounting than earlier definitions. He stated:

---
[1] Accounting Principles Board. *Statement No. 4: Basic Concepts and Accounting Principles Underlying Financial Statements of Business Enterprises.* New York: American Institute of Certified Public Accountants, 1970. p. 6.

The APB definition of accounting is goal oriented rather than process oriented. It emphasizes economic decision-making activities rather than the recording, classifying, summarizing and interpreting process of accounting. This interpretation emphasizes the true role of accounting in its modern setting.[2]

Accounting is a discipline with an established body of generally accepted accounting principles. Understanding the theoretical foundation for these principles gives meaning and rationale to the tasks that engender from the application of these principles. Thus, understanding theories underlying accounting tasks will foster mastery of the tasks.

As in most professional fields, the amount of basic accounting information is proliferating at such a rapid rate that it has become almost impossible to include all necessary material within the confines of traditional accounting courses. Therefore, to be effective, accounting concepts and principles must be taught in terms broad enough to apply to any business type or combination and to any system of data accumulation, processing, analysis, storage, and retrieval.

Accounting principles—like principles governing any science or discipline—are formulated or developed to govern different situations. If students learn a general principle behind a task and then have an opportunity to apply this principle to many different types of problems and situations, they will be able to apply it to any new and unfamiliar problem or situation that may be encountered. If courses are to be called "accounting principles," theory must be taught. Otherwise, we have a systematic application of bookkeeping procedures.

EARLY BEGINNINGS OF ACCOUNTING EDUCATION

The first form of accounting education was the apprenticeship system. For centuries this was the only form of instruction in bookkeeping. This system, however, became inadequate to prepare bookkeepers needed for the expanded business activity generated by the Industrial Revolution. As a consequence, the need arose for formal training in bookkeeping procedures. To satisfy this need, private business schools developed and, by 1850, were a well-established segment of the U.S. school system.

With the expansion and proliferation of American business, accounting education soon evolved from formal training in bookkeeping procedures to formal training in accounting theories and concepts. Due to the increased demand for accounting education, and business education in general, the public schools began to absorb the courses from private business schools and include an increasing number of these courses in their curriculums.

As accounting education moved into public institutions, increased attention was placed on methods of instruction and output from the course. As the body of accounting knowledge grew, formal educational requirements were adopted. The body of accounting knowledge continues to grow and the structure of accounting practice continues to change in response to advances in technology and the complexity of modern business combinations. Account-

---

[2]Woelfel, C.J. *Accounting: An Introduction.* Pacific Palisades, Calif.: Goodyear Publishing Co., 1975. p. 8.

ing educators today are challenged to maintain the level and content of instruction that will adequately prepare graduates for entry into a vastly changing and diverse field.

CURRENT STATE OF ACCOUNTING EDUCATION

Accounting education, both as a major field of study and as support for other business disciplines, is available at a variety of postsecondary institutions. From a major field of study perspective, a variety of degree requirements are also evident, at both the undergraduate and graduate levels. What is not as varied is the delivery system for accounting education, which is dominated by the lecture method, routine problem solving, and to a lesser degree, class discussion.

The curriculums at most four-year institutions are similar in that most programs require approximately 30 credit hours of accounting instruction including principles, intermediate accounting, cost, systems, taxation, auditing, and advanced accounting. In addition to the accounting requirements, courses in general business and liberal arts are also required, leading to a total of 120 semester hours of credit needed for the baccalaureate degree.

The number of postbaccalaureate programs have increased significantly over the past decade. The majority of such programs can be classified into two types: master of accountancy (MAcc) and MBA with an accounting concentration. The typical MAcc programs requires 15 credit hours of accounting and 15 credit hours of general business administration. A specialization in specific accounting areas—for example, auditing or tax—is available in some MAcc programs.

The current curricular format, from the point of view of many accounting educators and practitioners, falls far short of what is necessary to adequately cover the expanding body of knowledge. Consider that 40 years ago most four-year programs included a two-semester sequence for intermediate accounting. A two-semester sequence for intermediate is still the norm, yet today's accounting students encounter Accounting Research Bulletins (ARB's), Accounting Principles Board Opinions (APB's), and Statements of Financial Accounting Standards (SFAS's), none of which existed in the late forties. Add to this the impact of the computer on accounting education and one can understand the opinion held by many, both inside and outside public accounting, that today's curriculum is inadequate.

The computer has impacted accounting education more than any other factor over the past 40 years. We are now living and working in what has been called the "information age." Within the next few years the computer will become a tool with the universal application of the calculator. No longer is the computer confined to the data processing department. It has moved into the office, the small retail store, the service establishment, the school, and the home. In offices today, microcomputers are as commonplace as typewriters. It has been estimated that over 70 percent of the country's largest corporations use microcomputers. This availability of computing power did not exist 15 years ago. Consider that only a decade ago most computing was done on large computers that could cost in excess of $4 million. The minicomputer, costing about $50,000, brought computing capabilities to many companies that could not afford, and probably did not need, a large computer. The computing revolution, however, did not truly start until 1977 with the introduction of the first microcomputer or desktop computer. Desktop computers were to become known as personal computers (PC's).

With reduced costs brought about by improved technology and increased production, even the smallest business is able to afford a PC. Based on current sales projections, it is estimated that by 1990 there could be over 50 million personal computers in use in the United States. Considering a national population of approximately 220 million people, this works out to be a computer for every 4.5 persons.

An accounting information systems course, or integration of the computer into existing courses, was mandated by the American Assembly of Collegiate Schools of Business (AACSB) in the late seventies. Proponents hoped the use of computers would revolutionize accounting education by improving student learning and reducing the cost and time of instruction.

Borthick and Clark point out that progress toward achieving these goals has been mixed, with integration being time-consuming and costly, and with modest improvements in learning, at best, being achieved.[3] This does not mean, however, that integration of the computer into the accounting curriculum has not occurred. The literature is replete with articles describing various pedagogies, experiments, applications, and research involving the use of computers in accounting education. Popular methods for integration include spreadsheet programs and computerized practices.

Concerning the impact of PC's, the EDP Technology Research Subcommittee of the AICPA made the following statement in its response to the issue "Widespread Computerization and Automation of Business Operations" published on July 10, 1985:

> The enormous growth in the use and availability of personal computers has significant implications for both the processes of organizational computing and of personal computing. Personal computers have also provided the tool for individual or personal computing tasks. The availability of the hardware and software (spreadsheets, word processors, graphics, communication packages) systems for personal computers at sufficiently low costs, make it economically feasible to use these systems for individual workstations. Thus, analysis requiring multiple iterations or multi-dimensional comparisons can be performed more rapidly on a much larger scale than previously possible. . . .
>
> Another impact of the growth in personal computers has been the significant reduction in the scale of operations for which in-house computerization of the accounting and management information systems is not only feasible, but advantageous. This means that virtually all clients—large and small—will have computerized functions requiring universal computer literacy within the profession.[4]

---

[3]Borthick, A.F., and Clark, R.L. *Issues in Accounting Education.* American Accounting Association, 1987. Vol. 2, No. 1, pp. 13-27.

[4]EDP Technology Research Subcommittee. *Widespread Computerization and Automation of Business Operations.* New York: American Institute of Certified Public Accountants, 1985. p. 5.

Considering the current and future impact of computers, it is imperative that current accounting graduates have a thorough understanding of computer hardware and software. Further, graduates must accept the concept of lifelong learning because continuing education will be essential to maintain computer skills current as breakthroughs and advances in technology continue to occur.

EMERGING TRENDS IN ACCOUNTING EDUCATION

Outside of curriculum and computer considerations, there are two relatively important issues that are currently being addressed concerning education and the accounting profession. These issues are the design of a uniform CPA examination and the requirements for professional certification, both under the aegis of the AICPA.

Uniform CPA examination. The CPA exam has been a four-part, two-and-one-half day exam for many years. Currently the exam consists of multiple-choice questions and problems over four areas: accounting practice, accounting theory, business law, and auditing. The AICPA is faced with the challenge of grading an ever increasing number of exams and appears to be on the verge of altering the format of the exam to include only multiple-choice questions. In addition, a change to a two-day format with the following schedule is also being considered:

Accounting Practice and Accounting Theory (combined)

Business Law

Auditing.

Adoption of these changes would only affect the structure and length of the exam. Individual state boards of accountancy will continue to prescribe requirements for obtaining a certificate in their respective states. Requirements by individual states vary. Requirements typically include a college degree in accounting (or equivalent) and a prescribed amount of work experience in public accounting. A few states do not have a public accounting experience requirement to obtain certification. And some states that have the experience requirement allow certain nonpublic accounting experience. In Georgia, for example, the experience requirement can be met by working in public accounting for two years or by teaching upper-level accounting courses in a senior college for five years.

The five-year accounting curriculum. The second issue, the five-year accounting program, has received considerable attention. Many accounting practitioners and educators feel strongly that entry-level accountants need five years of college study. The AICPA has sponsored several studies concerning needed accounting education. Both the Perry Commission (1950's) and the Beamer Committee (1969) recommended postbaccalaureate education for CPA's which led to a resolution by the AICPA endorsing the five-year education requirement and suggesting that it be passed by 1975. In 1967, Robert H. Roy and James H. MacNeill chaired the AICPA study of the common body of knowledge for accounting, cosponsored by the Carnegie Corporation, entitled "Horizons for the Profession." This report stated that accounting was a separate and distinct discipline and not just a service function for management. The report also recommended postbaccalaureate education. The Albers task force (late 1970's) confirmed the AICPA resolution for a five-year curriculum and recommended immediate implementation of the five-year requirement. Additionally, in 1978 the AICPA's Cohen Commission published a report dealing with the responsibilities of independent auditors. This report stated that the current content of accounting education did not adequately prepare students for careers in public practice, thereby placing a burden on public accounting firms to fill the gap by on-job training programs.[5]

In 1985 the Board of Directors of the AICPA attempted to further the postbaccalaureate issue by encouraging states to pass legislation requiring 150 semester hours of college study. As of this writing, only four states have passed legislation requiring a fifth year of accounting education to become a licensed CPA.

Proponents of the additional 30 semester hours of college education feel that graduates will be better prepared to accept the challenges of the accounting profession, will have a better chance of passing the CPA exam, and will have a better chance of promotion after initial employment. Additionally, the extra 30 hours will add maturity and foster better communication skills.

The 30 additional semester hours do not have to result in a master's degree. In 1984, the AICPA adopted "The 1984 Model Public Accountancy Bill," which advocated that the education requirement for entry-level CPA's should be a baccalaureate degree plus at least 30 additional semester hours of college study, with the toal academic program including a concentration in accounting.[6]

FUTURES COMMITTEE REPORT

The final section of this chapter is a brief overview of the American Accounting Association's (AAA) Futures Committee Report, Part III: The Future Scope, Content and Structure of Accounting Education. The committee suggests that, due to already evident changes and expected future changes, accounting education will need to revise and expand the current curriculum, design and implement a more effective delivery system, and develop a more distinct structure for the administrative units offering the programs. The curriculum should include strong general education in order to develop the critical thought process necessary for successful accountants. The report stresses that general education should be just that, general and not specific, but should include courses in calculus, statistics, economics, and computers. General professional education's primary purpose is to provide students the means to ". . . acquire both (a) the knowledge, techniques, sensitivities, and abilities all accountants should have for entry into the

---

[5]Langenderfer, H.Q. "Accounting Education's History—A 100-Year Search for Identity." *Journal of Accountancy*, May 1987. pp. 302-31.

[6]Ellyson, R.C.; Nelson, A.T.; and MacNeill, J.H. "Educating Tomorrow's CPA's." *Journal of Accountancy*, October 1987. p. 8.

accounting profession, and (b) the capacity to apply these qualities under reasonable supervision."

According to the committee report, the components should include education in the design and use of information systems, communication, decision problems and information in organizations, financial information and public reporting, and knowledge of the accounting profession. A passage from the report represents the embodiment of accounting education:

> . . . when accounting faculty accept a greater responsibility for student learning at the general professional accounting education level, they are also implicitly assuming a responsibility to recognize, foster, and encourage the following personal capacities in students:
> - Ambition and persistence
> - Empathy
> - Creative thinking
> - Understanding of cultural and intellectual differences
> - Logical reasoning
> - Sensitivity to social responsibilities
> - Leadership.

The curriculum must also include specialized professional accounting education in existing and emerging areas. This portion of the curriculum must be offered at the graduate level, as the undergraduate level already includes sufficient rigor and content to fill a four-year program.

Other recommendations from the committee stress the fact that post-secondary accounting education should prepare accounting students for the future. This could be achieved by, among other things, designing programs that ". . . help students learn to learn, to think, and to be creative . . ." and ". . . emphasize the skills and capacities needed for lifelong learning." In summary, the Futures Committee Report is a challenge to higher education to totally revamp the undergraduate curriculum, the structure of the delivery unit, and the design of the delivery system.

CHAPTER 21
Management Systems

GAIL L. FANN
Arizona State University, Tempe

Managers are facing more rapid changes than at any time since the industrial revolution. Major corporate restructuring, globalization of markets, rapidly changing technology, intensified competition, and increased demands by customers and employees create the most volatile and dynamic business environment in recent history.

Attempting to meet these changes, management education has evolved over the past 30 years. Management education has been and continues to be a growing major at postsecondary institutions. In 1961, business accounted for 15 percent of all undergraduate degrees. By 1981, business had increased its share of the degrees to 22 percent or 215,000 undergraduate degrees. A recent study of fall 1987 freshmen by the American Council on Education and UCLA found that 24.6 percent of the college freshmen hoped to pursue a business career.[1]

This chapter focuses on the evolution of management curriculum, the changes in management, the adaptation of management education, and finally, the challenges which face management educators.

EVOLUTION OF MANAGEMENT CURRICULUM

Present day business programs stem from the developments of the mid-twenties. Interestingly, the business school curriculum of today closely resembles the business curriculum of the twenties. One must look to developments of the past to clearly understand the purpose and problems of management education today. Perhaps it is easiest to divide the earlier years of management education into two periods—pre- and post-World War II.

Management education before 1940. During the industrial revolution, management had been strongly influenced by engineering. The study of organizations at this time was production and shop oriented, and managers were primarily concerned with the economics of production.

The 1900's ushered in the movement of scientific management. Frederick Taylor, the father of scientific management, provided direction in a search for efficiency and systematization in management thought. Others who supported and encouraged this movement included Carl Barth, Henry Gantt,

---

[1]*The American Freshman: National Norms for Fall 1987*. Los Angeles: Higher Education Research Institute, Graduate School of Education, University of California at Los Angeles.

Harrington Emerson, Morris Cooke, and Frank and Lillian Gilbreth. These people made significant contributions to the study of management and their teachings continue to influence management education today.

As the engineering community began to lose interest in management, business schools began to flourish. The year 1881 marked the opening of the first business school, the Wharton School of Finance and Commerce. The Amos Tuck School of Administration and Finance at Dartmouth College, founded in 1990, was America's first graduate school of business administration; the second graduate school of business was founded in 1908 at Harvard University. While the formalization of industrial management was becoming increasingly evident, no standard curriculum for management existed. Curriculums tended to be practical in orientation, specializing in business functions such as accounting, transportation, banking, marketing, and finance.

Management education after 1940. World War II mobilized vast production capabilities in American industries. The American economy accelerated with the rise of purchasing power, a baby boom, an increase in new technology, and the introduction of numerous new products into the market.

About this time industry began to turn away from shop-level management to general management theory. The proliferation of staff specialists, increased governmental regulations, the growth of unions, and the advancement of technical developments contributed to the changes in management philosophy.

In 1941 the Academy of Management was formed. The purpose of the organization was to promote the necessity of teaching management and to encourage the search for a unified management theory. It was not until 1949 that Henry Fayol first proposed a general theory of management. He defined theory as "a collection of principles, rules, methods, and procedures tried and checked by general experience."

Until the sixties, business education primarily had a vocational orientation. Most business schools were focusing on business practice and entry-level job skills. In 1959 the Gordon-Howell report, sponsored through the Ford Foundation, produced an extensive study of the nation's business programs. Concurrently, Frank Pierson's report for the Carnegie Foundation outlined reforms to make management education "more academically respectable and professionally relevant."[2] These reports molded management education for the years to come.

Gordon and Howell leveled criticisms that business schools: (1) lacked focus and purpose; (2) were not preparing competent, imaginative, flexible managers for a changing environment; (3) were overemphasizing vocational training for specific jobs rather than a broad education for maximum future growth in a business career; and (4) lacked professionalism.[3]

As a result of this reform, business programs became more heavily based

---

[2]Pierson, Frank C., and others. *The Education of American Businessmen: A Study of University-College Programs in Business Administration.* New York: Columbia University Press, 1959.

[3]*Ibid.*

in managerial problem solving through the scientific method and quantitative analysis, organizational theory, management principles, and human relations.

CHANGES IN MANAGEMENT

Rosabeth Moss Kanter, professor at Yale University's School of Management and author of *The Change Masters,* provides a splendid explanation of the changes which are taking place in American business. Kanter sees yesteryear's postindustrial organization characterized by less educated and less skilled workers, simple and physical tasks, mechanical technology, mechanistic views, stable markets and supplies, and a sharp distinction between workers and managers. Clearly, business today has changed in response to several striking social transformations. Among these are the introduction of a transformed business organization, high technology, and a changing work force.

Transformed business organizations. Books abound which extol the transformation of business organizations. Some of the more popular ones include Rosabeth Moss Kanter's *The Change Masters,* John Naisbett and Patricia Aburdene's *Re-inventing the Corporation,* Thomas Peters and Robert Waterman's *In Search of Excellence,* and Peter Drucker's *Innovation and Entrepreneurship.* All of these authors divulge a new business environment—one we have never seen before.

Naisbett and Aburdene explain how the new corporation differs from the old in both goals and basic assumptions. The strategic resource of the industrial era was capital. Today, in the information era, the strategic resources are information, knowledge, and creativity. Today, human resources are an organization's competitive edge.

The transformed business organization values people—the stakeholders on whom a business depends. Customers, employees, shareholders, suppliers, and members of the financial community all help an organization achieve its goals or send the organization to its grave.

The introduction of high technology. Technological advances have transformed the workplace. Managerial workstations, telecommunications, robots, and other forms of computerization require a new way of managing businesses. Managers must keep abreast with state-of-the-art technology. Monitoring functions, training employees, dealing with suppliers, and daily decision making are all affected by technological change. Technology creates new tools which in turn create new procedures. Even something as fundamental as communicating with one another takes on new dimensions with the advent of electronics.

Technology will require managers to cope with more complex problems than ever before. Technological changes can drastically alter power sources, communication, production, and transportation. Technological inventions require today's manager to be creative, innovative, and able to solve problems which never existed before.

The changing work force. In addition to managing in a transformed organizational structure and understanding new technology, managers must also deal with a changed work force. A key element to organizational success—employees—has taken on new dimensions. Several major social changes have contributed to this transformation; an increased proportion of women in the work force, an overall increase in the educational level of the labor force, more dual income families, a call for reduced work weeks and flexible scheduling, an increase in concern for the "quality of work life," and an aging work force. Successful managers must be creative and innovative to attract and keep productive employees.

MANAGEMENT EDUCATION ADAPTS

Today's business students are the managers of the next century. As business educators, we must provide a strong educational foundation which will allow students to become responsible leaders for the 21st century. Accordingly, business colleges must continue to refine and develop courses to meet the needs of the public and private sector. Specifically, management educators across the nation are responding to these changes by introducing internationalization, integrating high technology, introducing entrepreneurship, and reemphasizing small business management.

Introducing internationalization. The global marketplace has emerged. At current growth rates, U.S. international trade will exceed $4 trillion by the year 2000.[4] Nearly one of three jobs will be involved in international commerce. One glance at the daily newspaper illustrates the critical need to understand and adapt to increased internationalization. Today's business manager must have an understanding of global issues including economic, political, and cultural differences.

Economic considerations must include an understanding of economic development in various foreign countries around the world, markets, sources of supply, competition, infrastructures, exchange rates, interest rates, and economic growth. Political concerns include an understanding of the governmental laws and regulations, as well as the political systems in various countries.

A nation's culture is defined as the shared knowledge, beliefs, and values of a society. Culture is often difficult to grasp because it is intangible. However, successful business relationships depend on realizing the significance of local cultures. Cultural concerns include a knowledge of a society's religious beliefs, languages, attitudes, and social customs.

Increasingly, business schools are offering courses and programs intended for undergraduates and graduates. New courses in international management are being introduced in business schools across the nation. Content might include business strategies, policies, risks, organizing, directing, and controlling in developed and developing countries. Some universities and colleges offer certificates or special programs of study for international business. Additionally, most business course content and textbooks are integrating international issues into the existing materials.

---

[4]Report of the President's Commission on Industrial Competitiveness. *Global Competition: The New Reality.* Vol. 1. Washington, D.C.: U.S. Government Printing Office, January 1985.

Opportunities abound for students to study abroad. Cooperative international business programs are designed to offer students an opportunity to examine the economy and business management of foreign countries in a political, historical, and socio-cultural context.

Generally, college and university curriculums are becoming more internationalized. The general core curriculum often requires students to include courses which would expose them to international issues. Existing courses in foreign language, comparative political systems, comparative religions, history, geography, anthropology, and sociology are valuable to the future business manager.

Integrating high technology. We live amidst an electronic era. Changes ushered in by electronics have made a major impact on society, perhaps an impact greater than that of the original industrial revolution. Recent advances in electronic technology have also resulted in dramatic changes for business managers. Today's manager is likely to encounter word processors, local area networks (LAN's), telecommunication, electronic mail, micrographics, executive workstations, and teleconferencing. These technological advances require tomorrow's business manager to understand modern concepts and acquire new skills.

The information era has created new ways of doing business. New technology is not simply the application of new tools to old methods. Technology coupled with the transformation of business organizations changes methods of communicating, planning, controlling, organizing, and managing human resources. Business students must be introduced to modern organizational theory and understand the implications of new technology on business organizations. For instance, technology has introduced numerous avenues for communication such as electronic mail and teleconferencing. Effective use of technology requires not only a knowledge of electronic mail and teleconferencing, but a knowledge of the most effective means of communication based on an understanding of organizational dynamics.

Additionally, managers entering the world of business will be expected to have skills related to these technological advances. Specifically, the use of word processing, graphics, spreadsheets, and electronic mail might be expected.

How, then, are these concepts and skills being integrated into the management curriculum? Course content and current texts are integrating technology. Technology is introduced either as a separate topic or may be interspersed throughout. Current journal articles also provide relevant information for classroom discussion. Skills are being introduced throughout students' college education. Professors often encourage or require the use of microcomputers for word processing, graphics, spreadsheets, and/or electronic mail. Teleconferencing, simulations, local area networks, desktop publishing, and managerial workstations may also be demonstrated to or used by students.

Entrepreneurship. In 1967 only six universities had courses or research centers on entrepreneurship. By 1984 there were more than 150 colleges offering courses in entrepreneurship, including a course on entrepreneurial management at the Harvard Business School. Moreover, literature related to entrepreneurs and entrepreneurship has burgeoned during the past ten years.

The term enterpreneurship is used to describe businesses which are innovative, experience high growth, and create wealth. Fred Smith of Federal Express and Steven Jobs of Apple exemplify successful entrepreneurs. These men were able to coordinate people, resources, and capital to create successful businesses. Their ingenuity and creativity demonstrates the entrepreneurial spirit which is necessary in today's fast-paced information society.

Intrapreneuring—entrepreneurship within the corporation—is another popular concept. Many large bureaucratic organizations are fostering employee efforts to develop new products and adapt to changing markets. More employers are looking for employees who are able to think creatively and solve complex problems.

Academic institutions are responding to this entrepreneurial shift by offering a variety of courses in entrepreneurship. Introductory entrepreneurship courses generally include a study of high growth markets, start-up capital, venture capital, equity sources, form of ownership, business life cycles, and exit modes. Other courses include the development of business plans, industry analysis and competitive strategies, and venture management. Videotapes, simulations, and guest speakers are excellent resources for presenting concepts related to entrepreneurship.

Several academic institutions throughout the country have established entrepreneurial incubators. Incubators are created in conjunction with the business community and offer inexpensive rental space and business services to potential entrepreneurs. With start-up support and an entrepreneurial environment, new ventures have shown a higher success rate than those without such support.

Small business management. Business start-ups, which averaged 1,800 a day in 1950 and 4,000 in 1960, increased to an estimated 12,000 a day in 1983. From 1970 to 1980 small new businesses added 20 million new jobs, while the *Fortune* 500 companies added none. *Fortune* 500 companies lost 3 million jobs from 1980 to 1983, while companies less than ten years old added 750,000.[5] Small businesses comprise an important portion of today's economy. Successful operation of small firms is increasingly important to our nation's economic health. The small business owner/manager must respond rapidly to a changing economic and social environment. Moreover the owner/manager must adjust to shifts in consumer demands, competitors, and shifts in markets.

Traditionally business schools have focused on education for managers in large corporations. Today, moreover, it has become increasingly clear that many college students will become owner/managers of small firms, or they most likely will encounter business associates and competitors who are owner/managers of small firms. Research indicates that small businesses are not little big businesses. Therefore, students need to be able to compare and contrast the management strategies in large and small firms.

---

[5]Solomon, Steven. *Small Business USA*. New York: Crown Publishers, 1986.

Small business management has been included among the courses in business schools for many years. However, the recent shift toward entrepreneurship and the realization of the importance of small firms to our economy has created a renewed interest in small business management. Courses and certificates in small business management are offered at some colleges and universities. Typical content in an introductory course would include the causes of business failures, means to business ownership, legal organization of the firms, franchising opportunities, location of the firm, staffing, operations, marketing, accounting systems, forecasting, budgeting, purchashing, inventory control, and taxation. Small business owners, bankers, laywers, marketing consultants, accountants, and small business consultants are usually willing to serve as guest speakers.

Several universities cooperate with the local small business administration office to offer consulting services to small, local businesses. This cooperative effort allows business students to gain an awareness of the typical problems which face small business owner/managers.

CHALLENGES WHICH FACE MANAGEMENT EDUCATORS

While no one can accurately predict the future, we do know that the business manager will continue to face a climate of rapid change. Social, economic, and political forces will exert tremendous influence on the organizations of tomorrow. Management educators will continually encounter the issue of focus and purpose. Finally, academic research is becoming increasingly important.

Social, political, and economic forces. Social values shape business activities. Employee work ethic, profitability, social responsibility, and business ethics are strongly influenced by social values. Products and services introduced into the marketplace are also vulnerable to social changes. For example, the emphasis on health in our society has had a major impact on the introduction of food products, exercise equipment, and services related to health. Undoubtedly as social values shift, managers must be able to forecast and comprehend the impact of these shifts on the organization.

Managers in tomorrow's organization cannot afford to be myopic about the economy. An understanding of how global markets and economics influence organizations will be essential. The picture will become increasingly complex as we become more entrenched in a global economy.

Political concerns will have an increasing role as societies become more complex. Major shifts in political policies are a given. Managers must be able to foresee and adapt to changes in government policies and regulations, both domestic and foreign. These might include trade and tariff policies, foreign policy, defense spending, product regulation, wage/price guidelines, antitrust legislation, employment practices, or pollution control.

Focus and purpose. Management education has continually dealt with the issue of focus and purpose. The relationship between management education and managerial performance is weak if not nonexistent. Business professionals and academicians debate the priority of skill development and the teaching of theoretical knowledge. What constitutes a well-educated manager?

The focus and goal of management education used to be vocational. Management educators' goals were to prepare their students for entry-level jobs. Rapid obsolescence, however, will not allow management educators to teach short-run practical relevance. Many colleges and universities are attempting to shift their curriculum to more generalized understandings of principles and practices. Perhaps the more applicable knowledge and skills might include problem-solving skills, communications skills, creative thinking, and managerial decision making, leadership, human relations, personnel management, information systems, financial analysis, and organizational theory. Integrating technology and internationalism has become standardized procedure in most managerial courses throughout the nation.

Emphasis on research. Entry into the information era has put the spotlight on research. Management educators will be expected to continue to add to the knowledge base. The discipline will depend on credible research in the field of management. Without it, management education will lose respectability.

SUMMARY

The Gordon-Howell report ushered in a new era of management education. Until the sixties, the business curriculum was vocationally oriented and focused on entry-level skills. The resulting reformation promoted business programs with increased emphasis in managerial problem solving through scientific method and quantitative analysis, organizational theory, management principles, and human relations. As business organizations take on new meaning in the information era, management educators must reassess the goal and content of management education. The adaptation of management education includes the introduction of internationalization, the integration of high technology, the introduction of entrepreneurship, and the reemphasis of small business management.

The business organization will continue to grow and change at a rapid pace. Management educators must understand the role of management education within the framework of an ever changing society. Educators must adapt curriculum to meet the needs of managers for the 21st century.

EPILOGUE
Business Education in the Years To Come

BURTON S. KALISKI
New Hampshire College, Manchester

In the preceding pages, you have read a wealth of ideas about business education, ideas ranging from the philosophical to the historical, from the presecondary school to the university, and from the factual to the controversial. In sum, they show a picture of what we know as business education at the end of the 1980's.

A snapshot at one point in time, however, leads to thoughts of how the same scene might look at another point in time. One can ponder, for example, if Frederick Nichols would recognize business education as it is today. In line with this thought, will we recognize business education 70 years from today? Will there even be a business education 70 years from today?

Both questions posed can be answered with one of three choices: yes, maybe, or no. All three alternatives are possibilities. However, it does appear to be clear, based on what you have read in the previous chapters, that the answer to the first question *must be no*, for if it is answered with either remaining choice, then the second question will be answered with a resounding *no*. If we do not change what we do today, we will not survive long into the 21st century. It must no longer be "business as usual."

Happily, as attested to in the chapters of this yearbook, there are many alternatives to business as usual. What all of these alternatives have in common is that they are things that we *can* do, not things that are completely out of our control. They are ways in which we can assert ourselves in new directions and reassert ourselves in those areas in which we have done so well in the past. We should never change our mission of educating students for and about business. We must change our ways, and perhaps even our level of school, in reaching this mission. Change is very much within our hands. We can indeed be managers of change and not its victims.

It is a sobering thought that hardly any of us will be active viewers of business education as it will appear in 70 years. This does not in the least reduce our responsibility to those business educators who will follow us— our students and our students' students. If we do assert and reassert the role of business education, we can assure a vibrant, challenging, and contributing business education in the years to come. Shall we all rise to the responsibility?